DENG XIAOPING
SHAKES THE WORLD

YU GUANGYUAN

DENG XIAOPING
SHAKES THE WORLD

An Eyewitness Account of
China's Party Work Conference
and the Third Plenum
(November–December 1978)

EDITED BY

EZRA F. VOGEL AND **STEVEN I. LEVINE**

INTRODUCTION BY **EZRA F. VOGEL**

Eastbridge
BOOKS

Published by Eastbridge Books, an imprint of Camphor Press Ltd

83 Ducie Street, Manchester, M1 2JQ
United Kingdom

www.eastbridgebooks.com

23 22 21 20 19 18 17 2 3 4 5

ISBN   978-1-910736-93-7 (pbk)
        978-1-910736-94-4 (cloth)

Contents

INTRODUCTION TO THE ENGLISH EDITION
Ezra F. Vogel

In 1978 China initiated changes that altered not only its own course, but the relationship between China and the rest of the world. We have known that changes began when Deng Xiaoping emerged as China's preeminent leader and launched the era of reform and opening, but we have known very little about the turning point itself, a 36-day Chinese Communist Party Work Conference that commenced on November 10, 1978. We have also known little about what went on behind the scenes at the Third Plenum (of the 11th Central Committee) that began immediately after, on December 18.

Fortunately for those who wish to understand these momentous changes, in 1998 on the 20th anniversary of these events, one of the last remaining key participants in these meetings, Yu Guangyuan, then age eighty-three, wrote a book describing the background and the contents of both the Party Work Conference and the Third Plenum. Yu was a regular participant at the Party Work Conference. Although he was not a member of the Central Committee, he attended the Third Plenum as a staff member. Yu based his book on detailed notes he had taken at these meetings.

I have had the good fortune to know Yu Guangyuan as part of my research on the era of Deng Xiaoping. Although he does not walk easily and is a bit hard of hearing, his mind and his memory remain today as clear as a bell. He still sparkles, and a continuing stream of visitors come to his home to visit "Yu Lao," as they affectionately call him, and to listen to his historical recollections. His run-down home not far from Zhongnanhai is covered with books and manuscripts that his research assistants help him locate. In his writings Yu Lao is careful to rely on what he personally saw and recorded and to document carefully his source for conclusions not based on direct observation. It is easy to see why serious Party historians working on the period regard Yu Lao as a favorite interviewee in their effort to reconstruct and preserve the history of the time.

Yu Guangyuan was one of the key people in charge of preparing Deng Xiaoping's speech for the Party Work Conference and therefore met with Deng, Hu Yaobang and others during the course of the Work Conference to prepare and review various drafts. Deng's speech was the only document issued by the Work Conference, and it became the key document for the Third Plenum.

Thanks to Yu's account, we now understand the nature of the Party Work Conference and the drama that took place there. Until Yu's book appeared, it was possible for Western scholars to argue that the turning point in reform and opening was at the Third Plenum of December 1978. We now know that the key debates were held at the 36-day Party Work Conference that began on November 10, 1978, and that the Third Plenum that followed immediately after was essentially ceremonial, officially approving the new consensus worked out at the Party Work Conference.

When Yu Lao first raised with me the possibility of publishing this book in English, I suggested that he find a translator in Beijing and told him I would be happy to take responsibility for finding a publisher and for editing the translation for a Western audience. Yu Lao agreed and he adapted his book for a Western audience and found a translator.

❦ ❦ ❦ ❦

Born on July 5, 1915, in Shanghai, Yu Guangyuan was a participant in the December 9th movement (1935) in Beiping, which mobilized young intellectuals to the nationalist cause. He graduated from Qinghua University in 1936, three years behind Qiao Guanhua, who became foreign minister during the Cultural Revolution. Yu graduated from Qinghua in physics, a student of the distinguished physicist Zhou Peiyuan, who later became president of Peking University. By the time he graduated from Qinghua, Yu decided to dedicate himself to the revolution rather than to physics.

In 1935, when the Communist Youth League was replaced by the "Minxian" (the Minzu jiefang xianfengdui (National Liberation Pioneers), to broaden the anti-Japanese alliance beyond communists, Yu Guangyuan was one of its original organizers. After graduation, Yu Guangyuan was sent south to help expand the Minxian. He went to Lingnan University, Guangzhou, as a member of the teaching staff, but his main activity was to help organize the Minxian. When the KMT (Guomindang) in Guangzhou broke up the Minxian organization in January 1937, he returned to Beiping and began to work full time as a revolutionary in Minxian. Yu became a Communist Party member two months later, shortly before the Japanese invasion.

Between 1937 and 1982, Yu held a variety of positions. In 1941 he was assigned to the Northwest Bureau to work on economic issues of the Shenganning Border area. After taking part in the Rectification Campaign, he joined the faculty of the Communist-led Yan'an University. He later worked for Communist newspaper *Jiefang ri bao*. In 1947 he took part in land reform work in a number of different localities. In 1948 he was assigned to the Propaganda Department of the Central Committee to work on Marxist theory and to take part in formulating Party policies toward philosophy, social sciences, and natural sciences. In 1956 Yu was head of the Science Section of the Central Committee Propaganda Department under Lu Dingyi, and concurrently served as deputy bureau chief of the Senior Specialists Bureau of the State Council, along with Fei Xiaotong and Lei Jieqiong. From 1966 to 1975, during the Cultural Revolution, Yu was the object of criticism and struggle. He "studied" at a May 7th Cadre School.

In 1975 when allowed to return to work Yu was assigned as one of the seven senior members of the Political Research Office under the State Council. In June 1975 when the Political Research Office was officially established, the State Council was under the direction of Deng Xiaoping. In 1975 Deng Xiaoping acquired a broad range of responsibilities. Deng therefore drew on the seven senior members of the Political Research Office of the State Council who became key drafters under his direction. Deng was not known as a specialist in theory, but in this Office he could draw on a number of specialists who could speak authoritatively about Marxism-Leninism and the Thought of Mao Zedong, even if some of them turned out to be more conservative than Deng in pushing the cause of reform and opening in the 1980s. In addition to Yu, the other six were Hu Qiaomu, Wu Lengxi, Hu Sheng, Xiong Fu, Li Xin, and Deng Liqun. When Deng was ousted from his positions after the April 5, 1976, demonstrations,

Yu Guangyuan also came under criticism for supporting Deng in trying to achieve the so-called rightist reversal of verdicts.

When Deng returned in 1977, Yu Guangyuan began working for him again, this time as one of the three senior members of the Political Research Office and concurrently as a deputy president of the Chinese Academy of Social Sciences and as a deputy director of the Science and Technology Commission of the State Council. Yu Lao thus had a distinguished career as an official concerned with policy in science, technology, and other academic areas.

In 1982 although Yu Lao took part in the 12th Party Congress, it was decided before the Congress that no one over sixty-six would be added to the Central Committee. Like a number of prominent people over sixty-six, Yu was selected as a member of the prestigious Central Advisory Committee. Yu welcomed going to the second line, saying that many people should no longer work as officials and they could still make a contribution in their role as private citizens working for the increase of people's rights and for the material and spiritual betterment of the people. Yu has since said that he has enjoyed far more freedom since 1982 than he did as an official, that he has not had to do unnecessary boring work, and that no one has to obey him just because of his position but only because of the value of what he says. Yu says this freedom has enabled him to accomplish a great deal more in the last twenty years as a non-official than he accomplished in his almost half a century as an official. During these twenty years Yu has authored a large number of important publications but had he written only this history of the Party Work Conference and the Third Plenum, one would still find it hard to disagree with his judgement about the value of his contribution after retirement.[1]

This volume was translated by Fang Yinong and edited by Ezra F. Vogel and Steven I. Levine

---

[1] For accounts of some of Yu Guangyuan's roles in domestic intellectual debates in the 1980s, see Merle Goldman, *Sowing the Seeds of Democracy in China* (Cambridge: Harvard University Press, 1994); and Joseph Fewsmith, *Dilemmas of Reform in China* (Armonk, NY: M.E. Sharpe, 1994).

At the beginning of the last decade of the twentieth century the world's economic and social systems underwent earth-shaking changes. The Soviet Union dissolved and East European countries changed their basic orientation. On May 3, 1996, The Pacific Studies Association of China convened an international forum to analyze the deep layers of causes that gave rise to these changes.

In the early part of the twentieth century, the entire world was under the sway of capitalism. After the First World War a socialist state, the Soviet Union, appeared. As a result of evolutionary historical changes, in 1939 World War II broke out. After World War II, in Eastern Europe and in Asia a group of socialist countries appeared. The weakening of capitalism and the splits between capitalist countries after the war made it necessary for capitalist states to follow a path of readjustment. One after the other various capitalist states took steps to lessen domestic class struggles, to reduce the tensions between themselves and their former colonies and countries dependent on them, and to adjust their relations with other capitalist countries.

As a result of these adjustments, the capitalist countries were revitalized. Their economies and culture advanced rapidly. At the same time the leaders of socialist nations, dizzy with success and convinced of their inevitable advance forward, announced that, "Socialism will be better day by day, and capitalism will decay day by day." They failed to take measures to resolve the serious economic and political problems they faced. The Soviet Union was absorbed in military competition with the United States. It was not concerned with raising the standard of living of its people, and the common people became very dissatisfied. While capitalism was continuing to advance, the Soviet Union and East Europe lost out in the competition. Therefore the Soviet Union and Eastern Europe, which had not previously experienced domestic upheavals and turmoil, underwent, respectively, dissolution and basic change of orientation.

In China as well, we had some problems that were almost the same as those in the Soviet Union and Eastern Europe. It is not necessary to trace the origins of these problems for they are clear if we examine the 20 years after 1957 and before China terminated its emphasis on class struggle. China tried to "expand the class struggle" even where objectively there was absolutely no class struggle, thereby carrying on the "class struggle" against its own people. China wasted so much time, missed so many opportunities, and expended so much energy, even to the extent of ruining China's productive forces and the livelihood of the people. Because of this, during this period that extended over 20 years, the Chinese economy stagnated and culture withered. There were daily calls to "surpass England" and "catch up with the United States," but in fact we fell further behind. Some people were thoroughly convinced that China would become more like the Soviet Union or like Eastern Europe. Fortunately, things did not turn out that way.

I believe we should pose the question: "Why did China not undergo the changes like those in the Soviet Union and Eastern Europe?" The answer lies in the concrete process of historical change that China underwent. In 1966 in the great proletarian Cultural Revolution, China's "class struggle" against its own people deepened. In this unprecedented "great revolution" Mao Zedong relied on the Lin Biao and Jiang Qing cliques to attack "those in authority taking the capitalist roads" who were actually cadres faithful to the Chinese people, faithful to the course of advancing society, and faithful to the Party's correct line. In this campaign, these cliques trampled on the state Constitution, betrayed the Party's Constitution, and oppressed cadres and ordinary Party members, going so far as to remove the state chairman Liu Shaoqi and persecute him to death. After the Ninth Party Congress in April 1969 there was another sharp struggle in which the Lin Biao and Jiang Qing cliques competed to usurp the highest state authority. One aspect of the Cultural Revolution was that of a domestic struggle, and in this period it was the struggle between the Lin Biao and Jiang Qing cliques. After the Lin Biao Clique collapsed, many cadres who had been overthrown returned to work. Then the struggle within the Communist Party was between those old cadres who had regained some authority and the Jiang Qing clique.

A few weeks after Mao died in September 1976, the Jiang Qing clique was smashed, and only then could the old cadres rise to the positions in which they could provide normal leadership for Party and government work. But in some areas such as the ideological and political lines and the selection of personnel, they were still many problems waiting for resolution.

This is a brief outline of the course of historical development of socialist China. Only at the end of this period, after they had been struggled against for ten years, did senior cadres really reflect on the Cultural Revolution. A majority of them realized that it was necessary for China to undertake large-scale reform. This is the historical background for the Central Work Conference and the Third Plenum called by the Chinese Communist Party in 1978.

As one of those accused of being "an authority taking the capitalist road," a "counterrevolutionary revisionist," and a "reactionary capitalist academic authority," I received ample criticism. I not only personally witnessed this "Great Cultural Revolution," I was deeply affected by it. In July 1975 when I formally returned to office, I worked directly for Deng Xiaoping who had just returned for the first time. I became one of his seven assistants responsible for the Political Research Office of the State Council. In 1976, in the campaign that Mao initiated to "Criticize Deng and oppose the rightist reversal of verdicts," I was one of the major targets subjected to criticism. In the farce that constituted the final stage of the Cultural Revolution, I gained further experience as a participant. In addition I later approached this period as a scholar conducting historical research. In response to the question, "Why did China not undergo those changes found in the Soviet Union and Eastern Europe?," based on an analysis of the specific historical events I can give the following reply: In our country, from 1966 to 1976 the unprecedented Cultural Revolution pushed developments to an extreme.

In ancient China there was an old expression, full of wisdom, "When things reach an extreme, they must swing back." The destruction by the great proletarian Cultural Revolution caused many people who had accepted in varying degrees Mao's individual infallibility to wake up and gain the ability to do their independent thinking. Increasingly more people realized that China must carry on reform in the area of social and economic systems. At the same time, with the smashing of Lin Biao's and Jiang Qing's cliques, it was possible to do away with the obstacles to this kind of reform. Meanwhile some old comrades in the Communist Party who were loyal to the Chinese people were successively liberated in the latter part of the Cultural Revolution and returned to their leadership work. Thus they could take the main role in carrying on this reform.

In November and December 1978 there was a 36-day "Central Committee Work Conference" and, immediately following, the five-day Third Plenum of the 11th Central Committee. This was the starting point of one of the great turning points in Chinese history that "turned misfortune to good fortune."

When the Jiang Qing Clique was smashed and Deng Xiaoping returned for the second time, I was still working at the State Council Research Office. Beginning in March 1977, Deng Xiaoping frequently came to the Research Office to have discussions with the responsible leaders. In the year and a half between that time and the end of 1978, I had an opportunity to know quite clearly much of Deng Xiaoping's thinking and his activities. At the Work Conference in late 1978 I took part as one of the responsible people in the Research Office of the State Council. In order to draft his speech for the closing session of the Central Work Conference for a number of days Deng Xiaoping had daily talks with Hu Yaobang and me. I kept detailed notes at the time on the main content of our conversations. I was not a member of the Central Committee, and I was only an auditor at the Third Plenum, but I was familiar with all the circumstances of the entire meeting. Because of this I was deeply aware of the great historical significance of these two meetings.

In 1998 on the 20th anniversary of these two meetings, I reflected on the fact that there were very few elders who had taken part in those meetings and were still in good health and there were even fewer who like myself had a deep understanding of the circumstances not only of the public meetings but of the discussions behind the curtains. I was also aware that in 1998 there was no one still working in the Party Central Committee leadership who had taken part in those two meetings twenty years earlier. They had all left their positions. I felt that my writing about this period of history could be of some assistance to those who had not had this personal experience.

I myself have felt distant from those events that I did not personally experience. For example, although I had participated in land reform and gone to the Soviet base areas before Liberation, I had not taken part in the 8,000 mile Long March. Therefore, I felt that I should make special efforts to study the history that I had not personally experienced. We should make every effort to understand important historical events in order "to take history as a mirror" to guide our policies.

Therefore in 1998, on the eve of the 20th anniversary of the Third Plenum and the Party Work Conference that preceded it, I wrote a book with others titled *Gaibian Zhongguo mingyun de 41 tian* [The forty-one days that changed the fate of China] by Yu Guangyuan, Wang Enmao, Ren Zhongyi, Li Desheng and others to describe the Party Work Conference and the Third Plenum of the 11th Central Committee that had taken place 20 years before. The Central Compilation and Translation Publishing House published the book in October of that year. I have drawn on that volume to prepare the present volume.

I know that there are an increasing number of foreign scholars and officials interested in the present situation in China. The effort to grasp the current issues in China cannot be achieved without an understanding of contemporary Chinese history. Therefore, in order to be of service to the foreign reader, I decided to have the book translated into English.

Before passing the volume to the translator I excised a few passages of little interest to foreigners and added some new content, supplementing the text for the foreign reader, hoping that the English version of this work will have additional value. I originally had no intention of making these additions, but after I completed them, I felt that it improved the work.

Yu Guangyuan
September 19, 2001

This year marks the twentieth anniversary of the convocation of the Third Plenum of the 11th Central Committee of the Chinese Communist Party (CCP) and the Central Work Conference at which full preparations were made for the plenum. As a witness to this historical turn, I have not forgotten my own social responsibility. I deem it necessary to write down what I personally experienced and my own opinions then and now. So, in April and May of this year I wrote a series of articles to commemorate the twentieth anniversary of the publication of the article, "Practice Is the Sole Criterion for Testing Truth."[1] I wrote most of these articles hastily, at the request of newspaper and magazine editors, and as soon as I finished writing them, I sent them to the newspapers and magazines for publication. After almost half a year of writing, I completed a short book, titled *An Historical Turning Point I Personally Experienced*. This brief book totals about 200,000 characters. At first I did not plan to publish it. Later, I decided that since I had written so much, I should try to see if a publishing house would like to publish it. As a result, I obtained support from the Central Compilation and Translation Publishing House, and this book will become available to readers.

While writing the book, I became deeply aware of how quickly people forget history. Perhaps there is a law governing social and historical development: the faster history progresses, the more people's access to communications increases, and the more they come into contact with newly created things, the faster they forget history. Therefore I believe it is all the more imperative to study and understand history. The lessons from historical experience are the wealth created by mankind, sometimes a precious wealth obtained at through huge costs. Forgetting repeated historical experience and its lessons is an enormous loss to humanity. I watched a film from the former Soviet Union entitled *Dawn over Moscow*, in which Lenin was quoted as saying, "Never forget the past. Forgetting the past is betrayal." This remark is not contained in the *Complete Works of Lenin* and perhaps was fabricated by the playwright. At any rate, the remark is very apt. Assuming that Lenin really made the remark, he mentioned only the past—not the future. I prefer to change Lenin's remark to "Never forget the past. Forgetting the past means failing to grasp the future." I added the word "future" for if the past is forgotten, some people will likely repeat past mistakes, thus damaging a future world that might have progressed more smoothly.

I feel a responsibility to spend some time "looking to the past"— reviewing history. In the meantime, however, we should also "Look to the future" to learn new circumstances and study new problems. Written on the three pages of the outline that Deng Xiaoping[2] gave me at the Central Work Conference were the words "looking to the past will help people look to the future." Later, the words in his speech were changed to the more specific "handling problems left over from the past will help people look to the future." But I committed to memory the words contained in Deng's original outline because they convey the significance of all historical studies and education.

Many people have too little knowledge of the specific circumstances of and the ideological background for the historical turn that occurred in 1978. They really should increase their understanding in this regard. For instance, many only know of the Third Plenum of the 11th Central Committee and yet do not know the plenum lasted only five days. Still less do they understand why the five-day plenum could solve so many problems or why the plenum did not produce a thematic report. In my view, since we mark the plenum, we should relate more of the historical facts. If we clarify the circumstances, people will realize that before the Third Plenum there was a Central Work Conference, which lasted 36 days, a large-scale conference with a high level of discussion. The full preparations for the Third Plenum were made at the work conference. The Third Plenum was actually a meeting without a thematic report. Hua Guofeng presided over the Third Plenum and delivered a speech at the opening session on the evening of the first day of the Third Plenum.[3] However, in keeping with the arrangements for the plenum, the Central Committee members who had not attended the Central Work Conference but did attend the Third Plenum spent the entire day reading the texts of the speeches given by Hua Guofeng, Ye Jianying,[4] and Deng Xiaoping at the closing session of the Central Work Conference. Since Deng Xiaoping's speech was considered the most comprehensive and profound, people later agreed that his speech should become the main report for the Third Plenum.

Take another example. Many people believed that since a success was scored at the conference in opposing the "two whatevers," it should follow that it would be easy to correct the mistake of making rural units "large in size and collective in nature,"[5] so that rural reforms could be carried out quickly and smoothly. They did not realize that the success in opposing the "two whatevers" lay merely in resolving the reversal of the verdict on the nature of the 1976 Tiananmen Incident[6] and certain major problems left over from the Cultural Revolution. However, even after the Third Plenum, it was not yet possible to correct many past mistakes, including the mistaken guidelines for rural work. Many assume that measures to develop China's agriculture and improve farmers' living standard could be taken immediately. But this was not the case.

On many occasions Mao Zedong had firmly opposed the practice of assigning rural output quotas "down to the household."[7] Therefore, the drafters of the document on agriculture did not yet dare to write in the document the idea of setting rural output quotas down to the household. Instead they specifically wrote in the document on agriculture distributed at the Third Plenum that it was not permitted to "fix farm output quotas down to the household or divide land for individual farming." This mistake was corrected step-by-step two to three years after the Third Plenum.

Take still another example. At the Central Work Conference, several central leaders such as Ye Jianying and Deng Xiaoping and even Hua Guofeng all emphasized the need to give full scope to democracy. The speeches of Deng Xiaoping and Ye Jianying contained many brilliant remarks on fully carrying forward the pursuit of democracy. I believe it is timely to introduce this background to our readers.

I was lucky to have experienced personally the historical turn that occurred in 1978. Moreover, although I am now eighty-three years old, I am still in fairly good health and can still write. I would not be able to justify myself if I did not record what I know and what might be useful for today and precious for the future. That is why I have written so many articles. Yet it was too late when I started to do such things. Although I have tried my best to be accurate, after all, I did write in a hurry, so that it is inevitable that my knowledge of some issues is not deep enough and may not be completely accurate on some points. Besides, I certainly have made many omissions. Fortunately, many veteran comrades are now writing articles in commemoration of the Third Plenum, which will help me recollect and clarify more matters, so that I will be able to supplement what I have written.

Yu Guangyuan

October 25, 1998

DENG XIAOPING
SHAKES THE WORLD

CHAPTER 1

CONVOCATION OF THE CENTRAL WORK CONFERENCE

Historical Background of the Central Work Conference November 10–December 15, 1978

Most Chinese readers who are concerned with politics and history know that in 1978 the 11th Party Central Committee held its historic Third Plenum that was constitutionally mandated and well-publicized. But few people know about the Party Central Work Conference that preceded the Third Plenum. Many do not know that full preparations for the Third Plenum were made at the Central Work Conference or that it solved a host of problems. Central work conferences are more flexible than plenums and are held by the Party Central Committee to discuss important issues concerning work. The topics for discussion were usually national issues. Central work conferences are attended by many people, usually including the number one and number two leaders of various central departments and all provinces and municipalities under the direct administration of the central government as well as of autonomous regions, many of which are members of the Party Central Committee. All members of the Political Bureau of the Party Central Committee are also likely to attend.

Work conferences are generally equivalent in status to enlarged meetings of the Political Bureau but lack the powers of the Party Central Committee. For instance, the conference could not make a decision that the whole Party must abide by or elect a certain number of new members of the Central Committee as permitted by the Party Constitution. Yet it had its own advantages: A work conference could be called when convenient and it allowed free deliberation among a fairly large number of senior Party cadres seeking to reach consensus on important issues.

The 1978 Work Conference was unusual. The conference continued for an exceptionally long time—36 days—and discussions

1

were fruitful.   After 36 days of discussions that were often confrontational, the participants reached consensus on the cardinal policies and principles that would guide the Party's work in the future. They expressed the hope that the consensus reached on the basic line and principles that had been reached through their deliberations would shape the Party's formal resolutions. This new consensus required the adjustment of the institutions of the Party Central Committee and the appointment of additional leaders like Hu Yaobang. For this reason, a decision was made to convene the Third Plenum promptly to enact the changes formally.   The Work Conference also decided not to prepare a separate overall theme report for the Third Plenum. The Central Work Conference made full preparations for the issues to be solved at the Third Plenum. The Third Plenum lasted only five days, one-seventh the length of time of the Central Work Conference.

What was the background for the Central Work Conference and the Third Plenum? To fully understand them, it is necessary to examine the situation in China between 1976 and 1978. In 1976, three events of paramount importance took place in China:

The first event was the movement that grew out of the crowds of people who gathered in Tiananmen Square to mourn Zhou Enlai, support Deng Xiaoping, and oppose the "Gang of Four." This movement commenced in March 1976 and continued through April. Because it peaked on April 5th, it is referred to as the "April 5th Movement." The event demonstrated the thinking and courage of the vast number of cadres, intellectuals and youth.

The second event was the death of Mao Zedong on September 9, 1976. Mao could no longer carry out real work in 1976, but his wife Jiang Qing,[1] his nephew Mao Yuanxin,[2] and others were able to manipulate him at will. Taking advantage of the people's total lack of knowledge of Mao Zedong's health condition and Mao's complete ignorance of what was going on beyond his ward, Jiang Qing did things in Mao's name that were detrimental to the interests of the state and the people. Mao's death made it impossible to continue to cover up this situation. Changes therefore became inevitable.

The third event occurred on October 6, 1976. With the support and cooperation of Ye Jianying, Li Xiannian,[3] and others, Hua

Guofeng took resolute measures to arrest the "Gang of Four" and place them under "isolated examination."[4] The "Gang of Four" was the term used by Mao Zedong, who warned Jiang Qing, "You should not act as a gang of four." The "four" he referred to were Jiang Qing, Zhang Chunqiao,[5] Yao Wenyuan,[6] and Wang Hongwen.[7] Mao Zedong's wife, Jiang Qing, was the ringleader of the group. These four were all members of the Political Bureau of the Party Central Committee. Zhang Chunqiao was also a Standing Committee member of the Political Bureau of the Party Central Committee, and a vice-premier of the State Council. Wang Hongwen was a vice-chairman of the Party Central Committee. After being placed under house arrest, the four together were called the "Gang of Four." Hua Guofeng and others drove these evil people who brought calamity to the country and people out of power. The entire nation was relieved to be freed of their leadership and expressed deep joy. Hua thus performed a deed of great merit. In examining this historical turn in China, we must acknowledge that Hua's action was a precondition for later progress.

However, Hua Guofeng, who then wielded the supreme power of the Party and state, did not fundamentally change his stance or respond adequately to the new situation. He continued Mao's personality cult. After all, he had risen to power in the Party by being personally selected by Mao Zedong during the Cultural Revolution. To uphold his position, he could not, and dared not, thoroughly negate the theory, line, principles, and policies of the Cultural Revolution.

Hua was also unwilling to let Deng Xiaoping return to lead the Party and country because Deng was immeasurably higher than he in terms of political and ideological levels, wisdom, and the ability to govern the Party and the country. Consequently, in the months from October 1976 to March 1977, on the one hand, Hua stressed the need to expose and criticize the "Gang of Four," with criticism focusing on the "ultra-Right line" of the "Gang of Four." On the other hand, although the "criticism of Deng Xiaoping" could not, in fact, be carried out thoroughly, he still insisted on "continuing to criticize Deng Xiaoping and attack the Right-deviationist tendency toward reversing the verdicts" of veteran cadres. The man he relied on as his

3

closest assistant was Wang Dongxing,[8] who had risen to become a member of the Party Central Committee during the Cultural Revolution.

Wang became an alternate member of the Political Bureau at the Ninth Party Central Committee in 1969 and a member of the Political Bureau in 1973. He participated in the operation to smash the "Gang of Four." After the "Gang of Four" was destroyed, he became one of the vice-chairmen and the Political Bureau Standing Committee member of the Central Committee, and served concurrently as the director of the General Office of the Party Central Committee and the secretary of the Party Committee of the General Office, the director of the Central Guards Bureau and the secretary of the Party Committee of that bureau, and the political commissar of the 8341 Unit and the secretary of the Party Committee of that unit. Wang also assumed a new post as the director of the General Office of the Committee for Compiling and Publishing Chairman Mao Zedong's Works and the secretary of the Party Committee of the committee. Hua Guofeng authorized him to take charge of the "Central Publicity Department."[9]

Wang Dongxing also led two smaller groups; one was headed by Li Xin,[10] the other by Guo Yufeng.[11] Li Xin's group was in charge of ideology and was responsible for taking care of Mao Zedong's manuscripts and speech records and compiling Mao Zedong's works. (At the time this was a source of great power because one word of Mao Zedong was then regarded "as good as 10,000 words." Whoever wielded this power mastered "truth.") The group headed by Guo Yufeng was in charge of organization and personnel. So, we can say that Wang Dongxing was Hua Guofeng's "deputy commander-in-chief."

These three events and the development of the political situation in the following two to three years necessitated the convocation of the Central Work Conference and shaped the agenda for discussion and resolution at the Conference. Of course, changes in the rest of the world had an extremely significant impact on China, but the impact was less direct.

Unprecedented Cultural Revolution

When the Central Work Conference opened in November 1978, slightly more than two years had elapsed since the downfall of the "Gang of Four." Over a year had also passed since Hua Guofeng declared the end of the Cultural Revolution at the 11th Party Congress. However, the adverse effects of the Cultural Revolution continued. Its monstrous shadows still menaced people. The Cultural Revolution that Mao Zedong, as supreme leader of the Chinese Communist Party, had initiated in 1966 aimed at "continuing the revolution under the dictatorship of the proletariat" against "capitalist roaders inside the Party" and "counterrevolutionary revisionists." The driving force behind the "revolution" were the "five red elements,"[12] "rebels," and red guards.[13] The slogans of the "revolution" were: "to rebel is justified," "bringing down capitalist roaders to the ground and planting one foot on them," "destroying the "four olds" (old ideas, old culture, old customs, and old habits),"[14] and "appraising Legalists and criticizing Confucianists."[15] The basic tactic was to destroy and punish one by one the targets to be overthrown. For over two years after the "Gang of Four" was smashed, the "theory," policies, and slogans of the Cultural Revolution were neither criticized nor removed. Some were still used in the Party's documents. The people's revolutionary action — gathering in Tiananmen Square in April 1976 — was still regarded as a counterrevolutionary incident. At the time this was a force preventing China's society from advancing and, as such, was absolutely unacceptable to the vast number of the ordinary people, cadres, and intellectuals.

**Mao Zedong's Last Years and the "Final Phase"
of the Cultural Revolution**

Many Chinese researchers define the "late Mao era" as beginning in 1966 or slightly earlier when Mao initiated the Cultural Revolution. They share the view that prior to this, although Mao Zedong had made some mistakes, he was on the whole correct. After he initiated the Cultural Revolution, his mistakes predominated. I do not agree with such a demarcation of the late Mao era. I define the late Mao period as beginning in 1971 after Mao dealt with the Lin Biao anti-

Party Clique. Mao was then weak and advanced in age. He was suffering from a variety of diseases and was sometimes muddleheaded. No one outside of Mao's inner circle knew this. Foreigners, the Chinese people, and even senior Party cadres were in the dark. Mao was still worshiped as the top leader of the Party and state and the supreme commander of the army. His remarks were still taken as the "supreme directives." The state of Mao Zedong's health was kept strictly confidential.

Later, I obtained some reliable data concerning Mao Zedong's later years. One was a set of notes taken after the Tiananmen Square incident in 1976 by Mao Yuanxin, Mao's nephew and "liaison official." On April 7, 1976, the third day after the Tiananmen Square incident occurred, Mao Yuanxin reported to Mao Zedong what had happened on Tiananmen Square and voiced his own views before Mao Zedong made important decisions. Mao Yuanxin then took notes of that talk that were later released. It is clear from reading the notes that Mao Zedong's view of the incident was based entirely on the report of one person, namely, Mao Yuanxin, whose own views thereby determined the nature of the Tiananmen Square incident. While listening to his nephew, Mao Zedong expressed his views and position, but his mode of expression was quite simple, mostly using one character: "*hao*" (good), "*shi*" (yes), "*dui*" (right), "*kuai*" (quick), or two characters: "*shi de*" (yes), "*bu shi*" (no), and "*dengbao*" (have it carried in the newspapers), or three characters; "*gan chu qu*" (drive him out). The three characters "*gan chu qu*" meant driving Deng Xiaoping from the Party Central Committee. Mao did not make many complete remarks that day yet one remark was very important, namely, "retain Deng Xiaoping's Party membership to observe how he will behave." I tallied up Mao's words from the notes and found that he uttered fewer than 100 characters in his entire 70-minute talk. But what an important decision he made!

Another piece of information I obtained is material written by Zhang Yufeng,[16] Mao Zedong's personal aide. In this material Zhang wrote:

> In August of 1975, the Chairman was in increasingly poor health, was fidgety, and did not want to speak to or meet others. He

> inhaled oxygen every day. His speech became more inaudible. He had great difficulty eating food and drinking water. I had to feed him food or medicines mouthful by mouthful. Previously, he could eat one or two liang of rice a day (20 liang equals one kilogram). But in April and May of 1976, he could take only one spoonful or two spoonfuls of rice per meal. Furthermore, often because of difficulty in swallowing, he choked and sometimes coughed for a long time. It is precisely during that period that the Chairman said meaningfully many times: "I am an idol for exhibition." Once the Chairman suffered from bronchitis and was coughing very hard. A nurse put a clinical thermometer into his mouth, which made the chairman cough, and he bit off half of the thermometer and swallowed the mercury. Three days later, the Chairman discharged the half thermometer in his stool."

If someone who worked closely at Mao's side had not related this, such a thing would be unimaginable.

I also know of another episode. In 1974 when a meeting of the Political Bureau of the Party Central Committee was held, Mao Zedong had blurred eyesight from an eye ailment. The members of the Political Bureau shook hands with him one by one. While shaking his hand, Jiang Qing said, "How do you do, Chairman." Mao Zedong asked her: "Who are you?" Someone standing beside him said hurriedly: "This is Comrade Jiang Qing." This material shows that Mao Zedong in his last years could not even recognize the voice of his wife of many years.

The late Mao era basically coincided with the last phase of the Cultural Revolution. September 1971, the beginning of the late Mao era, also marks the last phase of the Cultural Revolution, the phase in which the genuine revolutionary cadres loyal to the people headed by Zhou Enlai, Ye Jianying, and – later – Deng Xiaoping waged resolute struggles against the Jiang Qing Clique. This phase marked the end of the short phase, from 1969 to 1971, in which the Lin Biao clique fought for power with the Jiang Qing clique. The late Mao era and the final phase of the Cultural Revolution ended with the death of Mao Zedong and the downfall of the "Gang of Four." In the five years of the final phase of the Cultural Revolution, Mao Zedong used people from both camps. From January to October of 1975, he let Deng Xiaoping take charge of the work at the central level for ten months before siding with the Jiang Qing clique in launching the movement to "criticize Deng Xiaoping." Nevertheless, of the fairly large number of veteran cadres liberated in these five years, some were allowed to continue working but some were overthrown once again because of their close relations with Deng Xiaoping. After all, the movement to "criticize Deng Xiaoping" lasted a very short time. The death of Mao Zedong changed the course of history.

"Two Whatevers" and Opposing "Two Whatevers"

After the downfall of the Gang of Four, Hua Guofeng led the Party in the final quarter of 1976 and throughout 1977. Hua Guofeng rose to prominence during the Cultural Revolution. When I went to Hunan in 1961 to carry out investigations, he was serving as a member of the secretariat of the Hunan Provincial Party Committee, in charge of financial and trade affairs. In 1968, he served as a vice-chairman of the Hunan Provincial Revolutionary Committee. He was elected to the Party Central Committee at the 9th Party Congress in 1969. Shortly after the Lin Biao Incident, he was transferred from Hunan to work in the Party Central Committee. From 1973 he served as a deputy head of the State Council Business Group and attended Political Bureau meetings as a nonvoting member. He was elected to the Political Bureau of the Party Central Committee at the 10th Party Congress in 1973, and became vice-chairman of the Party Central Committee and premier of the State Council in May 1976 after the 1976 Tiananmen Incident.

After Hua, Ye Jianying, and Li Xiannian smashed the Gang of Four in October 1976, a vast number of cadres hoped that Deng Xiaoping would be reinstated, but Hua would not give up power. Before the downfall of the Gang of Four Mao Zedong had chosen him to serve as the first vice-chairman of the Party Central Committee. He therefore considered himself Mao's handpicked successor. This circumstance led to the debate over the "two whatevers," a well-known term in Party history. It originated in Hua Guofeng's own speeches, articles issued with his approval, or the speeches of other leaders of the Party Central Committee delivered with his approval.

There are three versions of the "two whatevers." In sequential order, the earliest version appeared in the speech delivered by Wu

De[17] at the Third Session of the Fourth National People's Congress held on November 30, 1976, one month after the downfall of the "Gang of Four." Wu declared, "We must try to do whatever Chairman Mao Zedong instructed and whatever the Chairman decided, and try to do them well." When the Tiananmen Incident occurred on April 5, 1976, Wu De was serving as the first secretary of the Beijing Municipal Party Committee and the chairman of the Beijing Municipal Revolutionary Committee. After the downfall of the "Gang of Four," support for the rehabilitation of those criticized in the 1976 Tiananmen Incident both inside and outside the Party grew very strong. Wu made these remarks to counter this support, hoping to suppress the people's voice by waving the banner of Mao Zedong.

On February 7, 1977, the *People's Daily*, *Red Flag* magazine, and the *Liberation Army Daily* jointly issued an editorial titled "Study Documents Carefully and Grasp the Key Link." The editorial asserted: "We must resolutely uphold whatever policy decisions Chairman Mao made; and we must unswervingly follow whatever instructions Chairman Mao gave." Wang Dongxing finalized the editorial before submitting it to Hua Guofeng for approval. This is the second version, which is considered the standard one. In his speech at the Central Work Conference held in March of 1977, Hua Guofeng said: "We must uphold whatever policy decisions Chairman Mao made, and we must put a stop to whatever words and actions damage Chairman Mao's image." This became the third version.

The three versions are essentially identical despite minor differences. The term "two whatevers" is very clear in connotation. Opposing the "two whatevers" means disregarding the premise of the "two whatevers," viewing issues on the basis of facts and proceeding from the reality, spelling out that "practice is the sole criterion for testing truth," and opposing Mao Zedong's speeches and decisions as the criteria for determining truth.

But from the time when the "two whatevers" was put forward, the debate for and against the "two whatevers" was not only a debate over principle, but had specific contents. In practice, the debate was restricted to the instructions Mao Zedong gave during the Cultural Revolution, particularly those Mao gave while seriously ill. During that period, old and weak as he was, Mao Zedong was unable to carry out normal thinking and work. It was during that period that he made many important policy decisions. For example, he decided to launch the movement to "criticize Deng Xiaoping and strike back at the right-deviationist tendency toward reversing the verdicts." Another example, after the 1976 Tiananmen Incident, was his decision to remove Deng Xiaoping from all posts inside and outside the Party. Hua Guofeng was the successor hand-picked by Mao Zedong during his illness. After the downfall of the "Gang of Four," Hua needed to emphasize the "two whatevers" to uphold his position, whereas the vast majority of cadres and people demanded the reversal of the wrong verdict on the Tiananmen Incident. Opposition to the "two whatevers" was imperative in order to redress the cases of cadres who were framed and falsely accused and to correct Mao Zedong's erroneous guiding ideology of the Cultural Revolution.

As for those upholding the "two whatevers," after the two newspapers and one magazine jointly issued the February 7, 1977, editorial, Hua Guofeng convened a central work conference from March 10 to 22. In his report to the conference, he reiterated the "two whatevers" principle in the language of the third version referred to above. He pronounced the Tiananmen Incident a "counterrevolutionary incident," and also expressed the view that it was "correct" to "continue criticizing Deng Xiaoping and striking back at the right-deviationist tendency toward reversing verdicts." Li Xin, an assistant to Wang Dongxing, made a major speech at the conference, "Criticizing Deng Xiaoping," in a blatant attempt to obstruct Deng's return to work.

At this same conference, however, Chen Yun,[18] Wang Zhen,[19] and others opposing the "two whatevers" resisted Hua Guofeng's actions and earnestly proposed that Deng Xiaoping should be reinstated. On April 10, 1977, Deng Xiaoping wrote a letter to the Party Central Committee, sharply criticizing the "two whatevers" principle. Enclosed with this letter was another letter Deng Xiaoping had written to the Party Central Committee, dated October 10, 1976. On May 3, the Party Central Committee distributed Deng's letter. This marked a great victory for the forces opposing the "two whatevers." It was the result of the struggles waged by many veteran comrades inside the Party and the vast number of cadres and people. Hua Guofeng, the principal leader of the Central Committee, used a passive approach and delaying tactics to resist these pressures, but support for the reinstatement of Deng Xiaoping was growing. This compelled Hua Guofeng to put the issue of Deng's return high on the agenda. On the one hand, the 1977 work conference still affirmed the movement to "criticize Deng Xiaoping and attack the right deviationist tendency toward reversing verdicts." On the other hand, it also announced that at the Third Plenum of the 10th Party Congress, a formal decision would be made to let Deng Xiaoping come back to work. Distributing Deng Xiaoping's two letters was a step taken after the conference.

The Third Plenum of the 10th Party Congress, convened from July 16 to 21, subsequently confirmed Hua Guofeng as the chairman of the Party Central Committee and also adopted the decision to restore Deng Xiaoping to leadership positions. As a result, Deng Xiaoping resumed his posts as a vice-chairman of the Party Central Committee and a vice-chairman of the Military Commission of the Party Central Committee. At the plenum Hua Guofeng continued to preach his "two whatevers" and clung to the theory and line of the Cultural Revolution. Deng Xiaoping also addressed the plenum, stressing the necessity of having a comprehensive and correct understanding of Mao Zedong Thought. Both sides made their respective viewpoints known.

A Conversation with Deng Xiaoping

In mid-May of 1977, Feng Lanrui, wife of Comrade Li Chang,[20] and a colleague of mine at the State Council Political Research Office,[21] told me that on May 12, Deng Xiaoping asked Fang Yi[22] and Li Chang to come to his residence so that he might air his views on science, education, and other areas. This indicated that Deng Xiaoping would return to work very soon. Feng Lanrui suggested that the Political Research Office should contact Deng Xiaoping, too. After the movement to "criticize Deng Xiaoping" was launched, the Political Research Office had lost contact with Deng. Everyone became very excited at learning the new information about him and awaited his official reinstatement.

11

Through contacts, another leading official of the Political Research Office and I arranged to visit Deng Xiaoping on May 24. Wang Zhen, then a vice-premier of the State Council, was also present. The talk lasted one and a half hours, during which Deng Xiaoping spoke on many issues. He seriously criticized the "two whatevers," noting, "the 'two whatevers' were unacceptable. If this principle were correct, there could be no justification for my rehabilitation; nor could there be any for the statement that the activities of the masses on Tiananmen were reasonable."

Deng also said, "The Chairman said he too had made mistakes. If we say that every word of his is correct, then there could have been no mistakes. This is an important theoretical question, a question of whether or not we are adhering to materialism. A thoroughgoing materialist should approach this question in the way advocated by the Chairman. Neither Marx nor Lenin put forward any 'whatever' doctrine, nor did Lenin, nor did the Chairman himself. Mao Zedong Thought is an ideological system. We must hold high, study, and apply Mao Zedong Thought as an ideological system. I waged struggles against Lin Biao. I criticized him for vulgarizing Mao Zedong Thought instead of viewing it as a system."

Deng Xiaoping referred to the public discussion about his return to work. He said that it had been settled that he would come back to work. He also said humorously, "Anyway I will continue to be a senior official." As to the division of his work, he said that he would take charge of the army, but did not want to continue to be in charge of foreign affairs. Yet except for taking part in activities involving important foreign affairs, he no longer wanted to spend part of his time on foreign affairs. He said that he was then considering science and education.

Then Deng made a lengthy comment on science and technology. He said,"The key to achieving modernization is the development of science and technology. And unless we pay special attention to education, it will be impossible to develop science and technology. Empty talk will get our modernization program nowhere. We must have knowledge and trained personnel. Without them, how can we develop our science and technology? If we are backward in those areas, how can we advance? Now it appears that China is fully twenty years behind developed countries in science, technology and education. So far as scientific research personnel are concerned, the United States has 1.2 million and the Soviet Union, 900,000, while we have only some 150,000. As early as the Meiji Restoration, the Japanese began to expend a great deal of effort on science, technology, and education. Right now we must work in the spirit of the Meiji Restoration and Peter the Great. To promote scientific and technological work, we must improve education simultaneously."

Speaking of the need to create conditions for researchers to do research, he said, "We must create inside the Party an atmosphere of respect for knowledge and respect for trained personnel."

While talking about his possible work assignment, he expressed a desire to take charge of scientific, technological, and educational work. A few days after he was formally reinstated, he told us that he had volunteered to take charge of scientific, technological, and educational work, and that he had obtained approval from the Party Central Committee.

I took detailed notes of this talk and processed them. The processed text was later included in Volume Two of the *Selected Works of Deng Xiaoping*, titled "The Two Whatevers Do Not Accord with Marxism" and "Respect Knowledge, Respect Trained Personnel."

Deng Xiaoping Was Reinstated and Yet the Great Task to Draw Lessons from the Cultural Revolution Has Not Been Fulfilled

The Third Plenum of the 10th Central Committee held in July 1977 formally made the decision to restore Deng Xiaoping's positions. Meanwhile, Hua Guofeng still clung to the "two whatevers." To wage a tit-for-tat struggle against it, Deng Xiaoping also made his own views known. In August the 11th Party Congress was held. The First Plenum of the 11th Party Central Committee, convened immediately after the Party Congress, elected Hua Guofeng chairman of the Party Central Committee, and Ye Jianying, Deng Xiaoping, Li Xiannian, and Wang Dongxing vice-chairmen. These five people constituted the Standing Committee of the Political Bureau of the Party Central Committee.

The issue of Deng Xiaoping's reinstatement was thus resolved for the second time. But Hua Guofeng's report at the plenum contained a 2,000-character preface in praise of Mao Zedong, and another 5,000-characters describing the "11th line struggle" Mao Zedong waged against the "Gang of Four."[23] Hua simultaneously affirmed the criticism of Peng Dehuai in 1959 and the criticism of Liu Shaoqi during the Cultural Revolution as correct lines waged by the Party. Hua Guofeng described as the 11th line struggle Mao Zedong's criticism of Jiang Qing and her followers and Mao's personal struggle against the "Gang of Four." That meant, as a matter of course, that he accepted the correctness of the 10 line struggles. Then how could he rehabilitate Peng Dehuai and Liu Shaoqi? With this approach they could not thoroughly negate the Cultural Revolution that lasted over 10 years or draw the conclusion that China must carry out restructuring.

In the report delivered at the Party's Eleventh Party Congress Hua did not emphasize the four characters *"liang ge fan shi"* (the two whatevers), and he defended the "theory," the general line, and the slogans of the Cultural Revolution. Some important policies such as the policy in rural areas of criticizing the "fixing of farm output quotas for each household" should have been changed. But he did not want to do so, because Mao Zedong had been explicitly and resolutely against fixing farm output quotas for each household. Hua Guofeng also continued to support Mao's personality cult, but he could no longer use the "two whatevers" to block Deng Xiaoping's reinstatement. Yet the adverse judgment on the Tiananmen Incident in 1976 had not yet been reversed. On the issue of organizational line, there was no sign of vigorously rehabilitating the veteran cadres persecuted during the Cultural Revolution. On the contrary, many formulations used during the Cultural Revolution continued to be used. Wang Dongxing rose to the position of a vice-chairman of the Party Central Committee. Furthermore, he continued to wield the great power of publicity. Hu Yaobang,[24] recommended by Ye Jianying and others, first served as the vice-president of the Party School of the Party Central Committee and was appointed the head of the Organization Department of the Party Central Committee in November of 1977. This was a great blessing.

In short, although Deng Xiaoping was reinstated, there were still many unresolved problems that needed to be solved as soon as possible. This was why a debate among senior cadres of the Party to seek solutions was needed.

The Great Debate over the Criterion for Testing Truth

The debate about the question of the criterion for testing truth began in May 1978 when the *Guangming Daily* carried the article titled "Practice Is the Sole Criterion for Testing Truth." The Central Work Conference was convened in November of the same year, with only half a year between the two. We can say that this article and the Work Conference shared the same historical background. At the time the article "Practice Is the Sole Criterion for Testing Truth" was published, it was said this issue should be discussed for six months. Specifically, the discussion about the criterion for testing truth constituted a key reason for the convocation of the Central Work Conference. The result of the discussion served as the major guiding perspective for the Central Work Conference. Moreover, thanks to the efforts of Ye Jianying and Deng Xiaoping, the discussion about the criterion for testing truth made it possible to convene the Central Work Conference.

To support such a judgment, I offer the following historical facts. First, publication of that article by the *Guangming Daily* in May 1978 attracted the attention of Ye Jianying, who agreed with the views expressed in the article. After the publication of the article, the *People's Daily* and the *Liberation Army Daily* reprinted it immediately. The magazine *Red Flag,* however, followed Wang Dongxing's instructions "not to become involved" in the discussion. *Red Flag* published another article, "Study 'On Practice' Again," which also mentioned the issue of the criterion for testing truth. Yet the article erased edges and corners and did not touch upon the opposition to the "two whatevers." So, in the course of soliciting opinions about it, some people expressed opposition and made critical comments. The leading official of *Red Flag's* editorial board submitted this article to the Party Central Committee for examination, where it was passed on to Ye Jianying.

Then, enlightened by the success in the State Council meeting to discuss guidelines which was held with Li Xiannian presiding, Ye Jianying proposed at a meeting of the Standing Committee that the Party Central Committee should hold a meeting to discuss theoretical guidelines and settle this question.   On other occasions, he also proposed that the article carried by the *Guangming Daily* should be printed and distributed.   Many people, including me, had previously assumed that his proposal would be implemented at a work conference to discuss theoretical guidelines held in 1979. As a matter of fact, his proposal materialized at the Central Work Conference. This can be proved by the remarks Deng Xiaoping had made prior to the Central Work Conference.

At first Deng Xiaoping was not very clear about the origin of the process of drafting the article titled "Practice Is the Sole Criterion for Testing Truth." Viewed from the two talks he had had with me some time previously, we can see that he did not know that Hu Yaobang had arranged for this article to be drafted n the Party School of the Party Central Committee.   Nor did he have an accurate understanding of how the *Guangming Daily* published the article. He heard about the contribution of an article by Hu Fuming,[25] a resident of Nanjing. But he presumed that the contributor was a worker in Shanghai. He had a very high opinion of the article.

It was precisely on the 30th of May, the month when the article was published, that Deng Xiaoping delivered a speech at the All-Army Conference on Political Work. That speech was aimed at the then director of the Publicity Department of the General Political Department of the People's Liberation Army (PLA), who objected to the fact that the expressions used at the Political Work Conference of the PLA were not in total agreement with those of Mao Zedong and Hua Guofeng. The director also requested that the discussion about the matter be held at a meeting of the Party Committee of the General Political Department and at the Conference on Political Work. In the speech Deng Xiaoping said by way of criticizing some people, "Now a problem has cropped up—whether or not practice is the sole criterion for testing truth. This is simply baffling."

On another occasion Deng had a talk with the leading officials of the State Council Research Office. In my notebook I did not mark the exact date of the talk, but I am sure that it was sometime in May or June. Hu Qiaomu[26] reported to Deng Xiaoping that Zhang Pinghua[27] had told the secretaries of the provincial Party committees attending a conference on higher education held in Beijing that "there are two opinions on the article titled 'Practice Is the Sole Criterion for Testing Truth.' One is that the article is very good and the other is that the article is very bad. A very important article must be analyzed. Not all articles carried in the *People's Daily* are accurate. After returning home, please discuss this and air your views freely, whether you agree or disagree. Don't suppress debates."

Deng Xiaoping asked if all the secretaries from the various provincial Party committees had attended the conference. Hu Qiaomu did not reply to this question. Then he reported that Xiong Fu[28] had visited Hu Yaobang, saying that *Red Flag* was successful and relatively cautious in publishing theoretical articles. Then Xiong told Hu Yaobang that a cautious approach must be taken with regard to theoretical issues. Hu did not agree, noting that in putting forward a theoretical viewpoint one must be courageous. Hu Qiaomu also reported that at the recent conference on publicity the report originally contained the words "the Cultural Revolution is very timely and necessary." However, the heads of the publicity departments did not agree with this view. Having heard the briefing, Deng Xiaoping said, "This matter had been handled very well indeed. Just go ahead with the debate, but none of us should put a label on others. Instead we should hold theoretical discussions. We should proceed from reality and should not indulge in empty talk."

On still another occasion, probably slightly earlier than the previous talk, Deng Xiaoping said to us, "Now there are many different views. There have been different views on the articles pertaining to the issue of 'to each according to his work.' Especially there have been different views of the article stating that practice is the sole criterion for testing truth. The view that practice is the sole criterion for testing truth is widely acknowledged as a basic tenet of Marxism. This is not debatable." In this light, he said that to solve problems, it was imperative to take a broad theoretical perspective. He told us, "The Chinese Academy of Social Sciences is an institution studying and expounding theories. You should not make concessions

17

theoretically. I do not advise you to give in theoretically, because giving in will lead to the loss of principle." In this talk, he said that in his view, the Party Central Committee should discuss this question and clarify it. Maybe this was the "origin" of the decision to convene the Central Work Conference.

Of course, Hua Guofeng also had his own needs and considerations for convening the Central Work Conference. In the second part of a report, "Situation and Tasks," delivered to the 11th Party Congress, Hua spoke of 8 questions. Later the 2nd Plenum of the 11th Party Central Committee and the 1st Plenary Session of the 5th National People's Congress were convened. In 1978, Hua himself felt that some changes were necessary. He came to realize that from 1979 the focus of the Party's work should be shifted to economic development. Ye Jianying, Deng Xiaoping, and Li Xiannian all agreed. Furthermore, a very long State Council meeting to discuss guidelines was held, with Li Xiannian presiding. Since Hua Guofeng had such a need, the Central Work Conference was convened very soon. The questions that Ye Jianying and Deng Xiaoping raised could be presented along with Hua's agenda for discussing economic development. For several months discussions of the criterion for testing truth continued — in the academic community, press circles, among "dukes and princes"[29] from all over the country, and army generals — that provided support for placing the issue on the Central Work Conference's agenda. I believe that Ye and Deng must have made it clear to Hua Guofeng beforehand that they believed it important to discuss the issue, but Hua would have had some understanding of his own of the importance of discussing that issue. I heard nothing specific from Hua about this. The above thoughts represent my analysis and judgment. Perhaps a better understanding of real circumstances will emerge from additional recollections.

Participants in the Central Work Conference

Thus I learned that a central work conference would be held soon, and I received the notice to attend. I went to the Jingxi Hotel to check in before the conference was held. Upon registering, I received the general list of participants as well as a list of participants divided into various groups. I hastened to "study" the list of participants carefully, one by one.

Twenty-three full members and three alternate members of the Political Bureau of the Party Central Committee elected at the First Plenum of the 11th Party Central Committee had been invited to attend the conference. Among these full members were five Standing Committee members of the Political Bureau, namely, Hua Guofeng, Ye Jianying, Deng Xiaoping, Li Xiannian, and Wang Dongxing. The eighteen others were Wei Guoqing,[30] Wu Lanfu,[31] Fang Yi, Liu Bocheng,[32] Xu Shiyou,[33] Ji Dengkui,[34] Su Zhenhua,[35] Li Desheng,[36] Wu De, Yu Qiuli,[37] Zhang Tingfa,[38] Chen Yonggui,[39] Chen Xilian,[40] Geng Biao,[41] Nie Rongzhen,[42] Ni Zhifu,[43] Xu Xiangqian,[44] and Peng Chong.[45] The alternate members were Chen Muhua,[46] Zhao Ziyang,[47] and Sai Fuding.[48]

I was familiar with the positions of these people in normal times and had a fairly good impression of most of them, but I strongly resented the behavior of some of them during the Cultural Revolution. Wu De was a good example. Although some on the name list, like Chen Yonggui, were in power during the rule of the "Gang of Four," they did not arouse strong popular indignation. I thought that after Chen Yonggui was promoted to such a high position he became giddy. All his comments were directed to support the campaign to "learn from Dazhai." Dazhai must be studied not only in agriculture, but also politically. However, I personally heard him make comments that showed he recognized the priority that should be given to production. He just had a distorted model for agricultural production.

It seemed to me that several members of the Political Bureau lacked ability and independent opinions and were incapable of making significant contributions. But they were not the cause of the failure. Of course, having read this name list, I noticed one point very clearly: there existed a great difference between the members of the 11th Political Bureau and those of the 10th Political Bureau. Since Deng Xiaoping served as a vice-chairman of the Party Central Committee, he would certainly be able to control the situation in the conference and make it a complete success. The name list also contained Ye Jianying, whose role in smashing the "Gang of Four" reminded me of

Mao Zedong's assessment of his role in the Long March. In addition to Deng Xiaoping and Ye Jianying, there were Nie Rongzhen and others under whose leadership I had served. Furthermore, I had served under Deng Xiaoping and Nie Rongzhen for quite a long time. The name list of the members of the Political Bureau also contained quite a few people with whom I had contacts and whom I understood quite well.

Also listed were the Standing Committee members of the Military Commission of the Party Central Committee, Wang Zhen and Su Yu; the vice-chairmen of the Standing Committee of the National People's Congress, Chen Yun, Tan Zhenlin, Li Jingquan, Zhang Dingcheng, Cai Chang, Deng Yinchao, Liao Chengzhi, Ji Pengfei, and Zhou Jianren; the vice-premiers of the State Council, Gu Mu, Kang Shi'en and Wang Zhen; the Vice-chairmen of the National Committee of the Chinese People's Political Consultative Conference, Song Renqiong, Kang Keqing, Wang Shoudao, and Yang Jingren; the president of the Supreme People's Court, Jiang Hua; and the procurator of the Supreme People's Procuratorate, Huang Huoqing. These are what are known today as the "*san fu liang gao* (three types of vice and two types of supreme). Those in this category had all been invited to attend the conference. Of the people included in the name list, it was not necessary to mention Chen Yun. I also had a favorable impression of many others, who were well-respected senior revolutionaries. I had also worked together with some of them. I considered the material Gu Mu had offered recently at a State Council meeting to discuss guidelines quite good. Only a few who had praised Hua Guofeng to the skies and supported his personality cult left a bad impression on me.

From the Chinese Academy of Sciences there was Fang Yi and Li Chang. Li Chang was an old friend of mine. When I was transferred to the State Science and Technology Commission to serve as a vice-minister, Fang Yi served as the minister in charge of the commission. From the Chinese Academy of Social Sciences there was Hu Qiaomu. The presidents and vice-presidents of the two academies were appointed by the National People's Congress. Only one person from each unit was invited to attend the Central Work Conference. Yet two members of the Chinese Academy of Sciences were invited. To my understanding, this was because Fang Yi was a Political Bureau member. That was why Li Chang was invited too.

Next were the leaders of various provinces, municipalities under the direct administration of the central government and autonomous regions, as well as various military area commands. From the name list I could see that both the No. 1 and No. 2 leaders of each locality were invited to the conference. Next were the leaders of the departments of the Party Central Committee, state departments at the central level and the departments directly attached to the Military Commission of the Party Central Committee. From the name list I could find that either the No. 1 or No. 2 leader of each department was invited to attend the conference. I was familiar with many of these people, and had a good understanding of their views except for those belonging to the army system.

Two hundred nineteen people were on the list. From studying the list, I had two impressions. The first was that the conference was large and of high quality. The other was that the participants in the conference were of very high quality. Some central work conferences convened in our Party's history were much larger. For instance, the 7,000-person conference held in 1962 was very large.[49] Yet many conferences were smaller in scale. All Political Bureau members were invited to attend. Consequently the conference was big enough to match the level of an enlarged meeting of the Political Bureau.

Most participants were veteran comrades persecuted during the Cultural Revolution. Although some incurred the displeasure of the "Gang of Four" when it was in power and some had supported the "two whatevers," they were not the majority. Therefore, after reading the list, I had a pretty good idea of what would happen. I expected there would be a serious debate, and I thought the conference would accomplish a great deal.

I made marks on the list as to whether the participants were the Central Committee members elected at the Eleventh Party Congress. I counted the members and alternate members of the 11th Central Committee who were on the name list and found that there were 137 such members and alternate members, accounting for 63 percent of those invited to attend — nearly two thirds of the total. They comprised 42 percent of the 333 members and alternate members of

21

the 11th Party Central Committee. The list contained 82 people who were not members of the 11th Party Central Committee, or slightly less than 37 percent of the 219 people invited. Those who were not members or alternate members of the 11th Party Central Committee were all veteran Party members taking up leading posts in various localities, army units, and departments at the central level.

So far as I could remember, those who were members and alternate members elected at the 8th Party Congress convened in 1956 included Xi Zhongxun,[50] Song Renqiong,[51] Huang Huoqing, Hu Qiaomu, Hang Guang, Hong Xuezhi, Jiang Nanxiang, and Li Chang. There were also those who were elected Party Central Committee members at the Second Plenum of the 8th Party Congress, such as Wang Renzhong.[52] The members and alternate members of the 8th Party Central Committee who would attend the conference accounted for 29.6 percent of all participants. All this indicated that this was a very high-level conference.

While reading the list, I anticipated that some people invited to attend would be unable to come because of illness. The number of the participants would be fewer than 219. Judging from the group name lists, I saw that they would add up to 211. Adding the five Standing Committee members, who would not be included in small group discussions, the total number of participants would be 216. Hua Guofeng said on the day when the conference opened that 12 people had asked for leave. This was the case before the conference was held. How many people were really present, and who was present and who was absent? I am uncertain because I neither obtained relevant data nor specially spent time studying the matter.

CHAPTER 2

THE FIRST GENERAL MEETING AND DISCUSSION ABOUT SHIFTING THE FOCUS OF WORK

Speech by Hua Guofeng

Although the Central Work Conference lasted a long time, only four plenary meetings were held. No preparatory meeting was held for the conference. Immediately after the opening ceremony Hua Guofeng delivered a speech in which he declared the conference open and announced the three topics to be discussed. The first was how to further implement the principle of taking agriculture as the foundation of the national economy and promptly promote agricultural production. Two papers on this topic had been prepared for discussion at the conference: "The Decision on Accelerating the Agricultural Growth Rate" and "The Rules Governing the Work of Rural People's Communes" (Draft for Trial Implementation). The second topic was arrangements for the plan for national economic development for 1979 and 1980. The conference had a document on this topic. The third was the speech delivered by Vice-Chairman Li Xiannian at the State Council meeting to discuss guidelines.

After announcing the three topics, Hua Guofeng noted that this was a very important conference. He added that before discussing the three topics, the participants should discuss one question: namely, under the guidance of the general line for the new period, to begin January 1979, how to shift the focus of the whole country's work to the socialist modernization drive. He announced that the participants would discuss the question of the shift in the focus of work in the first two to three days of the conference and that the entire meeting was expected to last twenty or more days. He also told the participants that they would be divided into six discussion groups.

There seemed to be no secretary general for the conference. The name list did not have the name of a secretary general and at the conference I never heard anyone mention the secretary general.

According to some articles, Wang Dongxing served as the secretary general, but I did not read or hear anything that might indicate that this was so. In his speech at the opening ceremony, Hua Guofeng said what a secretary general ordinarily says. None of the four vice-chairmen addressed the opening ceremony. Hua Guofeng's speech was not long, in fact less than 5,000 characters. In the course of his speech, he departed from the text, and according to my notes, these extempore remarks contained almost 2,000 additional characters. He spoke slowly for one hour or a bit longer. I listened carefully. I was then not as hard of hearing as I am today. I heard him very clearly. I noticed that in his speech he no longer mentioned the "two whatevers."

I did not have excessively high expectations for his speech. The reason why I listened to his speech carefully was that I wanted to learn about the objective situation and to find out what level of understanding he had achieved. I also noticed that in his speech he once again used the wording of the 11th line struggle. As I mentioned above, Hua Guofeng used such a concept at the 11th Party Congress convened in August of 1977. In his speech at the Central Work Conference, he still used this wording, which grated on my ears. This was because mentioning the 11th line struggle meant affirming all previous 10 line struggles and affirming the eighth struggle against the "Peng Dehuai Right opportunist anti-Party clique and the ninth struggle against Liu Shaoqi's counterrevolutionary line." These two line struggles involved a large number of veteran comrades who were then alive and had been criticized and persecuted during the Cultural Revolution. In the early period of the Cultural Revolution, the rebels used expressions like the "Liu Shaoqi-Deng Xiaoping Line." In 1978, many people still remembered this.

Hua's words regarding the ninth line struggle represented by Liu Shaoqi meant acknowledging the struggle against the "erroneous Liu Shaoqi-Deng Xiaoping Line." This had profound implications, because by using such a term, he could elevate himself because he "had never committed mistakes in line struggles in history and had been always correct," or could belittle or suppress many veteran comrades who had committed "political mistakes" in line struggles. He did not say this clearly, however, and such conclusions could only have been deduced indirectly from his comments. Moreover, even if that were so, he could be excused, as what he said was merely repeating what was in the report delivered to the 11th Party Congress, and the text of his speech was written by skillful writers. I only observed him and considered what he said. I did not want to lay bare the truth, as this would have upset many cadres.

Regarding the shift in the focus of work announced by Hua Guofeng, some people today may misunderstand and assume that he referred to the shift from "taking class struggle as the key link" to the socialist modernization drive. If he had stated that the focus of the Party's work should be shifted from Mao Zedong's emphasis on "taking class struggle as the key link" to an emphasis on the tasks of development, that would have been viewed as a matter of great historical significance. Yet his speech did not touch upon such a matter of principle. Only after citing the three topics for the conference did Hua Guofeng say, "the Political Bureau of the Party Central Committee has decided that before discussing the above three topics, we should discuss one issue, that is, under the guidance of the general line and overall task for the new period, from January of next year, to shift the focus of the work of the whole Party to the socialist modernization drive."

Hua told the participants in the Central Work Conference that the Standing Committee of the Politbureau and the Politbureau itself unanimously believed that to conform to the development of domestic and foreign situations, it was entirely necessary promptly and resolutely to end the mass movement to expose and criticize the "Gang of Four" and to shift the focus of Party work to the socialist modernization drive. Then he asked the participants to consider how much the movement to expose and criticize the "Gang of Four" had accomplished. He said, "Properly assessing the development of the movement constitutes an important basis for us to propose shifting the focus of the work of the whole Party." He then offered his personal evaluation, saying that the mass movement to expose and criticize the "Gang of Four" would achieve its historical mission and successfully conclude by the end of 1978.

What Hua Guofeng put forward in his speech was only the issue of the phase of work. He said that historical experience indicated that "once major issues in one phase are resolved, the phase will evolve into a new one." The problems that he mentioned as needing solution were the problems destined to crop up on the basis of the work principle formulated for the period starting in 1979 and those arising with regard to specific work in specific conditions. He then expounded on the domestic economic situation and the international situation before eventually returning to the issue of shifting the focus of work. He said:

> The participants will spend the first three days of the current conference discussing the issue of shifting the focus of Party work. Starting from January of next year, the shift will be practiced in the work of the whole Party. Is this practice proper or not? How will the Party Committees at all levels implement this shift in their work? With the shift, what major matters shall we focus on next year? How will our Party's ideological building and organizational building, our work in agriculture, industry, finance and trade, science and technology, culture and education, military affairs, politics and legal affairs, and the work of mass organizations for workers, youth and women, adapt to the shift? Please offer your advice, think about ways and air your views freely, so that we can draw on collective wisdom and absorb all useful ideas. After this the participants will discuss the three topics mentioned above. These discussions will all focus on the central issue of shifting the focus of the work of whole Party to the socialist modernization drive.

These remarks demonstrated that the shift of the focus of work he stressed referred to the specific questions of how to do specific work in specific time and in specific conditions.

At this point in his speech, Hua interposed a paragraph of remarks pertaining to the question of whether the focus should be shifted or not. He said, "As for the 'double attacks,'[1] I have considered carrying out a movement from the highest organizations to the grass-roots unit and from the grass-roots units to the highest organizations." He said, "I have considered this question many times. I think this practice is not good because at the mention of carrying out a movement, the leaderships will once again concentrate attention on the movement, which will impede all provinces and municipalities in promoting the modernization drive." He said he had considered "that all provinces and municipalities may carry out the movement in line with their local conditions [and] attack the already-exposed elements," yet "we should not adopt this approach nationwide and should not carry out a nationwide movement," because once a movement was launched, either central authorities or local authorities would have to spend either half a year or a whole year on it. It was better for the whole Party to concentrate its attention on the modernization drive.

Hua said, "We should advocate doing things within the range of a legal system. Holding mass criticism meetings is necessary, but should be subject to approval by court. Don't parade somebody through the streets on a truck to expose him before the public. We should not adopt this method." Here, what he spoke of was the struggle against the lackeys of the "Gang of Four." "Of course, we do not mean that the movement cannot be carried out. For example, rectification meetings can be held in the course of consolidating the leadership at various levels." He also said, "systematic exposure and criticism should be carried out for a long time and, although Wang Ming's line has been criticized for a long time, it is still necessary to criticize it now." Today, I copied this paragraph of his remarks from my notebook to show that he had repeatedly considered this issue.

Then Hua discussed the issue of economic development, expounding on the domestic economic situation and the favorable international conditions. He emphasized the need to become skilled at using these circumstances to absorb foreign funds and technology. (In finalizing the text of his speech, he accepted Li Xiannian's view by adding before this sentence the words "on the basis of acting independently and keeping the initiative in our own hands, and self-reliance.")

At this point he inserted some other comments. He began by saying, "Because of the interference and sabotage by Lin Biao and the 'Gang of Four,' some people dare not import goods. Once they import goods, they are vilified for 'betraying the country' and 'worshiping foreign things and toadying to foreign powers.'" Hearing this remark reminded me of the well-known "snail incident." During the Cultural Revolution, while a Chinese company negotiated with a United States company on importing color TV tubes, the

American, in a good-will gesture, presented a delicate snail-shaped carved decoration to their Chinese counterparts. In Jiang Qing's view, this gift was meant to satirize China for its low growth rate. She said that U.S. imperialists meant to mock China's economy, implying that it grew as slowly as a snail crawled. She severely reprimanded the Chinese negotiators for accepting such a gift and ordered that the gift should be returned and protests lodged against the American negotiators. Consequently, the development of China's TV industry was delayed for many years.

Hua Guofeng gave several specific examples. He commented that during the Cultural Revolution, seeing China in chaos, foreigners did not dare support China with funds and technology. After the downfall of the "Gang of Four," China first signed the Sino-Japanese long-term trade agreement, valued at 20 billion U.S. dollars. After signing the agreement, the Japanese deemed the amount of 20 billion dollars too small and proposed increasing the amount to 100 billion dollars from 1980 to 1990. After negotiations, Comrade Deng Xiaoping agreed to increase the amount by 10 to 20 billion dollars beyond the initial 20 billion dollars. Comrade Deng said,

> Japan is now on fire in both economic and political terms, and the masses are also enthusiastic. After signing of the Sino-Japanese long-term trade agreement, Western Europe became anxious. France announced its intention of signing a similar agreement with us, saying that the quality of Japanese goods is lower than that of French goods. France is active in expanding trade with us. This is also true of West Germany, which also intends to open up a market in China. We now have agreed to sign long-term trade agreements with France, Britain, the United States, West Germany and Italy. Foreign companies are also actively investing in China. They have built mechanized chicken farms, wristwatch factories, and power plants in Guangdong Province. The international situation is excellent. It is precisely because of this situation ... [that] a task has been spelled out for us, namely, we should be skilled at using this situation to absorb foreign technology and funds to greatly accelerate our development.

These remarks confirmed my impression that Hua Guofeng was indeed bent on development, that he was well informed, and that he was open-minded. After the "Gang of Four" was smashed, he really wanted to accomplish a great deal.

Toward the end of his speech, Hua returned to the agenda. He said, "Originally, the conference was set to last twenty days. We are afraid that might not be enough. The Political Bureau has discussed the matter twice, in a lively manner." In conclusion, he elaborated on the question of some cadres who did not have a clear understanding of the "four modernizations." He cited as an example some cadres in Shihezi and Nanshan counties in Xinjiang Province who had a poor understanding of the "four modernizations." He pointed to the problem of bureaucracy in economic and government units unsuited to modernization. He cited as an example the fact that nineteen official seals had to be affixed to an application for the import of a single piece of equipment into Shanghai. He also gave many examples to show that China's superstructure was in bad shape. He said that he completely agreed with Ye Jianying's view that it was imperative to achieve a marked improvement in enterprise management. Calling attention to the many "ridiculous mistakes" in China's economic practices, he particularly criticized some cadres for neglecting market competition. I thought that his remarks were to the point. Despite some ill-advised sections in Hua Guofeng's speech, such as the "eleventh line struggle" I mentioned above, on the whole, all the participants, including me, were fairly satisfied.

Discussion about Shifting the Focus of Work

After Hua Guofeng completed his speech, the participants were divided into smaller discussion groups comprising six major regional groups. Group lists had been distributed to all participants prior to the opening ceremony. Four co-chairs were appointed for each group:

1. *The North China Group*:

Lin Hujia[2] (from Beijing), Liu Zihou[3] (from Hebei), Luo Qingchang[4] (from the Investigation Department of the Party Central Committee), and Qin Jiwei[5] (from the Beijing Area Command)

2. *The Northeast China Group*:

Wang Enmao[6] (from Jilin), Ren Zhongyi[7] (from Liaoning), Tang Ke[8] (from the Ministry of Metallurgical Industry), and Yang Yong [9] (from the General Staff Headquarters)

3. *The East China Group*:

Peng Chong (from Shanghai), Wan Li[10] (from Anhui), Bai Rubing[11] (from Shandong), and Nie Fengzhi[12] (from the Nanjing Military Area Command)

4. *The Central-South China Group*:

Duan Junyi[13] (from Henan), Mao Zhiyong[14] (from Hunan), Huang Hua[15] (from the Ministry of Foreign Affairs), and Yang Dezhi[16] (from the Wuhan Military Area Command)

5. *The Southwest China Group*:

Zhao Ziyang (from Sichuan), An Pingsheng[17] (from Yunnan), Zhang Pinghua (from the Publicity Department of the Party Central Committee), and Liang Biye (from the General Political Department)

6. *The Northwest China Group*:

Wang Feng[18] (from Xinjiang), Huo Shilian[19] (from Ningxia), Hu Yaobang (from the Organization Department of the Party Central Committee), and Xiao Hua[20] (from the Lanzhou Military Area Command)

Of the four conveners for each group, two were leaders of a province, a major municipality directly administered by the Center, or an autonomous region; one was either the leader of a regional military command or the leader of a department attached directly to the Military Commission of the Party Central Committee; and the fourth was the leader either of a department of the Party Central Committee or of a department of the State Council. The five Standing Committee members were not assigned to a regional group. The other members and alternate members of the Political Bureau were assigned to regional groups as ordinary group members. There were only two conveners who were also a member or an alternate member of the Political Bureau: Peng Chong in the East China Group and Zhao Ziyang in the Southwest China Group. The leaders of all provinces, of major municipalities and autonomous regions, and of regional military commands were all assigned to regional groups. All the participants in the work conference were also assigned to regional groups. Each group had an average of 33–35 members.

Because of my own work, I took a special interest in colleagues who were engaged in ideological, scientific research, and press work. From the group lists I could see that Li Xin was in the North China Group; Hu Qiaomu and Zhang Xiangshan[21] were in the East China Group; Zeng Tao,[22] Hua Nan[23] and Hu Sheng[24] were in the Northeast China Group; Wu Lengxi[25] was in the Central-South China Group; Xiong Fu, Hu Jiwei,[26] Zhang Pinghua, and Zhang Yaoci[27] were in the Southwest China Group; and Yang Xiguang,[28] Wang Huide,[29] and I were in the Northwest China Group. Li Xin, Wu Lengxi, Hu Sheng, and Xiong Fu, who had worked together with me in the State Council Politics Research Office, were also in this last group. They had been involved in the compilation of the *Selected Works of Mao Zedong*. Li, Wu, and Hu attended the conference in their capacity as leaders of the General Office of the Committee for Compiling and Publishing Chairman Mao Zedong's Works. Xiong Fu attended in his capacity as the editor-in-chief of *Red Flag* magazine. Zeng Tao, Hu Jiwei, Yang Xiguang, Hua Nan, Zhang Xiangshan, and Wang Huide attended in their capacity as the leaders, respectively, of the Xinhua News Agency, the *People's Daily*, the *Guangming Daily*, the *Liberation Army Daily*, the Central Radio Administration, and the Central Compilation and Translation Bureau. Since Zhang Pinghua then served as the head of the Publicity Department of the Party Central Committee, he was involved in many matters. Although Zhang Yaoci then served as a deputy director of the General Office of the Party Central Committee, ideological matters were beyond his reach.

I was assigned to the Northwest China Group. In addition to the four conveners, members of our group included three Political Bureau members— Fang Yi, Ji Dengkui and Xu Xiangqian, and three who belonged to the "three types of vice and two types of supreme," namely, Wang Zhen, Zhou Jianren, and Song Renqiong. Coming from provinces, major municipalities, and autonomous regions or regional military commands were Li Ruishan,[30] Wang Renzhong, and Yu Mingtao[31] from Shaanxi; Song Ping[32] and Li Dengying[33] from Gansu; Shao Jingwa[34] from Ningxia; Song Zhihe [35] from Xinjiang; Tan Qilong[36] and Zhao Haifeng[37] from Qinghai; Liu Zhen[38] and Guo

Linxiang[39] from the Xinjiang Military Area Command; and Han Xianchu[40] from the Lanzhou Military Area Command. Coming from the departments of the Party Central Committee were Yang Xiguang (of the *Guangming Daily*) and Wang Huide (of the Central Compilation and Translation Bureau). Attending from the departments attached directly to the Military Commission of the Party Central Committee were Li Shuiqing[41] and Chen Heqiao[42] (both from the Second Artillery forces) and Mo Wenhua[43] (from the Armored Forces). Representing the State Council departments were Liu Wei[44] (from the Second Ministry of the Machine-Building Industry), Zhan Zhen[45] (from the Fifth Ministry of the Machine-Building Industry), Zhang Jingfu[46] (from the Ministry of Finance), Jiang Yizhen[47] (from the Ministry of Health), Yao Yilin[48] (from the Financial and Trade Group of the State Council), and Li Renjun[49] (from the State Planning Commission). I attended in my capacity as the leader of the State Council Political Research Office. Many members of the Northwest China group were acquaintances and friends of mine, but several I met for the first time. I got on very well with them at the conference. Some, such as Jiang Yizhen, became my friends. Jiang and I became colleagues while working for the Association for Promoting the Development of Hainan. He passed away a few years ago.

All speeches were made in these group meetings. Except for the small number of general meetings, all participants had no other meetings. Group meetings were usually held in the mornings and in the afternoons. The participants were usually off on Sundays. Bulletins summarizing all group meetings were distributed daily to all Work Conference participants, enabling everyone to follow the discussions of all groups.

In the first couple of days of group discussions, almost all speakers, in line with the requirements set forth by Hua Guofeng in his speech, declared their stand on the issue of the shift in the focus of work. With respect to the issue of the shift in the focus of work, many of those attending the conference, including me, shared the view that it was necessary to shift the focus of work to development. Hence they supported that wording. But it was imperative to remind people that there remained a host of problems from the "Gang of Four" and we needed to expose and criticize them and ferret out their lackeys. The criticism of the 1976 Tiananmen Incident had not been reversed. Many incorrect viewpoints and theories released in Mao Zedong's name that had been put forward during the Cultural Revolution were not yet clarified. The cases of many people who had been falsely framed had not been redressed. People who had done evil things under the "Gang of Four" would likely go into hiding to evade criticism and exposure only to reemerge in the future. Solving these problems required that we continue to wage struggles and remain vigilant. In his speech Hua Guofeng made a remark related to this issue, "As for the problems that we have not had enough time to finish tackling, we should continue to do meticulous work and seek appropriate solutions." He also mentioned that the systematic criticism of Lin Biao and the "Gang of Four" would require a longer time. But he mentioned this in an overly abstract way. He did not give adequate weight to problems that needed to be solved and therefore there was a danger of failing to complete the task of thoroughly exposing and criticizing the "Gang of Four." After hearing Hua's speech, while expressing support, conference participants were worried and indicated they were not fully satisfied.

On November 13, Hu Yaobang gave a speech made to our Northwest China Group on the shift in the focus of work. In his view, shifting the focus of work, as Hua had suggested, belonged to the issue of the work principle and work arrangements. He quoted Mao Zedong's remark, "Hardly has one wave subsided when another rises," i.e., don't set new tasks until one wave subsides. Then he said the "wave" of exposing and criticizing the "Gang of Four" had not subsided, but had reached its crest, which was precisely the time to spell out tasks for development. Meanwhile, he noted that the shift in the focus of work did not mean that the task of exposing and criticizing the "Gang of Four" had been completed. He also stressed that the cardinal issues of right and wrong must be resolved thoroughly. I was in total agreement with his view. In discussing the shift in the focus of work, many speakers took a similar stand, favoring the shift in focus for the following year to the modernization drive. They also shared the view that it was imperative to solve correctly those problems that needed solutions.

Here, I want to add something related to the question of "resolutely ending the use of the slogan 'taking class struggle as the key link'." Later, in June 1981, the Sixth Plenum of the 11th Party Central Committee adopted the "Resolution on Certain Historical Questions of Our Party Since the Founding of the People's Republic of China." In summarizing the results of the Third Plenum, the Sixth Plenum cited the sentence "resolutely ending the use of the slogan of 'taking class struggle as the key link.'" The Sixth Plenum declared that "class struggle as the key link" was not suited to socialist society or to the strategic decision on shifting the focus of work to the socialist modernization drive. While discussing the draft for the Sixth Plenum's Decision, I was aware that their reference to the Third Plenum did not fully accord with what actually happened in the Third Plenum.

I would like to voice my own opinions based on the data from the Third Plenum and my own recollections. As I mentioned above, Hua Guofeng's speech on the shift in the focus of work failed to give full expression to the issue. What he said was just to end "resolutely" the nationwide mass movement to expose and criticize the "Gang of Four," but he did not say that it was imperative to end "resolutely" the use of the slogan "taking class struggle as the key link." What he said with regard to class struggle was to "pay equal attention to the three revolutionary movements, that is, class struggle, the struggle in production, and scientific experiments," with "class struggle" still placed in the forefront. It is not true that he really did not use the expression "taking class struggle as the key link." He did not refer favorably to the class struggle but in our group's discussions nobody interpreted Hua Guofeng's speech as a speech on "resolutely ending the use of the slogan of taking class struggle as the key link." Hu Yaobang's speech to the Northwest China Group can be considered representative in showing that Hua Guofeng had not yet declared an end to the use of "class struggle."

Perhaps at the Third Plenum some people did propose resolutely halting the use of the slogan "taking class struggle as the key link," and perhaps others echoed their remarks. If so, their proposal would have been discussed and written into the communiqué. But I remember that nobody made a speech to that effect. The relevant sentences in the communiqué of the Third Plenum concerning the issue of class struggle also did not contain that meaning. Those sentences contained in the Third Plenum communiqué read:

> Internally, there are still a tiny number of counterrevolutionaries and criminal offenders hostile to and sabotaging China's socialist modernization drive. We should never relax class struggle against them nor weaken the proletarian dictatorship. But just as Comrade Mao Zedong stated that large-scale, turbulent class struggles of the masses had in the main come to an end, that with regard to class struggle within a socialist society, we should resolve them in accordance with the principle of strictly differentiating and correctly handling the two types of contradictions (between ourselves and the enemy and among ourselves) different in nature and in accordance with the procedures as stipulated by the Constitution and laws, that we should never permit the confusion of the limits of the two types of contradictions different in nature nor allow damage to the political situation of stability and unity as required by the socialist modernization drive.

The communiqué of the Third Plenum is now 20 years old. At that plenum, I was not involved in drafting the communiqué; nor did I join discussions about the communiqué at the group meetings. (I did not intend to make any speech on this in the group discussions.) After reading this paragraph of the communiqué, I did not agree with the content. That paragraph was quoted from the speech titled "On the Question of Correctly Handling the Contradictions among the People" made by Mao Zedong in February of 1957. The main idea was to point out that there was no contradiction between the fact that "class struggle in ideology will last a long time and be tortuous and sometimes even violent," and "taking class struggle as the key link." It was, therefore, wrong to interpret this as calling a halt to the use of the slogan 'taking class struggle as the key link." The slogan 'taking class struggle as the key link" was put forward several years later after the speech was delivered, i.e., in 1963.

I know there were quite a few participants in the Work Conference who believed in resolutely stopping the use of the slogan "taking class struggle as the key link," but I don't remember anybody having made a speech to this effect. At the Work Conference the participants frequently expressed their opposition to the "two whatevers" in general terms. As realistic people, they usually talked about problems calling for urgent and immediate solutions. They did not touch upon basic theory, basic concepts, and basic slogans that were somewhat removed from the problems requiring urgent and immediate solutions. "Taking class struggle as the key link" was regarded as a question falling under the category of basic theory, basic concepts, and basic slogans. Under the assumption of not openly criticizing Mao Zedong's basic viewpoints, an assumption I believed erroneous, it was, of course, better not to touch on problems of this type.

I did not approve of ascribing all wrong viewpoints to Kang Sheng[50] and the "Gang of Four." Some people believed that this approach should be taken to protect Mao Zedong. I think, however, that this only results in ideological confusion. For instance, on January 3, 1979, less than 20 days after the conclusion of the Third Plenum, Hu Qiaomu delivered a speech titled "On the Question of Some Wordings of Class Struggle during the Socialist Period." I thought that speech reflected an inappropriate approach to protecting Mao's reputation and allowing the class struggle to continue. For example, Hu raised the question of "how we should understand 'taking class struggle as the key link'." He noted, "The meaning of this wording becomes clear only by judging in what sense and in what range it was used. Failure to make this clear will cause ideological confusion and confusion in our practical work," and "will inevitably cause the artificial expansion of class struggle." Another example he gave was that the "Gang of Four" and Kang Sheng revised and distorted Mao Zedong's original remarks at the 10th Plenum of the Eighth Central Committee. These remarks were, "In the historical phase of socialism, there exist classes, class contradictions and class struggle, the struggle between two roads, the socialist road and the capitalist road, and the danger of capitalist restoration." They revised and distorted Mao's remark by inserting the two characters "*shizhong*" (in this historical phase) before the word "exist" in the sentence that reads, "In this historical phase of socialism, there exist classes, class contradictions, and class struggle." As a consequence, they significantly altered Mao Zedong's remarks.

In my opinion, it was bad to add the two characters and yet the addition of the two characters written by Hu Qiaomu less than two weeks after the adoption of the communiqué of the Third Plenum, does provide evidence that the Third Plenum did not yet make a decision to halt the use of the slogan of "taking class struggle as the key link."

CHAPTER 3

SECOND GENERAL MEETING AND DISCUSSIONS ABOUT THREE TOPICS

Explanations by Ji Dengkui
and the First Topic: Agriculture

The second plenary session was held in the afternoon of November 13, the fourth day of the conference. There was only one item on the agenda: the presentation by Ji Dengkui, a member of the Political Bureau and a vice-premier of the State Council, concerning two documents dealing with agriculture. For China, with its low level of economic development and huge population, the issue of agriculture was obviously linked closely to social stability and development. In the 10 years that followed the Cultural Revolution natural disasters linked with manmade calamities made it particularly difficult for China to feed its 700 to 800 million citizens. As food supplies were very limited, it was extremely crucial to develop China's agriculture capabilities.

Hua Guofeng placed great importance on the issue of agriculture. When Mao Zedong inspected his home province of Hunan, Hua, then a member of the Secretariat of the Hunan Provincial Party Committee, talked about agriculture at such length that Mao Zedong had to remind him to "say something about politics." At the general meeting on November 13, Hua made only brief introductory remarks. For the important issues he turned to Ji Dengkui to explicate the documents on agriculture.

Ji's explanation had five parts: (1) The current state of agriculture; (2) The principle of taking agriculture as the foundation; (3) Arousing the initiative of farmers; (4) major measures to speed up agricultural development; and (5) the issue of leadership.

By way of introduction, Ji asserted that the conference participants warmly supported the shift in the focus of the Party's work. Then he said, "To build China into a strong, modern socialist country, first of all, we must promote the development of agriculture.

This is an issue with which the whole Party is very concerned and an issue about which many comrades are worried because the four modernizations cannot be based on backward agriculture. It is precisely because of this that the Party Central Committee has included how to make a success in agriculture as an important topic for the current conference."

The two documents on agriculture that Ji explained were the "Decision on Accelerating the Agricultural Growth Rate" and the "Rules Governing the Work of Rural People's Communes" (Draft for Trial Implementation). In the part titled "On the Current State of Agriculture," Ji emphasized the problem of low agricultural growth rate, the enormous pressure resulting from a growing population, and the necessity of importing grain because of insufficient domestic supply. He said that China had to import more than 10 million tons of grain the next year (1979), noting, "The biggest bottleneck is agriculture.... Because of the insufficient grain supply, laborers who newly migrated to the cities cannot be employed fully, [and] we cannot do many things that we should do." Farmers must sell the state nearly 50 million tons of grain a year, but "this amount has actually exceeded their current capability [and has caused] strains. The problems of state grain purchase reflect a relationship between our Party and farmers that is tense." If the annual grain ration for each farmer averages less than 150 kilograms [300 *jin*], then "Farmers do not have enough to eat," and "They should be given an opportunity to rest and build up their strength." In 1977, on average, one brigade (equivalent to a village today) had less than 10,000 yuan in its collective accumulation fund, not enough to buy a medium-sized tractor. Nearly one quarter of all production teams throughout the country had an annual per-capita income of less than 40 yuan. Calculations by comparable prices showed that farmers' income rose at an average annual rate of only 0.5 yuan. "Farmers can hardly afford to have children." In his view, the way out was to enhance agricultural productivity and accelerate the growth rate to a new target of four to five percent per year. Ji Dengkui's explanations did not conceal facts or cover up the truth. He made very clear the severity of the current state of agriculture.

In the second part of his speech, Ji Dengkui said, "The principle of taking agriculture as the foundation" was not seriously implemented in either theory or practice. "As Chairman Hua said, the agricultural problem has not been completely solved." In the third part, Ji Dengkui emphasized egalitarianism and supported the principle of "from each according to his ability, to each according to his work." Speaking of the campaign to "learn from Dazhai," he said, "In some localities, at the mention of learning from Dazhai, some people cut off the capitalist tail.... This means that they learn from Dazhai in a wrong and distorted way."

In the fourth part, Ji laid out major measures to speed up agricultural development. In addition to stepping up capital construction for farmland and giving priority to the supply of seeds and chemical fertilizers, he called for increased investments in agriculture. "From now until 1985, the ratio of investment in agricultural capital construction should rise to between 16 to 18 percent and the amount given in loans to agriculture should double. The Bank of Agriculture will be established." The purchase price of grain would be raised by 30 percent. In the fifth part, Ji stressed the importance of "maintaining the stability of the Party's policy."

> We must unswervingly implement all the Party's current policies concerning agriculture. We should never issue an order at dawn and rescind it at dusk. This would lose the confidence of the people. Our experience has proved that making unpredictable changes in policy, giving bad ideas, doing things not in line with local conditions, prescribing a single solution for diverse problems, issuing arbitrary and impracticable directives, and infringing upon the ownership and decision-making authority of local collective accounting units have seriously dampened farmers' initiative and hence are the archenemy of agriculture. We should never repeat such mistakes.

Ji Dengkui's speech served to launch discussion about agriculture.

Agriculture was also the first of three topics in Hua Guofeng's speech. Agriculture was of concern to all participants. Local cadres had a good knowledge of actual agricultural conditions and knew that the situation was very serious. There had always been a serious drawback in China's agriculture: agriculture was emphasized to the point that the areas of forestry, animal husbandry, sideline production, and fisheries were neglected and sometimes even destroyed. The rural industrial sector and transport industry had been neglected as well. Grain production was emphasized to the neglect and even destruction of cash crops such as cotton, edible oils, and sugarcane. Even so, grain production lagged because of policies encouraging units "large in size and collective in nature," "cutting off the capitalist tail,"[1] "struggling against privatism and revisionism," criticizing "the theory of the unique importance of productive forces," and issuing arbitrary and impracticable directives. However, those responsible had refused to sum up experience on the basis of facts. Instead they blamed natural disasters, China's huge population, and other factors. In the two years after the downfall of the "Gang of Four," there was no significant improvement in agricultural production. In rural work, many people's minds were still seriously shackled. Not all the participants were satisfied with the two documents prepared for the conference and Ji Dengkui's explanations. At the conference, not only did various local "dukes and princes" speak out on the issue of agriculture, but also comrades from the army and from central departments (many of whom had taken or were currently in charge of agriculture in localities) were heavy-hearted and talked at great length. From the bulletins, I could see that this was also true in all six regional groups.

Almost all the members in our Northwest China Group gave speeches about agriculture. The following persons, as far as I can remember, were among those participants who made systematic speeches. Li Dengying had been engaged in agricultural work for a long time. In 1956, when the 12-year long-range plan for science was formulated, he was deputy director of the State Council Office of Agriculture, the 10-member group responsible for drawing up the plan for science, under the leadership of Fan Changjiang and me. At the time of this Central Work Conference, he worked in the Gansu Provincial Party Committee. At the group meetings Li made comprehensive presentations on agricultural issues. Jiang Yizhen, who was also quite familiar with agricultural issues, had served as a secretary of the Hebei Provincial Party Committee before serving as the Minister of Health.

Xiao Hua was also familiar with agriculture, perhaps because, while working with the Lanzhou Military Area Command, he had visited rural areas in several provinces and autonomous regions in northwest China. His speech offered a comprehensive analysis of why China's agriculture had stagnated and had been in a backward state for over a decade. Li Renjun, a vice-minister of the State Planning Commission, expressed his opinions on agriculture from the State Planning Commission's point of view. In addition, various "dukes and princes," such as Shao Jingwa from Ningxia, Li Ruishan and Wang Renzhong from Shaanxi, Song Ping from Gansu, Zhao Haifeng from Qinghai, Liu Zhen and Guo Linxiang from the Xinjiang Military Area Command, and Song Zhehe from Xinjiang all aired their views on the documents regarding agriculture from the vantage point of their respective regions. I remember that all the "dukes and princes" took the floor on the issue of agriculture, but I don't remember what they talked about. Since I had taken part in drafting documents on agriculture on many occasions, I had my own views on the issue, which I expressed at length. Almost all participants were dissatisfied with the two documents distributed to them for discussion, and they expressed the view that these documents could not solve the present problems in agriculture.

Hu Yaobang expressed his deep concern with agriculture. In his speech to the Northwest China Group, he said that agriculture was the biggest concrete problem in our work and that faster development of agriculture would be a decisive link in accelerating China's modernization process. He said that the two documents could not resolve the crux of the matter. First, they did not show a thorough understanding of the issue. Second, they still reflected shackled thought. He maintained that some rural systems such as the "integration of government and people's communes" should be changed. He believed that the Cultural Revolution had seriously sapped our vitality, weakened laborers' strength, and dampened their initiative. In his view, promoting agricultural development depended largely on arousing the initiative of farmers and cadres in grass-roots units. He said that laborers' initiative was always of paramount importance, and that Lin Biao and the "Gang of Four" had dealt a devastating blow to the initiative of hundreds of millions of farmers and to millions of cadres. Hu said that describing the collective as "good" was an abstract phrase. If a collective economy was mismanaged, it would be impossible to fully arouse farmers' initiative, and the collective economy would have no superiority.

Hu Yaobang spelled out his views so fully that I realized that he was speaking of the necessity of "*bao chan dao hu*," fixing farm output quotas down to each household. Although he did not yet use that expression precisely, it was as if—with a light poke of the finger through a thin piece of window paper—the four characters would appear. Hu's remarks reflected a profound understanding of the basic issues confronting "agriculture." He disagreed with people who felt the issue could be explained by the fact that China fed one-fifth of the world's population with less than seven percent of the worlds' farmland. He said that there were various levels of "feeding." Feeding people with chaff and vegetables for half a year and grain for another half was one type of "feeding." Having enough to eat and wear, sufficient nutrients, and a good Constitution was also a type of "feeding." He said that the standards for feeding Chinese farmers were far too low. Meanwhile, he expressed the view that China's farmland acreage was actually much larger than the commonly used statistical figure. He maintained that once the farmers' initiative was aroused, China had enormous potential for increasing agricultural production.

I believe Hu's remarks were directed at those who, ignoring the most serious problems in agriculture, had covered up the facts and presented a false picture of peace and prosperity. I personally resented and disapproved of presenting a false picture of peace and prosperity. So, I felt that his remarks were excellent. Concerning the concept of "eating food," he told us a funny story. In the early years after the founding of New China, he and a veteran comrade had visited the Soviet Union. The Soviet Communist Party leaders invited them and their party to a Western meal. After a waiter had served the first course, Hu's comrade did not eat, expecting to begin eating after all the dishes had been brought out. Since he had not eaten the first dish, the waiter assumed that he did not want to eat. In the

Western fashion courses were served in sequence, with dishes removed when a new course was brought. Hu's comrade waited for all the dishes to arrive, but no food had come in the end. He had to leave hungry. I remember that funny story Hu told in the Northwest China Group to this day. He used the story to explain that many people had a very narrow understanding of the concept of "eating." This one-sided understanding meant that some people thought that solving the problem of "eating" would depend solely on planting and eating grain crops, unaware of the importance of developing diverse food crops.

The problem of agriculture was not fully solved at the Central Work Conference, and there was resistance to dropping the phrase "taking grain crops as the key link." Apparently the problem has not been completely solved even today. Some of us still equate grain with foodstuffs. Under the Guomindang, the term "U.N. Food and Agricultural Organization" was translated as "the U.N. Grain and Agriculture Organization." That translation has remained unchanged since New China was founded fifty years ago. The two issues Hu Yaoban raised in his speech, the lack of understanding and the mental shackles in our thinking, were both crucial ones for agriculture.

There was also the issue of importing some grain to supplement China's grain shortages. On this question Yao Yilin offered an excellent view. In his speech to the Northwest China Group, he said that in 1978 China imported 12 million tons of grain to ease the situation; one million tons were re-exported and the rest was used to supply the domestic market. He proposed importing 18 million tons of grain in 1979, to help China restore its cotton, edible oil, and sugar-bearing crop production and provide animal fodder.

All the comrades in the Northwest China Group eagerly expressed various views. On November 19, the Northwest China Group recommended that five group members — Hu Yaobang, Wang Renzhong, Jiang Yizhen, Li Dengying and Yu Guangyuan — form a group to revise the two documents presented at the plenary session in accordance with the discussions held at the group meetings. Their report was completed four days later and then submitted to the Party Central Committee. I don't remember what happened to our written report. As I recall, all groups were assigned the task of writing such reports

From the bulletins that summarized the other groups' sessions, I could see that the process was very similar. In the Southwest China Group, Zhao Ziyang delivered many speeches on the issue of agriculture. The keynote speeches given to various groups were much the same. On the whole, most participants in all the groups shared the view that the two documents could not solve the problems in agriculture. Yet nobody at the Work Conference dared openly to make a proposal that could genuinely solve the problems, namely, fixing farm output quotas for each household. Even if such a view had been expressed openly, the chances were that it would not have been adopted. Consequently, the reports on agriculture were slow in being issued. They were passed on to the Standing Committee members of the Political Bureau of the Party Central Committee.

Hua Guofeng made some brief remarks at the November 25 plenary session, at which the Standing Committee members listened to the committees' reports. Hua said that only a few people held the view that the documents concerning agriculture were feasible. The overwhelming majority of participants believed that the documents needed to be revised. Various groups continued writing. (I participated in writing the opinion of the Northwest China Group. Lin Hujia wrote a long statement for the North China Group.) Some comrades believed the documents should be completely redrafted.

The widespread criticism of the two documents caused Hua Guofeng to waver. He posed a rhetorical question: "Do we really need to have these documents from our conference?" He said that originally, he thought no documents should be written. Hua asked Hu Yaobang, who had advocated writing documents. Hu said: "We need to write them. If we do not make a decision, it will be hard to push ahead vigorously. With a written document we will be able to unify lines of action and solicit opinions extensively. This will be good for pushing ahead next year." After some hesitation, Hua finally agreed on a written document to unify thinking and solicit opinions. He asked the participants to make comments. The question of whether the current system of integrating the government and people's communes should be changed was an important matter. If the answer was yes, then how should it be changed? Should work be divided? Massive institutions would not do either. The rural economy should be managed by economic means.

When the committee reports were given, Li Xiannian also said that three different views on the documents concerning agriculture had been aired at a meeting that he had convened attended by thirteen people. The first was that the original documents were feasible. The second was that major revisions were necessary. The third was that the documents should be redrafted. He did not declare his own position, but he did remark that if "the revolution had not yet succeeded, comrades still needed to work hard." (Dr. Sun Yat-sen's words.) At the general meeting that followed on November 25, Hua Guofeng made his remarks on this question, "On the 'Decision on Accelerating the Agricultural Growth Rate.'" He said, "Some comrades favor making minor revisions, others call for major revisions, and still others propose that the document be redrafted. The Party Central Committee deems it better to write a new text."

I later learned about the circumstances surrounding the Standing Committee meeting referred to above. I learned that from the very beginning Hu Yaobang had vigorously advocated formulating a strong document on agriculture at the conference. One afternoon, both before and after the meeting for Standing Committee members to listen to the various group reports, he called Hu Qiaomu and me together to talk about the documents on agriculture. He explained why he felt it was imperative to have a forceful document on agriculture. He also expressed his hope that Hu Qiaomu would preside over the drafting of the documents, but Hu Qiaomu expressed his disapproval of Hu Yaobang's view and also indicated that he did not want this task. They argued with each other for some time, with neither succeeding in persuading the other. But Hu Yaobang still insisted that Hu Qiaomu should preside over the drafting of the documents. Because of Hu Yaobang's insistence, Hu Qiaomu reluctantly accepted this task. Under most circumstances, I should remember well the details of the argument between Hu Yaobang and Hu Qiaomu. But, no matter how hard I try, for some reason I cannot recollect the content. I just have the impression that they did not share the same views regarding how to resolve the question of agriculture.

To help Hu Qiaomu, the State Council Research Office then sent two comrades plus an assistant to the Jingxi Hotel. As I was busy with other business, I did not learn in detail about the work done by Hu Qiaomu and the two comrades.

A great deal of time and energy was devoted to studying the issue of agriculture at the Central Work Conference. Although I did not take part in drafting the documents on agriculture and devoted my energy to other matters, I still heard of and learned about many things. I learned that apart from Hu Yaobang, Zhao Ziyang played a significant role in drafting the documents. Hu Qiaomu praised Zhao in my presence more than once. I also learned about the real views of several comrades, which they did not air at group meetings. They expressed their critical comments on the comrades in charge of drafting the documents to me. They also told me they had learned that in fact there were insurmountable difficulties. Through talks with these comrades, I became aware that it was impossible at this conference to draft a document on agriculture that could really solve the problems. But as some of the "dukes and princes" who cherished the same ideals got together to exchange views, they came to a better understanding of what they should do in the future, after they returned to work. So for them the content of the final text of the documents on agriculture became a matter of little importance. They told me that no matter what the documents on agriculture said, they would act in accordance with the principles they had agreed upon among themselves. In short, they would take measures that could solve problems by proceeding from their local realities and would let practice prove them right or wrong.

The two documents, "The Decision on Accelerating the Agricultural Growth Rate" and "The Rules Governing the Work of Rural People's Communes (Draft for Trial Implementation)," were revised at the Central Work Conference and submitted to the Third Plenum and adopted in principle. I think that it is unnecessary to cite them in detail because their basic content can be found in a paragraph about agriculture in the communiqué of the Third Plenum. On the structure of rural ownership that paragraph merely said,

The ownership and decision-making authority of production teams, production brigades, and people's communes shall be protected effectively by state laws. It is impermissible to transfer, use, and possess for free production teams' laborers, funds, products, and materials. Communes' economic organizations at all levels shall earnestly implement the socialist principle of "to each according to his work" and calculate remuneration according to the amount and quality of labor, in order to overcome egalitarianism. Commune members' private plots, household sideline production, and market trading serve as a necessary supplement to the socialist economy, with nobody permitted to impose unwarranted interference. People's communes shall resolutely practice the system of ownership at three levels with the production team constituting the foundation, which will remain stable and unchanged. All people's communes' organizations at all levels shall resolutely practice democratic management, election of cadres, and making accounts open."

Most provisions contained in those sentences were good, yet they were just general principles. Even if they were implemented to the letter, they would only play a helpful role but not genuinely enhance farmers' initiative. The sentence that "people's communes shall resolutely practice the system of ownership at three levels with the production team constituting the foundation, which will remain stable and unchanged" was very conservative and lacked the spirit of reform.

Of course, the communiqué did not cover the entire contents of the two documents on agriculture. For example, the "two things not permitted" contained in the two documents — "not permitting the fixing of farm output quotas for each household" and "not permitting dividing farmland for individual farming" — were not included in the communiqué. What would have genuinely enhanced farmers' initiative for labor was fixing farm output quotas for each household. Judging by the prevailing mood, I supposed that it was impossible to have this written in. Before the documents were finalized, one day I heard that the documents on agriculture drafted by Hu Qiaomu did not contain the sentence that it was permissible to practice fixing of farm output quotas for each household. On the contrary, it contained the sentence "two things not permitted," that is, the sentences "not

49

permitting the fixing of farm output quotas for each household" and "not permitting dividing farmland for individual farming." Because of the prevailing mood at the conference, I was not surprised at all to learn this. So I did not want to blame Hu Qiaomu and other comrades in charge of drafting the documents on agriculture.

Given the prevailing mood, I knew that all that people could do, even those who then firmly stood for discarding the "two whatevers," was to oppose the directives Mao Zedong gave in the last few years of his life, to rehabilitate those accused in the Tiananmen Incident, and to solve some problems left over from the Cultural Revolution. Meanwhile, they had to uphold Mao Zedong's prestige to avoid a greater impact on thinking within the Party and in society. They could not then oppose the mistakes Mao Zedong had made before the Cultural Revolution. Fixing farm output quotas for each household was something that Mao Zedong unswervingly opposed many times from the 1950s. Therefore, they did not dare to demand that the sentence of fixing farm output quotas for each household be written into the documents on agriculture. Of course, I thought it was still desirable not to include the "two things not permitted."

At the time, I was still somewhat dissatisfied with those drafting the documents. But later, I thought that such a sentence did not really matter and was nothing terrible. I know that Chinese have many ways to deal with other Chinese. In ancient fables there was the story of *"zhao san mu si"* or *"zhao si mu san"* (both mean blowing hot and cold).[2] In the case of not permitting the fixing of farm output quotas for each household, the use of such words as "fixing farm output quotas for each group and defining responsibility for each household" or "defining responsibility for each laborer" could be regarded as not violating the provision of the "two things not permitted." As a result of the Cultural Revolution, all Chinese became much "smarter" than ever before.

There is one point that deserves attention. The slogan "In agriculture, learn from Dazhai," a model for collective agriculture during the Cultural Revolution, was no longer used. One of the documents cited in the editorial "Study the Documents Carefully and Grasp the Key Link" issued by the two newspapers and one magazine was the speech Hua Guofeng delivered at the Second

National Agricultural Conference on learning from Dazhai. The editorial became famous for a time for preaching the "two whatevers." Compared to the documents distributed shortly after the Central Work Conference was convened, the documents on agriculture that were finalized at the conference and adopted by the Third Plenum reflected great progress. From studying the documents concerning agriculture, we can conclude that the Third Plenum merely initiated the process of reform and opening. After the Third Plenum, this process encountered numerous difficulties that had to be overcome one by one.

Agricultural production is a complex issue requiring coordination with the rural industrial sector and the transport industry, and balancing agriculture, forestry, animal husbandry, sideline production, and fishery. Within agriculture there must be a balance between grain crops and cash crops. The innocuous sentence "resolutely and thoroughly implement the principle of paying equal attention to the development of agriculture, forestry, animal husbandry, sideline production, and fishery" and the 16-character principle of "taking grain as the key link, achieving all-round development, acting in line with local conditions, and exercising appropriate concentration" had already become an old saying before the Central Work Conference was convened.

The Second Topic:
The National Economic Development Plan
For 1979–1980

I did not think this was the place to discuss this topic. Since this topic was placed on the agenda of the Central Work Conference, cadres from various localities and departments took the floor at group meetings using the materials they had brought with them. Most participants basically accepted Hua Guofeng's proposal that from January 1979 the whole Party should shift the focus of its work to economic development. However, the participants all believed that next year's economic planning had already been covered in the "Government Work Report" that Hua Guofeng delivered at the First Plenary Session of the Fifth National People's Congress six months earlier. Hence they felt there was little point in discussing it again.

51

The participants in the current Central Work Conference were not interested in such concrete questions. So there were no discussions about this question at the conference. I don't remember anything on the topic that would be worth mentioning.

Although the discussions about plans were not of interest, the reports on what was happening in the economy turned out to be very interesting indeed. I personally paid close attention to economic work and had always been concerned about China's national economic development. So I attached great importance to an opportunity to listen to the reports on the economic situation given by various provinces, municipalities, autonomous regions, and government departments. Examining the notebook I had used then, I found it contained excerpts I had made from the speeches of leading comrades of many localities and departments that discussed the two-year plan. I had also written down many statistics.

I had previously attended many central conferences where I was often dissatisfied with such speeches because the leading cadres usually just cited the statistics, gave formal presentations on the state of affairs, and put forward requirements to the central authorities. Others usually did not offer comments after hearing their speeches. The leading cadres also usually often exaggerated the successes of their own regions or departments to the maximum, while minimizing as much as possible their problems. But the speeches I heard this time were better than those I had heard previously because a significant part of the speeches was devoted to talking frankly about problems. Listening to these speeches convinced me that the situation was quite serious.

For example, Ma Li said that the per-capita grain share in his province, Guizhou, was less than 250 kilograms a year, while production teams with per-capita annual grain rations of less than 150 kilograms accounted for 40 percent of the total in Guizhou. He also noted that the per-capita income of people's communes averaged 46 yuan a year. In the preliminary income distribution for 1978, some production teams produced only 0.02 yuan per workday. Wan Li from Anhui Province said that the province's per-capita grain share had not reached the level for 1955. The per-capita grain share had been 384 kilograms in 1955 but had fallen to 326 kilograms in 1977, a share only two kilograms more than in 1949, the year of the founding of New China. That meant a 2-kilogram increase in 28 years. Farmers living north of the Huai River received only 30-plus yuan per person each year from the collective. It was really heart-breaking that some farmers in the old revolutionary base areas of the Dabie Mountains were so poor that they didn't have trousers to wear or quilts to use. In my notebook I described scenes that left people deep in thought, as described in the speeches by Tie Ying[3] from Zhejiang, Peng Chong from Shanghai, Liu Zhen and Guo Linxiang from Xinjiang, Wang Qian[4] from Shanxi, Zhao Haifeng from Qinghai, Liu Xueping[5] from Inner Mongolia, Jiang Weiqing[6] from Jiangsu, Ma Xingyuan[7] from Fujian, Li Dengying, Han Xianchu and Xiao Hua from Gansu, Zhang Shiying[8] from Jilin, Ren Zhongyi and Chen Puru[9] from Liaoning, and Huo Shilian from Ningxia, as well as the leading cadres from various departments.

When the participants in the Central Work Conference discussed the two-year plan, they commonly focused on the destructive impact of the Cultural Revolution on the economy. The participants disliked talking about quotas and giving long, meaningless speeches. We could tell that our comrades wanted to go all out and achieve quick results. Facing reality, they were all thinking about how to advance along the road. None could come up with a clear method. The leaders from various localities did not ask for investments from the central authorities. The Work Conference participants felt that the critical issue of the moment was resolving the issues of the political and ideological lines. They did not comment on the two-year plan itself or on the documents related to the two-year plan distributed at the conference.

The Third Topic: The State Council Meeting
To Discuss Principles

A State Council meeting to discuss principles (*wuxuhui*) had been held prior to the Central Work Conference. The participants in that meeting were leaders of various ministries, commissions, administrations, and bureaus, as well as offices and groups attached to the State Council. Each unit was asked to send a principal leader to attend. This was also a long meeting, lasting over 60 days, and running from July 6 to September 9. Yet, as all the participants lived in Beijing, they tried to keep up with their work and the meetings. They did not stay in hotels. They continued to go to their offices and return to their homes. Sessions lasted only half a day and were not held on Sundays. In contrast, the Central Work Conference was full-time with no time to return home, even on weekends.

If I remember correctly, the Meeting on Principles was held in the Report Hall of the Huairen Auditorium in Zhongnanhai. There were 40 to 50 departments attached to the State Council. Including work personnel, the meeting room seated 60 to 70 people. Several rows of seats on the left and right sides of the meeting room were quite full. From the very beginning to the very end, the meeting was presided over by Li Xiannian, a vice-chairman of the Party Central Committee and a vice-premier of the State Council. Also present all the time was Vice-Premier Gu Mu. The meeting guidelines were discussed, but no decisions were made. The participants were asked to speak freely on the central topic of how to expedite the modernization drive. The State Council's economic and business institutions all prepared written speeches. Some of these were signed by the leading cadres; others were not. But all the speeches were studied in the units and were collective products.

During the meeting written speeches were periodically submitted to the organizers. All units focused on what was within their jurisdiction. Most units expounded their own problems in an all-round manner and some just dealt with a simple problem. The State Council Research Office wrote an overall document. These written materials were usually very long, so the speakers were not asked to read them at the meeting because that would have been very depressing. Instead they were required to speak briefly, concentrating on the main points. They were permitted to depart from their texts. For instance, Yao Yilin, who then worked with the Financial and Trade Group, which prepared the text of a speech on lowering grain prices, actually focused on the issue of grain imports. When one speaker addressed the meeting, the participants could raise questions freely, so that the meeting was lively and the participants aired many views and expressed ideas on reforms. The meeting proceeded that way until September 9, when Li Xiannian made a summary of the participants' views, including some ideas concerning reforms. For example, Li explicitly proposed reforming production relations that were not in conformity with productive forces and reforming the superstructure that was inconsistent with the economic foundation.

The participants were very satisfied with the State Council's meeting to discuss principles. When Li Xiannian reported this at a meeting of the Standing Committee of the Political Bureau of the Party Central Committee, Hua Guofeng and Ye Jianying also declared the meeting a success. Ye deemed this type of meeting to discuss principles very good and proposed convening another meeting to discuss theoretical principles. Later, the decision was made to convene the Central Work Conference. On the day the Central Work Conference opened, another topic was announced in addition to those of agriculture and the two-year plan, namely, Li Xiannian's speech two months earlier at the State Council meeting to discuss principles. As a participant, I knew a lot about that meeting, and believed it deserved a lot of attention.

Several things about it remain fresh in my memory to this very day. First, the participants criticized the past practice of not respecting objective laws governing economic development and imposing the "will of senior officials." They stressed the importance of improving people's consumption level. They noted that it was imperative to pursue the principle of "to each according to his work," paying great attention to commodity production and the law of value. They also reminded people of the necessity of seeking economic returns in doing economic work and of making economic calculations. Second, not long before the meeting was held, a Communist Party delegation headed by Li Yimang[10] with Qiao Shi[11] and myself as the deputy heads visited Yugoslavia. After returning home, we wrote a report to the Party Central Committee. Based on what we learned during our visit, we proposed restoring relations between the communist parties of China and Yugoslavia. A summary of the report was given at the State Council's meeting to discuss principles. The report said, "Stalin attempted to impose the Soviet economic model on Yugoslavia, but Tito firmly refused. Yugoslavia can still be regarded as a socialist country and the Communist Party of Yugoslavia as a party taking the socialist road. It is wrong for us to follow the Soviet Union in negating Yugoslavia as a socialist country." Our Central Committee approved the report. After our visit, we clarified our belief that there could be a variety of models for the same basic socialist economic system. We maintained that this could serve as a great enlightenment for China. The State Council's meeting to discuss principles paid great attention to the delegation's report on its visit to Yugoslavia. Some participants at the meeting expressed doubts about whether or not Yugoslavia was a socialist country, but most participants favored the Party Central Committee's approval of the delegation's view. Of course, many participants indicated they could not accept the social autonomous system practiced by Yugoslavia. The delegation did not advocate emulating Yugoslavia. However, we were of the view that any country should not mechanically copy the practice of other countries and instead should do a good study of the experience of other countries.

Not long before the State Council's meeting to discuss principles, Gu Mu led a Chinese government delegation to five countries in Western Europe. After returning home, he wrote a report that he submitted to the meeting, and this report also received close attention. Unlike previous reports, this one did not totally reject the experience of Western countries. Instead it maintained that China could draw a lot from the good experiences of Western countries. I still remember that Gu Mu's report noted that French farmers could not pass on their farms at will to their sons. To ensure that farms were run well, the government made it a rule that before a son could inherit his father's farm, he had to graduate from an agricultural school, do practical training for two years after graduation on a farm not belonging to his father, and receive certificates showing that he had passed his examinations. This showed all participants that capitalist countries did have some very good systems.

At the meeting the State Council Research Office distributed an article titled "We must Act according to Objective Law Governing Economic Development." Hu Qiaomu, Ma Hong,[12] and I jointly wrote this article. I was responsible for the section on the necessity of acting according to the basic law governing socialist economic development, and of clearly understanding that the purpose of production was to meet social needs, not simply for the sake of production. After discussions, we three writers reached a consensus. The part on the nature of the objectivity of laws adopted my viewpoint as expressed in a book. Ma Hong wrote the section on the law of value regarding commodity production. Hu Qiaomu made some changes in, and improvements, of the entire article.

Many enlightening speeches were delivered at the meeting. For instance, Yao Yilin quoted Lenin's remark "One must learn the wolf's howl when near a herd of wolves," meaning that since we had to deal with capitalist countries, we must know their common practices.

The State Council's meeting to discuss principles played a key role in broadening people's vision and enlightening people's thinking. In my view, we might as well say that it was from this meeting that our Party began to face squarely the problems in China's economic structure and attach utmost importance to reforms. Even earlier economists had started to touch on economic restructuring and to ponder and study related problems. But what they did had previously failed to attract the attention of the senior leaders of the Party and state. Of course, it was not possible to have the senior leaders accept the thinking on reforms before the downfall of the "Gang of Four." Previously, we had also used the language of "economic restructuring," for example, the reform of the taxation system, the labor system, the price system, and material system. As a result, people sometimes said that we had carried out restructuring many times over the previous twenty years. But the ideas on reform that were voiced at the State Council's meeting to discuss principles were not the ideas on reforms we had mentioned previously. True, in the 1960s, economists in the Soviet Union and Eastern Europe began to publish articles on the necessity of carrying out economic restructuring in socialist countries, and some countries started reforms. China had its own disastrous lessons and no longer regarded the Soviet Union's structure as sacrosanct. So far as the issue of the economic structure was concerned, it was at this meeting to discuss principles that new ideas began to emerge, and the emergence of new ideas caught the attention of some of the leaders at the highest level. There is no need to mention Deng Xiaoping. In addition to Deng and Li Xiannian who presided over the meeting,

Vice-Chairman Ye Jianying paid particular attention to the meeting. After hearing the report on the meeting, he considered it a complete success.

Nonetheless, it must be acknowledged that the ideas on reforms aired at the Work Conference were embryonic and the goals for reform still very low. The references to reforms contained in the communiqué of the Third Plenum were limited to the following:

> In accordance with new historical conditions and experience in practice, it is imperative to adopt a series of new important measures to carry out earnest reform of the economic and managerial structure and operational and managerial methods, and on the basis of self-reliance, vigorously enhance economic cooperation featuring equality and mutual benefit with all other countries.... Now a serious drawback in China's economic and managerial structure is the over-concentration of power. It is, therefore, necessary, in a guided way, to boldly delegate power to lower levels, so that localities and industrial and agricultural enterprises will, under the guidance of unified state plans, enjoy more operational and managerial decision-power authority. It is necessary to begin to energetically streamline economic administrative offices at all levels and transfer most of their functions and authority to specialized enterprise-like companies or joint companies. It is necessary to resolutely practice acting according to the law governing economic development, attach great importance to the role of the law governing economic development, take heed to combining ideological and political work with economic means and fully arouse the initiative of cadres and laborers for production. It is necessary, under the unified leadership of the Party, earnestly to resolve the phenomenon in which the functions of Party are not separated from those of the government and enterprises, and the functions of the Party are used in place of those of the government and enterprises, practice the assumption of responsibility at various levels, through the division of work and by assigning specific people, enhance the limits of authority and responsibility of managerial departments and managerial personnel, reduce the number of meetings and documents, improve work efficiency, and practice in real earnest the systems for assessment, rewards and punishment, promotion and demotion.

This paragraph was well written, but has not been fully implemented even to this day. But this paragraph did not yet contain the idea of establishing a socialist market economy; nor did it touch upon the issue of developing an economy of multiple types of ownership. Nor did it address the issues of the structural reform of the socialist ownership, reform of the socialist distribution system, or the issue that under the same basic socialist system within the same country, various localities might have diverse economic models. Of course, these issues could not yet be spelled out. More would have been said if the meeting's participants had had more time to discuss the issue of China's reforms and opening, but there were too many problems to be solved and more urgent questions that needed to be raised at the Central Work Conference. Consequently, although some speakers mentioned the State Council's meeting to discuss principles, they did not discuss the issue of economic restructuring.

Only a few participants in the Central Work Conference had attended the State Council's meeting to discuss principles. Li Xiannian's speech was written in a pedestrian way, and Hua Guofeng did not explain why the topic should be discussed. Nor did he urge the participants to study the issue of economic restructuring while discussing the topic. So, while discussing the topic, the participants usually held discussions on the second topic—the two-year plan. Furthermore, they did not make many remarks regarding reforms and opening. The communiqué's drafters summarized remarks about economic restructuring on the basis of views that were not fully aired at the conference. I thought that it should be acknowledged that the communiqué drafters played a very good role. As the communiqué was discussed formally and adopted by the participants in the Third Plenum, it should be acknowledged that the communiqué was a result of the plenum.

At the Central Work Conference, the leading cadres of various departments attending the State Council meeting to discuss principles did not speak of reforms, although they deemed the meeting very important. I did not use the opportunity to discuss this topic or to use the results of the meeting to discuss principles to deepen my understanding of reforms and opening. The fundamental reason lay in the fact that the focus of the meeting was still on political and ideological lines. The situation created after a breakthrough was achieved at the meeting in the political and ideological lines made it possible to make progress in reforms and opening after the meeting was over. Nevertheless, looking back, I deemed it necessary to bring up the topic at the State Council meeting to discuss principles and talk more about the question of reforms. Although I made many speeches at the Central Work Conference, I did not specially devote one to reform. This must be considered a shortcoming in my work.

Now everyone says that China's reforms and opening were initiated at the Third Plenum of the 11th Party Central Committee. This is quite correct. But we should not think that full discussions were held about reforms and opening at the Third Plenum of the 11th Party Central Committee or even at the Central Work Conference held before the Third Plenum. Still less can we say that the two meetings thoroughly resolved the issue of reforms and opening. From the facts cited in this chapter and the preceding chapter, we can see that this is not true. In particular, on rural reform, the document adopted at the conference specifically mentioned "no permitting the fixing of farm output quotas for each household." In fact, practicing the fixing of farm output quotas for each household marked the first step toward carrying out the rural reform. After the Third Plenum, reforms in enterprises as required by the communiqué were launched at an early date, but without a serious breakthrough. Yet, thanks to the efforts of Wan Li and other comrades, a breakthrough was later made in rural reform, after several years of work — fixing farm output quotas for each household and the all-round contract system was further introduced.

Here we point out the deficiency of the Central Work Conference and the Third Plenum in reform and opening. But this did not hinder us. While marking the 20th anniversary of the Third Plenum, we should make a full assessment of the significance of the Third Plenum to China's reforms and opening. We should acknowledge that the Central Work Conference and the Third Plenum convened toward the end of 1978 represented a great turn. The great significance of the two meetings lay precisely in the two characters of *"zhuan zhe"* (turn). The Third Plenum divided China's history after the founding of the People's Republic of China into two phases. The thirty years after New China's founding in 1949 until 1978 when the Third Plenum of the 11th Party Central Committee was convened were the thirty years that witnessed the People's Republic of China achieving tortuous advances along the socialist road before ultimately becoming aware of the necessity of reforms. Reforms were carried out right after the Third Plenum of the 11th Party Central Committee was over.

In the first 35-year phase, the period from 1949 to 1952 was one of recovery of the national economy. The years from 1953 to 1956 saw the hasty and unrealistic socialist transformation carried out in four years. In 1956 it was announced that China had become a socialist society. In the twenty-one years from 1957 to 1978 socialism in China was a prematurely delivered baby, congenitally deformed. If we say that China then entered the primary stage of socialism, the twenty years from 1957 to 1978 were an initial phase, one that witnessed economic stagnation, political disturbance, cultural withering, and people living in poverty and distress. After the Third Plenum of the 11th Party Central Committee, China entered the reform stage of the primary phase of socialism. After the Third Plenum, reform policy measures were introduced one by one and reforms were carried out at one tier after another. The success scored in reforms promoted economic and social development.

Where did this stage begin? It began precisely in the Central Work Conference and the Third Plenum of the 11th Party Central Committee convened toward the end of 1978. At the time it was so important that there was not yet an adequate understanding of the significance, range and degree of the depth of reforms and opening. What was important was that there was progress. Despite hesitation and twists and turns along the way, it was good that such hesitation and twists and turns could be overcome before advances were eventually made. The triumphant starting point of this reform is precisely the Central Work Conference and the Third Plenum of the 11th Party Central Committee convened twenty years ago. The slogan presented at the conference, "emancipating the mind, seeking truth from facts, and uniting as one in looking to the future," and the ideological line and the political line defined by the Party Central Committee with Deng Xiaoping at the core established at the conference have ensured advance in the cause of reform and opening. This is the most important point and it deserves our permanent commemoration.

CHAPTER 4

BREAKTHROUGH IN CHANGING THE AGENDA

The Speech by Chen Yun

At the Work Conference, immediately after group discussions began, a breakthrough was made. Discussion would go beyond the three topics originally set for the meeting. The speech that Chen Yun delivered to the Northeast China Group on November 12 was what produced the greatest impact. Chen maintained that to generate enthusiasm for next year's plan first we must deal with a wide range of unresolved problems remaining from the movement to expose and criticize the "Gang of Four." The Party Central Committee needed to consider these problems and make decisions. He cited the following problems as examples.

> First was the case of the so-called "renegade group"[1] of 61 members, including Comrade Bo Yibo.[2] They had departed from a self-examination center in accordance with the decision of the Party Organization and the Party Central Committee. So, they were not renegades. On July 7, 1937, the CC had approved the decision of its Organization Department (Chen Yun was not then the head of the Organization Department) regarding the so-called traitors. The CC also approved the decision, after Chen became the head of the Organization Department, on restoring, after examination, Party membership for those comrades who had completed the procedures necessary for release from a self-examination center and who had continued to make revolution. The comrades affected by these two decisions and those who had done revolutionary work in the situation of two types of political power were not renegades. They should have their Party membership restored.
>
> Comrades Tao Zhu,[3] Wang Heshou,[4] and others were members of a group of Party members who had been incarcerated in the Nanjing Army Prison and who adamantly refused to go to a self-examination center. Even after the War of Resistance against Japanese Aggression broke out on July 7, 1937, they still waged hunger strikes in the prison. These comrades are now either labeled as renegades or have resumed their organization life, and yet they still carry a "tail." Concerning the cases of Tao Zhu and

63

others, Chen Yun proposed that cases that were investigated by the Central Special Group for the Examination of Cases and classified as internal Party matters be handed over to the Organization Department, which should reexamine them before drawing conclusions based on facts.

Comrade Peng Dehuai[5] held important positions in the Party and army and made great contributions to the Party. Now he is dead. His ashes should be placed in the Babaoshan Revolutionary Cemetery.

The Tiananmen Incident (April 5, 1976) was actually a great mass movement in which millions of people in Beijing gathered to commemorate Premier Zhou Enlai and oppose the "Gang of Four" and the criticism of Comrade Deng Xiaoping. The Party Central Committee should affirm this movement.

In the early period of the Cultural Revolution, Kang Sheng was one of the two advisors to the Central Cultural Revolution Group.[6] Then he willfully attacked by name various revolutionary cadres and assumed great responsibility for causing paralysis of various ministries of the Central government and Party and government offices throughout the country. His mistakes were very serious. The Central Committee should make due criticism of his mistakes, at an appropriate meeting.

On the same day, some comrades in other groups made similar comments. For instance, the Northwest China Group stated that to make a success in shifting the focus of work, it was imperative to redress framed, wrong, and false cases, such as the case involving the 61 comrades who were not renegades and redressing the nature of the 1976 Tiananmen Incident. They also demanded that a thorough investigation of Kang Sheng's mistakes in the Yan'an Rectification Movement and during the Cultural Revolution be included in the agenda.

Comrade Chen Yun enjoyed high prestige within the Party, considered questions carefully, raised questions that were to the point, and was persuasive. Participants in all the groups echoed his remarks. Nie Rongzhen in the Northeast China Group, Kang Keqing in the North China Group, Song Renqiong and Xiao Hua in the Northwest China Group, and many others expressed their views on the problems raised by Chen Yun. They also cited a number of major cases that the Party Central Committee must consider redressing, such as the case of Peng Zhen, Lu Dingyi, Luo Ruiqing, and Yang

Shangkun.[7] By then Luo Ruiqing had passed away. Peng Zhen, Lu Dingyi, and Yang Shangkun had not been assigned work. Regarding the case of the "February Adverse Current,"[8] although Mao Zedong said during the Cultural Revolution "don't mention it any more," the case had not been redressed thoroughly. The case of Liu Shaoqi involved so many issues that many participants shared the view that it was premature to raise this case. Therefore, this case was not cited at the conference.

In addition to problems in redressing the framed, wrong, and false cases, there was also the issue of how to deal with those who had unfairly attacked others. Many participants considered it imperative to make a thorough investigation of Kang Sheng's mistakes. In addition, these participants laid bare many facts about some people who had followed the "Gang of Four" in doing many evil things, thus stirring widespread popular indignation. Among this group were Xie Fuzhi,[9] Wu De, Wu Zhong,[10] and Guo Yufeng who were all from the central departments. As for such people working in localities, the participants from Shandong Province listed Wang Xiaoyu[11] and those from Jilin Province cited Wang Huaixiang.[12]

Support for Thorough Rehabilitation of Officals in the Tiananmen Incident

The vast majority of people and cadres at grass-roots units always had had a clear and steadfast understanding of the April 5, 1976, Tiananmen Incident from the very beginning. Responsible cadres in leading departments and academics also viewed the incident positively. After the downfall of the "Gang of Four," the Party Central Committee reflected some change in its view of the decision made by the Political Bureau of the Party Central Committee on April 7, 1976, and the publicity about the Tiananmen Incident by the editorial of the *People's Daily* issued on the same date. At the Central Work Conference held in March 1977, Hua Guofeng acknowledged the positive evaluation of the Tiananmen Incident:

> On the problem of the Tiananmen Incident of April 1976 in which the "Gang of Four" suppressed the masses from mourning our beloved Premier Zhou Enlai who had been persecuted by the Gang of Four. It was reasonable for the masses to flock to

Tiananmen to mourn Premier Zhou. There were only a handful of counterrevolutionaries who turned their spearhead at our great leader Chairman Mao and took advantage of the opportunity to conduct counterrevolutionary activities, triggering off the counterrevolutionary incident at Tiananmen. But we should acknowledge that the overwhelming majority of the people flocking to Tiananmen are good and that they were there for the purpose of mourning Premier Zhou. Many of them resented and opposed the "Gang of Four." It is wrong to label them, including those detained or arrested purely for opposing the "Gang of Four," as participants in a counterrevolutionary incident at Tiananmen. After the downfall of the "Gang of Four," the Party Central Committee issued a circular on December 5, 1976, stating: "Those detained or arrested purely for opposing the "Gang of Four" should be released. Files on people from the incident should be rescinded; those being examined should have their examinations rescinded; those who have already been sentenced should have their prison terms revoked and they should be released; those who have been disciplined in Party membership or the Communist Youth League membership, should have these disciplinary actions rescinded." We should say that the actual problems in this respect have been solved.

In effect, although he made some changes in the conclusion that had previously, in late 1976, been announced by the Central Committee and the *People's Daily*, Hua still affirmed the existence of the counterrevolutionary incident at Tiananmen. Vast numbers of people and cadres were strongly dissatisfied with this description of the nature of the Tiananmen Incident. In particular, in his speech, Hua accused some people of putting up big character posters and delivering speeches in 1977 to attack by name leading comrades of the Party Center. He urged people to guard against the "scheme of counterrevolutionaries." (At that time, a young man who had put up a poster to criticizing Wu De was thrown into prison for the "crime of launching a vicious attack.") Under these circumstances, Hua said we should "not debate such problems as the Tiananmen Incident." People naturally could not agree with him. So, after he made the speech in March 1977, appeals by the people and cadres to rehabilitate cadres involved in the Tiananmen Incident continued.

In the several months before the Central Work Conference, many people were very active in gathering public support for reversing the decision on the nature of the Tiananmen Incident. There appeared on the streets big character posters calling for reversing the decisions on the Tiananmen Incident. Tong Huaizhou (a collective *nom de plume*, meaning "jointly cherishing the memory of Premier Zhou Enlai") from the Beijing No. 2 Foreign Languages Institute compiled, printed, and distributed poems in praise of the Tiananmen Incident. Workers in Shanghai wrote and performed a modern drama titled *In a Quiet Place*,[13] which was cited by Chen Yun in his speech. Many who had been persecuted on various occasions for their involvement in the Tiananmen Incident, made reports on their own struggles and experiences. Relevant articles were carried in the issue marking the resumption of the publication of *Chinese Youth*, the official magazine of the Central Committee of the Communist Youth League of China. The *People's Daily*, the official newspaper of the Party Central Committee, devoted a special page to the Tiananmen Incident. But the comrades in charge of publicity refused to allowthis special page printed. Comrade Yu Huanchun, an editor with the newspaper, delivered a speech at a meeting of the National Committee of the Chinese People's Political Consultative Conference, stating that the case had not been redressed completely. (Yu wrote an article on reversing the decisions and the nature of the Tiananmen Incident, which was carried in the second issue of the magazine *Hundred Year Tide* published in 1998. He introduced many facts he knew about the incident.) However, the activity to demand the rehabilitation of the Tiananmen Incident did not get high-level support until shortly before the Central Work Conference. The rationale that Wang Dongxing and others used after the downfall of the "Gang of Four" to obstruct the reversal of the decisions on the Tiananmen Incident against the will of the vast number of people and cadres was that "given Chairman Mao's directive, nobody can reverse the verdict on this case."

The issue of how to deal with the Tiananmen Incident was thus very alive when the Central Work Conference was held at this time. Comrades inside the Party and in society were universally concerned about this problem, and the participants enthusiastically took the floor at the conference while discussing the shift in the focus of work. According to the bulletin I saw, Chen Zaidao of the East China

67

Group gave the first speech on the Tiananmen Incident. He said, "Practice is the sole criterion for testing truth. We already have had the 'practice' and the 'truth' as well. The problem is that some people dare not 'test' — they dare not speak the truth. Practice has proved that the Tiananmen Incident and the activities mourning Premier Zhou and opposing the 'Gang of Four' were revolutionary actions. If we say that the Tiananmen Incident involved counterrevolutionaries, they are but the 'Gang of Four.' Once this problem is made clear to the entire Chinese people, they will be convinced."

From reading the bulletins I learned that the speech by Comrade Chen Yun in the Northeast China Group had played a central role in beginning discussion of the issue. The fifth of the six problems he cited was "the Tiananmen Incident." He said, "Now some people in Beijing have raised the problem again. In addition, the modern drama titled *In a Quiet Place* has been staged, and radio stations have broadcast revolutionary poems appearing at Tiananmen. This was a great mass movement launched by millions of people in Beijing to mourn Premier Zhou and to oppose the 'Gang of Four' and to oppose the criticism of Comrade Deng Xiaoping. Similar movements were also launched in many other big cities across the country. The Party Central Committee should affirm this movement." When a senior revolutionary like Chen Yun, who enjoyed very high prestige, addressed the issue, this raised it to a new level. He set a good example and greatly encouraged the comrades in all groups of the Central Work Conference.

In the Northeast China Group, Li Chang made a penetrating analysis of the Tiananmen Incident. He said that "the activity conducted by the masses at Tiananmen to mourn Premier Zhou was a great revolutionary movement. The 'May 4th' Movement (1919) was an enlightening movement during the new democratic revolution period. We can also say that the activity conducted by the masses at Tiananmen to mourn Premier Zhou is an enlightened Marxist movement during the socialist revolution period. This movement has since greatly promoted the trend of scientific thought featuring seeking truth from facts and the trend of strengthening people's socialist democratic thought. I think that we should continue to fully affirm and energetically support the movement. Now *In Quiet Place* is being performed. The Beijing Municipal Party Committee should vigorously support the 'April 5th' Movement."

In the East China Group, Lu Zhengcao took the lead in referring to this problem. "If we say there was a 'May 4th' Movement during the new democratic revolution period, the Tiananmen Incident is the 'May 4th' Movement during the socialist revolution period.... Nurtured by Mao Zedong Thought, it constitutes a great honor for the Chinese people. But then after the Tiananmen Incident was suppressed, a mass rally was held in Beijing in celebration of the victory. At the rally, a bad man had spoken at length, relating his criticism of Comrade Deng Xiaoping at a meeting of the Political Bureau. The remarks he made were all personal attacks. This is an unusual phenomenon that has never occurred inside the Party. Why did Comrade Wu De, who presided over the rally, permit the delivery of such a speech?"

In a joint speech delivered in the Northwest China Group on November 13, Wang Huide, Yang Xiguang, and I noted that in China it was necessary to give full scope to democracy. We said, "To realize the four modernizations, it is imperative to make corresponding changes in production relations, the superstructure, etc. According to Lenin, 'If full democracy is not practiced under victorious socialism, it will be impossible for socialism to retain the victory it has won and to guide mankind to the elimination of the state.' Here one viewpoint should be made clear inside the Party, that after our Party became a ruling party, it should still stand among the masses of the people and lead them in winning democracy. For this reason, the struggle to win democracy should continue. Moreover, democracy should not be bestowed because bestowed democracy is not solid. Only the democracy that the people themselves rise to win is solid. The people can win the victory in their struggle to win democracy only under the Party's correct leadership. Otherwise, it would be impossible. Proceeding from the revolutionary stand of leading the people in winning democracy, the Party ought to explicitly declare its stand on the 'Tiananmen Incident'."

We pointed out that "the Tiananmen Incident is a great revolutionary incident and should therefore merit our Party's high appreciation and full affirmation.... On the one hand, a ruling

Communist Party must stand among the people and continue to lead them in their struggle to win democracy. On the other hand, it must make full use of the political power it has seized to protect people's democracy and act in cooperation with the people in their struggle to win democracy."

Right after the Central Work Conference began, various participants in all groups proposed reassessing the nature of the Tiananmen Incident. On the morning of November 13, when we delivered our joint speech, Wang Huide, Yang Xiguang, and I did not know that the Beijing Municipal Party Committee was holding an enlarged meeting of its Standing Committee. On November 15, three days after our speech, the *Beijing Daily* carried a lengthy report on this meeting. The report contained the following paragraph about the Tiananmen Incident:

> On the Spring Grave-sweeping Festival of 1976, the masses of people gathered at Tiananmen to mourn our beloved Premier Zhou. Their frame of mind evinced a boundless love for Premier Zhou, they cherished infinite memories of him, and they engaged in profound mourning for Premier Zhou. They were gripped by a deep hatred for the hideous crimes committed by the 'Gang of Four' who brought calamity to the country. This action reflects the aspiration of hundreds of millions of people all over the country and is entirely a revolutionary action. All the comrades persecuted for their involvement shall be rehabilitated and have their reputations restored.

Compared to Hua Guofeng's speech at the Central Work Conference in March 1977, this paragraph in the *Beijing Daily* made progress in the following areas. First of all, it elevated the significance of the broad masses of people gathering at Tiananmen. In his March 1977 speech, Hua just said that the frame of mind of the masses (he did not say the broad masses of people) gathering on Tiananmen to mourn Premier Zhou was understandable. But the report stated that the broad masses of people gathering on Tiananmen to mourn Premier Zhou was a great revolutionary action. More importantly, in his March speech, immediately after the preceding sentence, Hua added, "There were really a handful of counterrevolutionaries who took advantage of the opportunity to create the Tiananmen counterrevolutionary incident." The November 14 article in the *Beijing Daily* did not negate the meaning of this second remark, but it did not mention it again.

This paragraph appeared in the newspaper on November 15, 1978. Even today I am still unclear about when these sentences were written into the report and what process led to their publication. This short paragraph was inserted in a report with a total of 3,000 to 4,000 characters and was not marked in the headline. So, that day it did not draw the attention of participants in the Central Working Conference meeting in the Jingxi Hotel. However, three comrades in the press community, Zeng Tao, the president of the Xinhua News Agency, Hu Jiwei, the editor-in-chief of *People's Daily*, and Yang Xiguang, the editor-in-chief of *Guangming Daily*, noticed it and took immediate action. They pulled this paragraph out of the text of the *Beijing Daily* report and released it as a news item under the headline "Beijing Municipal Party Committee Announces Tiananmen Incident Is Revolutionary Action." They drew attention to the description of how the masses had gathered at Tiananmen Square to mourn Premier Zhou and condemn the "Gang of Four." The Xinhua News Agency released a news item to that effect on November 15th. *People's Daily* and *Guangming Daily* gave this Xinhua news item a prominent place on their front pages.

When the comrades attending the Central Work Conference read this item in the morning, they were all overjoyed. When it released this news item, Xinhua did not submit it to the Political Bureau for examination and approval; nor did they report it to any of the Standing Committee members. Yu Huanchun recalled that afterward Hu Yaobang told Hu Jiwei that he had not been informed of such an important matter. Zeng Tao and others believed that it was better not to ask for instruction about this matter and that Xinhua should assume full responsibility on its own. Regarding this omission, Ji Dengkui of the Northwest China Group said it was not good that a matter of such importance had not discussed by the Political Bureau before the group meeting. Other participants in the group told him that this matter had already been clarified, so there was no need to discuss it. The comrades I talked with all praised Comrade Zeng Tao for his courage and resolute behavior. Of course, Hua Guofeng understood the situation very well.

This episode took place while the Central Work Conference was in session. It did not actually occur at the conference, but it had an impact on the conference. This was because three days after the Xinhua news item was released, on November 18, Hua Guofeng wrote the book name for the *Collection of Tiananmen Poems*[14] that had been submitted to him by Tong Huaizhou for publication at the request of the People's Literature Publishing House. It was in this form that Hua indicated support for the action of Zeng Tao and the other comrades. Meanwhile, Xinhua also reported the news that those sentenced to prison terms for their involvement in the Tiananmen Incident were all declared not guilty. But at the Central Work Conference some participants still hoped that the Party Central Committee would explicitly declare again its stand on the problem of reversing the decision on the Tiananmen Incident. They believed that after Hua Guofeng wrote the book name on November 18, the Tiananmen Incident should, in fact, be considered solved completely and that the only thing to be done would be to ask the Party Central Committee to formally issue another document to explicitly reiterate its stand.

Hua Nan in the Northeast China Group later remarked that "at the Central Work Conference held on November 25, Hua Guofeng made the following remarks on the TiananmenTiananmen Incident: "Shortly after the 'Gang of Four' was smashed, the Party Central Committee started to solve the problem of the [April 5, 1976] Tiananmen Incident and the problem of revolutionary masses persecuted for involvement in such incidents as the Tiananmen Incident. With the thoroughgoing movement to expose and criticize the 'Gang of Four,' most problems in this regard have been solved successively. Nevertheless, they have not been solved thoroughly and the nature of the Tiananmen Incident has not been reversed yet. The Party Central Committee holds that the Tiananmen Incident is entirely a revolutionary mass movement and that it is necessary to openly and thoroughly rehabilitate the people involved in the Tiananmen Incident."

Hua was very smart in making these remarks, because he defended himself while admitting that the judgment on the Tiananmen Incident had not been reversed. Finally, he accepted the views aired at the conference and announced on behalf of the Party Central Committee that the nature of the Tiananmen Incident had been reevaluated. In my opinion, this part of his speech should be welcomed. Indeed, it was high time to solve this problem. The actions of Zeng Tao and other comrades quickened the pace of the reevaluation so that the problem was solved before the conclusion of the Central Work Conference and before the convocation of the Third Plenum. This was the one major problem raised at the Central Work Conference that was solved before the conclusion of the conference.

Hua Guofeng continued to refer to the conclusion announced by the Beijing Municipal Party Committee on November 14. The announcement by the Beijing Municipal Party Committee, as transmitted by Hua, was consistent with the report of *Beijing Daily*. But I was not clear on one detail—when on earth was this meeting of the Beijing Municipal Party Committee held? Such a meeting should ordinarily be reported openly, but the report in the *Beijing Daily* did not mention it. This was very strange. As for when those sentences pertaining to the Tiananmen Incident were approved by Hua Guofeng, whether the Standing Committee of the Political Bureau of the Party Central Committee referred to Hua himself, to Wang Dongxing, or perhaps to someone else, these facts remain unclear. But one thing was indisputable, Deng Xiaoping was absent when those sentences were approved because he did not conclude his visit to Singapore and return to Beijing until November 14. He was given a warm send-off in Singapore on the morning of November 14. So, it was impossible for him to have been involved in "approving" the paragraph on November 14 as Hua Guofeng asserted. The declaration that approval had been given on November 14 was certainly a mistake because the *Beijing Daily* carrying these sentences was on the streets in Beijing by the early morning of November 14. Yet the dating was a detail of little importance.

Regarding the decision of the Beijing Municipal Party Committee to reevaluate the Tiananmen Incident, I published an article in the third issue of the *Hundred Year Tide* titled the "Truth about 'Beijing

Municipal Party Committee Reevaluating Tiananmen Incident' in 1978." In it I gave a detailed introduction to my "personal experience" then and did some "textual analysis" and made "some distinctions."

The Third General Meeting and
the Declaration of Hua Guofeng

The third plenary session of the Work Conference was held on November 25. Hua Guofeng delivered his second speech, expressing satisfaction with the previous two weeks of the conference. Hua also praised the participants for practicing democracy, engaging in lively discussion, airing their views, and speaking their minds freely. He said approvingly, "It is very good that all participants are discussing questions with open minds." His remarks served to further encourage the participants. Afterward they became even more open in their speeches.

Hua's speech evaded none of the problems raised by the participants. In fact, he discussed all eight problems and responded positively to the views of participants. Later, when the text of his speech was finalized, the reversal of the "criticism of Deng Xiaoping" was added, bringing the number of problems to nine. As for the Tiananmen Incident, he conceded, "The problem has not been fully solved and we have moved further to reevaluate the nature of the Tiananmen Incident." This was an appropriate reflection of the views expressed by the participants. On behalf of the Central Committee, he declared, "The Central Committee holds that the Tiananmen Incident is entirely a revolutionary mass movement and that it is necessary to reevaluate the Tiananmen Incident openly and thoroughly." This was the formal positive evaluation of the nature of the Tiananmen Incident and the first issue to be discussed.

Hua next spoke of the second problem. He acknowledged that "striking back the Right-deviationist tendency toward reversing the verdicts [in 1975 and after] was wrong." It had been decided to cancel all relevant documents of the Party Central Committee. Referring to the third problem, namely, the "February Adverse Current" (1967), he said that Chairman Mao had already reversed the verdict on the "February Adverse Current" in 1971. Hua said, "Now the Party

Central Committee has decided to restore the reputations of all the comrades who suffered injustice for their involvement in the case, and to rehabilitate all of those who were implicated and disciplined."

On the fourth problem, he said that in the case of 61 people, including Bo Yibo, it had been ascertained that a major incorrect judgment had been made, and the Party Central Committee decided to redress this incorrect judgment. On the fifth problem, the case of Peng Dehuai, Hua announced the decision that "his ashes should be placed in the first chamber of the Babaoshan Revolutionary Cemetery." Regarding the sixth problem, the case of Tao Zhu, he said: "It was wrong to label him a renegade and he should be posthumously rehabilitated." With respect to the seventh problem, the case of Yang Shangkun, Hua Guofeng said, "It was wrong to label him a conspirator opposed to the Party and to accuse him of having illicit relations with a foreign country. He should be rehabilitated. The Party Central Committee has decided to restore Comrade Yang Shangkun's Party organizational life and give him a new work assignment." On the eighth problem, the cases of Kang Sheng and Xie Fuzhi, he pointed out that the two men "had aroused great popular indignation.... it is correct to expose and criticize them.... The relevant materials for exposing them can be submitted to the Organization Department of the Party Central Committee for examination and processing." Finally, regarding the ninth problem, the problem of major local incidents, he said: "All should be handled by the Party Committees of various provinces, municipalities, and autonomous regions in accordance with specific circumstances and on the basis of facts." In short, in the view of the vast majority of participants, Hua gave satisfactory answers to all major problems cited in the discussions.

Hua Guofeng's speech must have been discussed and approved by the top central leaders in the Standing Committee members of the Political Bureau of the Party Central Committee. Hua Guofeng's attitude also deserves our praise. I had attended many meetings. But I had seen almost no top Party leaders who could solicit others' opinions in such a way and I had seen almost no problem solved so thoroughly and explicitly. Hua's speech was also pragmatic, not promising to do what could not in fact be done, and Hua listed a number of matters deserving attention. For instance, speaking of tackling local problems, he said that mass meetings could be held and documents could be issued, but they should not be carried in newspapers or broadcast by radio. He said that these problems involved the broad masses of people who had been split up into two factions during the Cultural Revolution, and that therefore they must be tackled cautiously and properly to avoid rekindling factional struggles. In short, this speech was excellent. After his speech, the third plenary session discussions proceeded in a more thoroughgoing way.

An Event Outside the Conference
That Was Reflected Inside

On the afternoon of November 25, immediately after the third plenary session, Hua Guofeng, Ye Jianying, Deng Xiaoping, Li Xiannian, and Wang Dongxing listened to reports on the opinions of the masses after the reevaluation of the Tiananmen Incident given by Lin Hujia and Jia Tingsan[15] from the Beijing Municipal Party Committee and by Han Ying[16] and Hu Qili[17] from the Central Committee of the Communist Youth League of China. After hearing the report, the Standing Committee of the Political Bureau of the Party Central Committee, collectively published an important speech by Deng Xiaoping, which contained the following remarks:

> We must hold high the great banner of Chairman Mao. Chairman Mao's banner is a banner of unity and revolution for the whole Party, the whole army, and the people of all ethnic groups across the country, and the banner for the international Communist movement as well. Now some people have raised historical problems. Some historical problems should be solved because not solving them will impose burdens on many people and make it impossible for them to forge ahead without any mental constraints. We cannot solve difficult historical problems in a brief period of time. If people of our generation cannot resolve certain matters, they should be left to people of the next generation to resolve. The longer the time, the more people can clearly analyze the difficult issues. Some problems can be resolved in a short while, and others cannot. Resolving difficult, divisive issues will divert the attention of the Party and people and is not in the essential interests of the state and people.

As for some problems that cropped up during the Cultural Revolution, Chairman Mao already pointed out the necessity of correcting the mistake of 'overthrowing everyone and launching an all-round civil war.' We are now redressing the framed, wrong, and false cases precisely to solve this problem. Furthermore, we are convinced that if Chairman Mao were still alive, these problems would be solved step-by-step. We must understand Mao Zedong Thought in an accurate and comprehensive manner and hold high Chairman Mao's great banner. Of course, 'there is no gold bullion that is 100 percent pure and there is no person in the world who is a perfect person." For some problems, there will invariably be a process of exposure and gaining understanding.

We should solve specific problems on the basis of facts and in accordance with the principle that practice is the sole criterion for testing truth. Now newspapers are discussing the issue of the criterion for testing truth and lively discussion is taking place. It is inappropriate to say that those articles are aimed at Chairman Mao, because that would constrain people from speaking their minds. But in dealing with problems, we must consider the context and the consequences as well.

In some matters, Chairman Mao's name should not be mentioned because mentioning him would be divisive. Newspapers must be very cautious. Once one exceeds the limit, truth will be turned into fallacy. Chairman Mao's great feats are enduring. Chinese history has proved that Chen Duxiu, Wang Ming, Li Lisan, and others could not have succeeded and that only Chairman Mao could have led us to victory. Without Chairman Mao, there would be no New China. Chairman Mao's greatness cannot be overestimated and cannot be adequately described with words. Chairman Mao was not without shortcomings and mistakes. Yet, they are insignificant when compared to his great feats. We should not require a great leader, a great person, and a great thinker to be free of shortcomings and mistakes, because whoever sets that requirement is not a Marxist. Chairman Mao said, while writing articles, even Marx and Lenin often made revisions. We cannot require Chairman Mao to be correct in every remark. If we did so, wouldn't that show that Lin Biao's 'theory of genius' was correct? Foreigners have asked me whether or not it was permissible to appraise Chairman Mao in the same way as to appraise Stalin when we say he had 70 percent achievements and 30 percent mistakes? I replied with certainty that it is wrong to do so. The Party Central Committee and the Chinese people will never do what Khrushchev did.

Deng Xiaoping's speech was not formally presented at the conference. However, the conference organizers printed and distributed it in the conference documents, the "Main Points of Notes of the Gist of the Directives of the Standing Committee members of the Political Bureau of the Party Central Committee." It was not distributed to participants until several days after the conference. When the document did become available, there was no time to engage in thorough criticism of the "two whatevers." In his November 25 speech, Hua Guofeng did not respond to the "two whatevers," and the participants were not enthusiastic about this omission.

Those who had read Deng's document and studied it carefully regarded it as a formal declaration of the stand by the Party Central Committee on the issue of the criterion for testing truth. Hua did not specifically refer to the Work Conference discussion about the criterion for testing truth. But he did acknowledge, "It is necessary to solve some specific problems on the basis of facts and in accordance with the principle that practice is the sole criterion for testing truth. Now newspapers are discussing the question of the criterion for testing truth, and lively discussions are taking place. It is inappropriate to say that those articles are aimed at Chairman Mao because that would constrain people from speaking their minds." These remarks could be viewed as a formal declaration supporting the article "Practice Is the Sole Criterion for Testing Truth" and the discussion that followed on that issue. But since events outside the conference were not related to the conference participants, many — including myself — did not take the floor to discuss it. But from the summary bulletins I learned that Zhang Pinghua in the Northeast China Group mentioned the event in which the Political Bureau Standing Committee members listened to reports. The comrades in the Northeast China Group criticized Zhang Pinghua, who, while head of the Publicity Department of the Party Central Committee, took a passive attitude toward the discussion of the issue of the criterion for testing truth. When criticized, Zhang defended himself by saying that he found it hard to declare his stand because the Party Central Committee had not formally declared its stand. He said that now that the situation was different, he would behave differently after the Political Bureau Standing Committee declared its stand on the afternoon of November 25. From his speech I deduced that he had attended the meeting to review the discussions. That was how he had come to know the content of the speeches of the Political Bureau Standing Committee members before the document was distributed to the participants. I first learned from the bulletins of the Southwest China Group about the speeches of the Political Bureau Standing Committee members. This was an event that occurred outside the conference and yet had an impact on our conference. I don't remember clearly what happened in other groups. So, I cannot say with certainty that no one aside from Zhang Pinghua mentioned the directive given by the Political Bureau Standing Committee members at that review meeting on the afternoon of November 25.

CHAPTER 5

THE CRITICISM OF WANG DONGXING, WU DE, AND KANG SHENG

The Criticism of Wang Dongxing

In the evening of November 25, following the plenary session, I went to Jiang Yizhen's room to discuss whether or not we should criticize Wang Dongxing by name. We all shared the view that Wang Dongxing in playng a significant role in smashing the "Gang of Four" had performed a deed of great merit. Without his active participation and without the deployment of the 8341 Unit under his direct command, it would have been impossible to smash the "Gang of Four" in a single stroke in October 1976. However, in his role as representing the Political Bureau on publicity issues, by clinging to the wording of the "two whatevers" and resisting the discussion about the criterion for testing truth, Wang was hindering the reevaluation of the Tiananmen Incident and the appointment of Deng Xiaoping to lead the state. Wang also adopted a passive attitude toward redressing the framed, wrong, and false cases arising from the Cultural Revolution and toward dealing with the Kang Sheng case. His stance was utterly wrong and his attitude was very bad. In clinging to the "two whatevers" he made many inappropriate remarks and served as a behind-the-scene boss for those insisting on the "two whatevers." If we did not mention him by name, many problems could not be explained clearly and resolved thoroughly.

In the first two weeks of group meetings all the participants had avoided mentioning Wang Dongxing by name in speeches touching upon areas he was in charge of. When reading the reports in the summary bulletins, we always felt that hiding some things did not conform to the spirit of fully carrying out democracy. Democracy was not bestowed, and we had to take vigorous action to achieve it. Moreover, Wang Dongxing was present at the conference, and, while he did not come to our group meetings, he would certainly read our criticism of him in the bulletins. If he thought that our criticism did not comply with the facts or contained parts that did not accord with the facts, he could issue a statement. If he thought that the reasons we referred to were incorrect, he could reply and both sides could hold discussions and debate. We had the right to democracy. As a vice-chairman of the Party Central Committee, of course, he also had his right to democracy. Having pondered the matter from all angles, we concluded that, since he was not following policies approved at the Work Conference, it was time to criticize Wang Dongxing by name. We thought that this would be good for the conference.

Of course, we were not without misgivings. We knew that what we intended to do was to criticize directly a vice-chairman of the Party Central Committee and a Political Bureau Standing Committee member at a large-scale meeting. The Party Constitution permitted such action. In fact, a Party member was duty-bound to make a stern criticism of anyone within the Party who had major shortcomings or committed mistakes. We considered the issue carefully and were convinced that our criticism would have a positive result. But this was a major matter and we did not know whether there was any precedent in our Party's history. We considered asking the leadership for approval before acting, but we deemed it might be awkward for them to take responsibility and therefore decided to take the responsibility on our own.

Jiang Yizhen and I decided to act immediately. Jiang Yizhen fired the first shot on the morning of November 26. He was the first to criticize Wang Dongxing by name, not only in our Northwest China Group, but also in the entire conference. In his speech Jiang said that he had marched together with Wang Dongxing in the Long March, that he reached Yan'an together with him, and that he had worked with him later. He said that he had had a favorable impression of Wang. He courteously praised Wang's merits in ensuring Mao Zedong's safety for years before smashing the "Gang of Four." Then he raised a series of questions. He questioned Wang's attitude toward Premier Zhou and Comrade Deng Xiaoping. He mentioned that Wang had said in November 1976, "Didn't Deng Xiaoping [in 1975] try his tricks? He is no good at all." He also criticized Wang's attitude in discussing the "issue of whether practice is the sole criterion for testing truth." He said that Wang had obstructed him when he redressed framed, false, and wrong cases in the Ministry of Health. He exposed Wang for harboring Liu Xiangping when the "Gang of Four" was exposed and criticized in the Beijing Hospital.

After Jiang made his speech, Yang Xiguang and I delivered a speech I had co-authored to the Northwest China Group. We emphatically criticized Wang Dongxing for clinging to the "two whatevers," impeding Deng Xiaoping from returning to work, and obstructing the discussion about the criterion for testing truth after the downfall of the "Gang of Four." Knowing a lot about Wang Dongxing, Yang spoke of matters in specific terms. For example, he could accurately relate the content of a speech Wang had made and could cite the names of those who were present and could bear witness. Quite a few people in our group had not previously known what Yang related and thus showed great interest.

When Jiang Yizhen, Yang Xiguang, and I criticized Wang Dongxing by name in the Northwest China Group, of course this caught our comrades' attention. Yet nobody publicly commented on this, as if they did not find it unusual. Only at the supper on November 26 and at the breakfast on November 27, did comrades say to me, "You were right to do so."

Of course, I paid close attention to the response of the conference leaders to our action. First I read the summary bulletins. The joint speech by Jiang Yizhen, Yang Xiguang, and Yu Guangyuan in the Northwest China Group was accurately recorded in the bulletins. Those in charge of compiling the bulletins did not delete our speeches just because we mentioned a member of the Political Bureau Standing Committee by name. Furthermore, judging from the speed at which our speech was carried in the bulletins, they apparently did not ask anyone for instruction, as this would have delayed the release of the bulletins. At the conference, I looked for responses from the five other groups to our criticism of Wang Dongxing by name. I noticed that although the speeches that echoed our speech did not appear at once, they did begin slowly to appear. I do not remember clearly the responses from all the groups. I only remember that the first person to criticize Wang Dongxing by name in the Southwest China Group was Hu Jiwei. In a long speech two days later, Hu made many references to Wang. The materials he cited in his speech were more specific and his criticism of Wang was more concentrated and forceful. Later, there was plenty of criticism of Wang in all the groups, with many veteran comrades revealing many of Wang's incorrect words and deeds. The criticism in some speeches was very sharp.

During the entire conference, not once was anyone accused for openly criticizing a vice-chairman at the conference. This demonstrated that democracy was practiced fully at the conference. Our previous misgivings proved unnecessary.

Wang Dongxing and the "Two Whatevers"

After Wang Dongxing was criticized by name, the issues related to the "two whatevers" and the criterion for testing truth could be resolved more clearly. Wang Dongxing was really a crucial case. If he had not been mentioned by name, it would have been impossible to trace the origin of many matters. The whole problem had started shortly after the "Gang of Four" was smashed. On November 18, 1976, Wang Dongxing, who was in charge of publicity, said at a national meeting of publicity departments, "It is only with the downfall of the 'Gang of Four' that the publicity work has been emancipated.... We have taken back the power to carry out publicity." People then hoped for a fundamental change in Party publicity work. Nevertheless, after relating a few things about the "Gang of Four," Wang Dongxing talked about Deng Xiaoping's "problems." He said:

> After October of last year [1975], Chairman Mao discovered Deng Xiaoping's mistakes, which were serious. He did what he had done previously. Seeing that Deng was no good, Chairman Mao singled out Hua Guofeng as his successor. Yet Deng Xiaoping's serious mistakes worsened until the Tiananmen Incident occurred.... If the Tiananmen Incident was intended to commemorate Premier Zhou, is there anything bad about it? What is wrong with it? But the incident was used by counter-revolutionaries. When we criticized Deng Xiaoping for his mistakes, counter-revolutionaries took advantage of this to launch a rebellion.

Then, after talking about how the "Gang of Four" used the Tiananmen Incident, Wang Dongxing returned to the criticism of Deng Xiaoping: "Chairman Mao issued the No. 4 document, whose content is correct because the document contains Chairman Mao's directives." Wang had said: "The current struggle is directed at the 'Gang of Four,' but it is also necessary to criticize Deng for his mistakes." Then he said, "Now there is a rumor that Deng has been reinstated." He called attention to the fact that "Chairman Mao said 'retain his [Deng Xiaoping's] Party membership to see how he behaves'." He said, "For his few tricks, Deng is far beneath Hua Guofeng. Deng Xiaoping was given the opportunity to show his ability but practice shows that he is no good at all!... He still does not have a good understanding of the Cultural Revolution and fails to do a good job in the "three correct treatments." This deserves the attention of our veteran comrades." Wang also said, "The case of Deng Xiaoping has not been designated as a contradiction between ourselves and the enemy. Who treated it so lightly? We must still 'see how he behaves.'" Throughout his speech Wang explicitly and firmly opposed the criticism of the "two whatevers" and Deng Xiaoping's return to work.

About half a month later, at the Third Plenary Session of the Standing Committee of the Fourth National People's Congress (NPC) held on November 30, 1976, Wang reiterated that it was wrong to oppose the "Gang of Four" concerning the Tiananmen Incident. "They [the "Gang of Four"] were still central leaders. Opposing them would mean splitting the Party Central Committee." He also said, "It is imperative to combine the criticism of the 'Gang of Four' with criticism of Deng Xiaoping." It was precisely at that NPC session that the first version of the "two whatevers" appeared. In his speech at the session Wu De had said, "We must try to do whatever Chairman Zedong instructed and whatever the Chairman decided, and try to do it well." The remarks Wang Dongxing made in his speech on November 18 were different from those in his November 30 speech. In the earlier speech, when speaking of the people opposing the "Gang of Four" at Tiananmen, he said, "The"Gang of Four" was still in power then. If you hated them in your heart, wore a look of indignation, and wrote about your hatred for them on the wreath, how can all this be distinguished? They were quite foolish in doing so. If you resented the "Gang of Four," you could have expressed your resentment and you should not have gotten mixed up with counterrevolutionaries." In that speech he did not label those people as "splitting the Party Central Committee" twelve days later.

A little over two months later, in February 1977, *Red Flag* magazine asked the Party Central Committee for instruction concerning the publication of the article by Zhang Chunqiao, "On Exercising All-Round Dictatorship over the Bourgeoisie," and the article by Yao Wenyuan, "On the Social Basis for the Lin Biao Anti-Party Clique." Wang Dongxing responded, "These two articles (the articles by Zhang Chunqiao and Yao Wenyuan) were approved by the Party Central Committee and read by our great leader Chairman Mao. So, it is permissible to criticize the erroneous viewpoints in the articles only without naming names." The obvious implication was that it was impermissible to criticize the two articles by name.

On February 7, 1977, two newspapers and one magazine jointly issued an editorial titled "Study Documents Carefully and Grasp the Key Link." This was the second version of the "two whatevers." The editorial asserted, "We must resolutely uphold whatever policy decisions Chairman Mao made; and we must unswervingly follow whatever instructions Chairman Mao gave." This is the standard version of the "two whatevers." The "two whatevers" that people mention now usually refers to this version of the "two whatevers." How was this editorial concocted? It was only after Wang Dongxing was criticized by name that people came to know that he had given a directive to the *People's Daily*: "I think that this article is all right after being discussed and revised repeatedly by Comrade Li Xin and the comrades of the Theoretical Study Group." He decided to issue the editorial in the two newspapers and in *Red Flag*. Geng Biao was then in charge of the publicity department. The editorial was distributed to various branches of this department. Several comrades in these branches, who had been asked by Geng Biao to discuss the editorial, said, "Carrying this article implies that the 'Gang of Four' was not smashed. If we acted according to the 'two whatevers,' we would accomplish nothing." Nevertheless, all the newspapers had no option but to carry this editorial because Wang Dongxing distributed it in the name of the Party Central Committee. Even Geng Biao could do nothing about it.

On May 11, 1978, the *Guangming Daily* carried an article on the criterion for testing truth. In less than one week, on May 17, Wang Dongxing said at a group meeting, "We must be cautious in handling theoretical questions. In particular, none of us had read the two articles—one titled 'Practice Is the Sole Criterion for Testing Truth' and another titled 'Implement the Socialist Principle of to Each According to His Work.' There are widespread comments on them inside and outside the Party. The two articles are actually spearheaded at the Chairman's Thought. Our Party newspapers cannot do this. Which Party Central Committee's view is this?" He added: "We must uphold and defend Mao Zedong Thought. We must examine, draw a lesson, and unify our understanding. This is not to be taken as a precedent. Of course, this enlivens our thinking. But the *People's Daily* must have the Party spirit and the Publicity Department of the Party Central Committee must examine articles before publication. "

Wang Dongxing understood clearly how the article in the *Guangming Daily* came to be written. He knew Deng Xiaoping's view on this issue and knew that it had been written in line with Hu Yaobang's proposal and under Hu's guidance. But he used such wording as "Which Party Central Committee's view is this?" to express his opposition. I also knew the circumstances surrounding the writing of the article "Implement the Socialist Principle of to Each According to His Work." This article was based on a number of speeches that had been delivered at the influential "symposia on the question of to each according to his work" that had been held many times in 1977 and 1978. In July and August of 1977, the *People's Daily* carried an article titled "Refute Yao Wenyuan's Fallacy that 'To Each According to His Work' Produces the Bourgeoisie" written jointly by Su Shaozhi[1] and Feng Lanrui.[2] After reading this article, Deng Xiaoping sent a memo to the State Council Research Office, saying that the viewpoint of the article was correct and yet the mind of the writers was not yet sufficiently emancipated. He asked the State Council Research Office to write another important article. So, the office arranged and organized Feng Lanrui and others to participate in writing an article, under Lin Jianqing's[3] leadership. Some experts on wages from other units were invited to participate and a writing group was formed. After the article was completed, it was sent to Deng Xiaoping for approval and was revised according to Deng's views before being finalized. Perhaps Wang Dongxing was unclear about the exact process by which the article came to be written. But at the meetings of the Party Central Committee, Deng spoke many times about the question of "to each according to his work." Wang knew that Deng approved the article and even knew it very well. That was why the remarks that Wang made were aimed completely at Deng and were designed to oppose him. Nonetheless, he had some misgivings and therefore he added the remark, "This enlivens our thinking." But Wang attempted to constrain people by saying, "The two articles are actually spearheaded at the Chairman." His intention to weaken Deng was quite obvious.

One month later, on June 15, 1977, Wang Dongxing called for a small-scale meeting of publicity departments in the Xinjiang Hall of the Great Hall of the People. Among the participants were Wu Lanfu, a member of the Political Bureau; the head and deputy heads of the Publicity Department of the Party Central Committee, Xiong Fu, Zeng Tao, Yang Xiguang, Hu Jiwei and Wang Shu who had assumed leadership in *Red Flag* magazine and been transferred to the Ministry of Foreign Affairs. Addressing the meeting, Wang Dongxing expressed his criticism at the beginning:

> Nowadays newspapers and magazines do not have a high sense of publicizing the Party spirit, of subordinating our individual characters to the Party spirit. Because some people were attacked in the Cultural Revolution, they are full of grievances and thus describe the Cultural Revolution as worthless. They will eventually direct their spearheads at Chairman Mao.... Some people now say the Cultural Revolution, personally initiated by Chairman Mao, was devoid of any merit. They also criticize Chairman Mao while criticizing the 'Gang of Four.'... Enemies at home and abroad will take advantage of our failure to do good publicity in our newspapers. They sow discord among the Standing Committee members of the Political Bureau of the Party Central Committee and aim to sow dissension between Chairman Hua and the memory of Chairman Mao. Failing to check articles before publication is a matter of overriding importance.

In that speech, Wang went on to make specific criticisms one by one. First, he criticized the special commentator of the *People's Daily* for writing several articles concerning the implementation of the policy on cadres. Second, he criticized Yu Huanchun of the *People's Daily* for his speech at a meeting of the National Committee of the Chinese People's Political Consultative Conference. Third, he criticized the *People's Daily* for writing a headline which stressed only that Deng Xiaoping brilliantly expounded Mao Zedong Thought, but did not stress that Chairman Hua had also brilliantly expounded Mao Zedong Thought. Fourth, he criticized Xu Chi[4] for writing two articles that incorrectly described certain people in the Cultural Revolution. Fifth, Wang criticized the *Changjiang Daily* for carrying the remark, "The counterrevolutionary line of the 'Gang of Four' is primarily ultra-left." He said that Hua Guofeng had not made such a remark. Sixth, he criticized the magazine *Minzu huabao* (Nationality Pictorial) for stating that both Kang Sheng and Xie Fuzhi were members of the "Gang of Four," noting that this would adversely affect Party unity. Seventh, he criticized Du Renzhi of the Chinese Academy of Social Sciences for his speech at a meeting of the National Committee of the Chinese People's Political Consultative Conference. Wang said that Du attempted to reverse the verdict on the "February Reverse Current" and the "May 16th Circular" and that Du had declared, "The verdict on the Cultural Revolution as a whole will soon be reversed." Wang also criticized Wu Shichang at a meeting of the National Committee of the Chinese People's Political Consultative Conference, for proposing the establishment of a "Committee for the Framed Tiananmen Case."

At group meetings of the Central Work Conference, those with a good knowledge of circumstances laid bare such matters by presenting the facts. As a result, people came to know why, with a certain person's backing, some people were not afraid to resist discussing the criterion for testing truth. They learned why some people limited discussion about the criterion for testing truth, issued an order to ban the discussion, and made sarcastic remarks about it. People learned why, at a meeting of the organizers of the national conference on the work to handle letters and calls, some people like

Zhang Yaoci (a Deputy Director of the General Office of the Party Central Committee) dared to irrationally criticize Hu Yaobang, then the head of the Organization Department of the Party Central Committee, for saying, "All unfounded remarks, no matter when and under what circumstances they were made and no matter by what organization at any level or by whomever they were determined and approved, must be corrected on the basis of facts." Zhang insisted that Hu's remark be deleted from the relevant documents.

Zhang Yaoci also said, "Now some people attempt to reverse the verdict on the Tiananmen Incident. Aren't they attempting to pressure the Party Central Committee?... Some articles are really problematic and some problems are very serious, with their spearhead directed at Chairman Mao. Some remarks contained in the article 'Practice Is the Sole Criterion for Testing Truth' are problematic. Some people disagreed with releasing the article, while others said that the article was very good and had it carried by newspapers one after another. Of course, we should let one hundred schools of thought contend. But some people use Chairman Mao's remarks to criticize the Chairman.... Some articles are spearheaded not only at Chairman Mao, but also at Chairman Hua.... This gust of wind is very strong and it is not easy to resist it.

I told Zhang Pinghua, 'You are the Head of the Publicity Department of the Party Central Committee and so you must keep to the orientation. Some people stress the need to understand Mao Zedong Thought in a comprehensive and accurate manner. But, when it comes to action, they do not act accordingly.'"

Zhang made these remarks on October 3, 37 days before theCentral Work Conference was convened. An assistant to Wang Dongxing really went to extremes. He went almost so far as to criticize Deng Xiaoping by name and he may have spoken that way to Zhang Pinghua, the head of the Publicity Department of the Party Central Committee.

Zhang Yaoci also attended the Central Work Conference. Yang Xiguang and I exposed this matter at a group meeting of the Northwest China Group. The members of the group agreed that Wang Dongxing's influence was reflected in Zhang Yaoci's remarks and that his remarks could be understood as Wang Dongxing's remarks. Zhang Yaoci had been placed in the Southwest China Group, the same group as Hu Jiwei. So, Hu refuted him to his face and of course, he had no way to defend himself.

As to the matters raised in connection with Wang Dongxing at the conference, Wang was a powerful and influential man, and if what others said contained anything that deviated from the facts, Wang was fully capable of offering an explanation. But he failed to explain one single matter where he was said not to have accorded with the facts. In exposing his mistakes, other participants gave specific time, place, and content. Furthermore, we can tell from they reported that his thoughts and actions were consistent. This caused people to believe that the exposures were convincing.

The Self-Criticism by Wu De

A day or two after the third plenary session of the Central Work Conference, Wu De delivered a speech pertaining to the Tiananmen Incident to the East China Group. He accounted for what had happened and conceded his mistakes. Since the nature of the Tiananmen Incident had been affirmed, his speech did not touch off any discussion. Nonetheless, his speech is historically interesting. (Wu De's speech was also distributed under the title "My Self-Criticism" to the participants in the Third Plenum of The 11th Party Central Committee.)

> The mourning activity in Tiananmen commenced on March 30. By April 3, there already had appeared many wreaths, poems, and memorial speeches around the Monument to the People's Heroes. Then we sent militiamen, police officers (some in plainclothes), soldiers from the Beijing Garrison, and government officials to maintain order, offer good advice, guard the wreaths, and prevent accidents from happening. At a meeting of the Political Bureau held on April 4, I reported what was going on at Tiananmen , explaining that circumstances were good and that since work was to be done there in a couple of days, the wreaths could be moved to the Baobashan Cemetery. It was precisely then that Lu Ying, an activist in the "Gang of Four," sent a secret report to Yao Wenyuan, telling him that in the southwestern corner of the monument someone made a speech cursing Jiang Qing. The 'Gang of Four' was infuriated and immediately forced us to arrest this man. Meanwhile, the 'Gang of Four' arbitrarily ordered that,

since the Spring Gravesweeping Festival was over, the wreaths be removed overnight. We proposed that we needed two days to persuade the people in the Square, but our proposal was rejected. I failed to resist the pressure of the 'Gang of Four' and had people arrested illegally and had the wreaths removed without the permission of the masses, thus arousing the greater indignation of the people. So, violent struggles to oppose the 'Gang of Four' erupted on April 5. The revolutionary masses raised the just slogan "return our wreaths and our comrades-in-arms". In indignation, they burned cars and a small building.

On April 5, Mao Yuanxin conveyed Chairman Mao's remark that the incident occurred first in the capital and second, at Tiananmen, and involved burning of cars and beating people. Therefore, the nature of the incident was changed into that of a counterrevolutionary incident. On April 5, a meeting of the Political Bureau decided first, to use militiamen to solve the problem, with militiamen being able to use wooden truncheons and second, to persuade the masses to leave the square by broadcasting a speech. The meeting decided to deploy 100,000 militiamen. We maintained that it was impossible to deploy so many militiamen in such a short time. So, we deployed only 30,000 militiamen.

After the speech was broadcast at 6:30 p.m., the masses gradually left. At nine o'clock that night, we turned lights on the square, signaling that the masses should continue to leave. But at 9:30, there were still over 200 people around the monument. Militiamen were dispatched to detain these people for examination. Following a day or two of examination, 100 people were released. But, in the end, scores of people were detained for examination. Broadcasting the speech and sending in militiamen were both designed to suppress the masses. People were beaten and injured both before and after the militia was sent in. We are responsible for this.

Broadcasting the speech was originally intended to persuade the masses to leave to prevent the situation from worsening. But it was seriously wrong politically. The speech asserted, "A tiny number of bad people with ulterior motives deliberately created a political incident by taking advantage of the Spring Gravesweeping Festival," and emphasized the need "to have a clear understanding of the reactionary nature of this political incident ... [and] to resolutely crack down on counterrevolutionary sabotage activities." It also made slanderous and unfounded remarks against Vice-Chairman Deng.

After the Tiananmen Incident, in accordance with the circular of the Party Central Committee dated April 8, we also arranged investigations and checks. We held meetings and issued a circular (on arranging the investigation into and checks of the so-called instigators of the counterrevolutionary incident, the creators of the poems and leaflets, and the behind-the-scene masterminds). We also detained and arrested a total of 260 people. Altogether, we detained and arrested 388 for examination, causing extremely serious consequences. Before the downfall of the "Gang of Four," 224 people had been gradually released. By the end of November 1976, another 140 people had been released. All had been released by the end of July of 1977. Arresting, investigating, and checking revolutionary masses have brought undue persecution to many comrades and made an extremely bad impression on the Party, causing serious consequences. I assume the enormous responsibility for this. When the leading comrades of the Jiangsu Provincial Party Committee and the Nanjing Military Area Command came to Beijing to report to the Party Central Committee, I made some extremely erroneous remarks: that the Nanjing political incident was a counterrevolutionary political incident as well; that it occurred earlier than a similar incident in Beijing; and that it had a great impact. Here, I would like to express my self-criticism to the comrades from Nanjing.

The Case of Kang Sheng

The case of Kang Sheng was the sixth and last problem raised by Chen Yun in his speech to the Northeast China Group on November 12. He said, "In the early period of the Cultural Revolution, Comrade Kang Sheng served as an advisor to the Central Cultural Revolution Group. He then cited by name leading cadres at will and assumed great responsibility for causing the paralyzed state of various central ministries and Party and government offices across the country. His mistakes were very serious. Therefore, the Party Central Committee ought to, at an appropriate meeting, make a due criticism of Comrade Kang Sheng's mistakes."

Chen Yun's speech caused great reverberations. At the conference those with a good understanding of the Kang Sheng case took the floor one after another. I made quite a few notes on the speeches regarding Kang Sheng from the summary bulletins.

The first speaker, Chen Manyuan,[5] said,

I hope that the Party Central Committee will make a thorough investigation into a number of problems concerning Kang Sheng. Kang Sheng knew that Zhang Chunqiao and Jiang Qing were renegades. Why was it that just before his death he reported this to Chairman Mao? (Chen Manyuan cited as proof the letter of Zhang Hanzhi,[6] which is one of the pieces of evidence for the crimes of the "Gang of Four.") While in the Soviet Union, Kang Sheng organized a small number of people in opposition to Chairman Mao serving as the secretary of the Party Central Committee. Instead he supported Wang Ming as secretary. Wang Ming and Kang Sheng concocted the pamphlet written by Wang Ming, "Work Hard to Make the Communist Party of China More Bolshevik." It is said that Kang chose the name of the book. While carrying out the qiangjiu (rescuing) movement in Yan'an, Kang Sheng erroneously singled out a large number of targets. Chairman Mao's nine-article directive to halt deviations was directed at correcting Kang Sheng's mistakes. Kang Sheng recommended that Jiang Qing marry Chairman Mao. When some people raised the question of Jiang Qing having problems in her record, Kang guaranteed that Jiang did not have such problems. While working in Shanghai, Kang Sheng was suddenly interrogated by Guomindang special agents for two hours before becoming a Guomindang special agent. Later, he did lots of bad things. The grandfather of Ding Zhaozhong[7] kept records on this. I heard that Ding Zhaozhong had handed over these materials to the Party Central Committee.

After China was totally liberated, Kang Sheng sent two workers from the Central Party School to scour the country for two Trotskyists. Later, he heard that while in Yan'an, the two Trotskyists had been executed on his own orders. He then felt reassured. During the Cultural Revolution, Kang Sheng wielded power over the publicity and organization departments of the Party Central Committee, and took charge of the No. 1, No. 2, and No. 3 offices. He also had many people arrested. I think it is better to make clear inside the Party what kind of man Kang Sheng was.

Cheng Zihua[8], who was also in the same Central-South China Group as Comrade Chen Manyuan, gave two examples of how Kang Sheng made others suffer. One was Wang Shiying[9] who was engaged in the students' movement like Cheng Zihua and who had been a loyal Party worker for dozens of years. After the Cultural Revolution started, Kang Sheng labeled him a renegade and persecuted him to death. The other was Yuan Xuezu, a leader of the Ningdu Uprising, who remained in Jiangxi Province after the Red Army began the Long March. Later, Yuan's troops were scattered in battle and he went to

Shanghai to make a living selling newspapers. He was arrested once in Shanghai and once in Ningbo. Later, he went to the Yan'an Party School to study. But Kang Sheng labeled him a renegade, and had him arrested and sent to the Security Headquarters. Yuan was not released until he wrote to Commander-in-Chief Zhu De. But his Party membership has been suspended ever since. In 1975, he wrote to Chairman Mao, who wrote and asked Kang Sheng to solve the problem, which remained unsolved. Cheng Zihua also spoke of what happened in the qiangjiu (rescuing) movement in Yan'an.

Lu Zhengcao said in the East China Group, "Some people say 'a dying person says kind words.' But it seemed to me that for Kang Sheng, 'even though he is dying, his tricks are still vicious.' While in Yan'an, Kang knew the real story about Jiang Qing, but he did not tell others. Finally, he made two young men his scapegoats. What a vicious man he was! At a meeting held in 1966, Deng Xiaoping confirmed that there was no 'February mutiny' at all. Later, Kang Sheng acknowledged that there was actually no such mutiny but held that theoretically it could happen."

Jin Rubo of the Southwest China Group gave another example of how, while at Haojiapo, Linxian County, in northeast Shanxi Province to carry out the land reform, Kang Sheng investigated three generations of villagers to increase the number of landlords and raised the slogan of letting poor peasants and farm laborers seize state power.

In the Northeast China Group Ma Wenrui revealed Kang Sheng's theoretical mistakes. He pointed out that at a meeting on cultural and educational work held in 1959, Kang Sheng said, "Mao Zedong Thought is the highest and final standard." As early as 1967 he said that to each according to his work "has a double nature and can produce bourgeois ideas." On the eve of the Ninth Party Congress, he instructed Wu Baohua, a rebel in the Party School of the Party Central Committee, to prepare materials for the Ninth Party Congress. In these materials, Kang cited 120 leading cadres by name. Ma Wenrui also exposed Kang for praising Lin Biao to the skies, and instructing Wu Baohua and others to compile the four-volume *Selected Works of Lin Biao* and one copy of *Quotations of Lin Biao*. He also supported Wu Baohua and others in writing, under the pen name

"Tang Xiaowen," a number of sinister articles, which were sent to Jiang Qing for examination. Ma also noted that a foreign book had said that Kang Sheng was arrested in Shanghai in 1930 and that he was quickly released, thanks to the mediation of a Guomindang official, Ding Weifen.

In the Northeast China Group Xiao Ke[10] revealed that while in Moscow serving as a member of the Chinese Communist Party delegation Kang Sheng was an assistant to Wang Ming and implemented the Wang Ming line. But nobody had ever heard him make a single remark of self-criticism. Xiao Ke also talked about the problem of "landlords in changed forms" that had been raised in carrying out the land reform in Yan'an.

Han Guang reflected further on how Kang Sheng persecuted comrades from the former Northeast Joint Army to Resist Japanese Aggressors. He said that from 1934 to 1936, quite a few cadres of the Northeast Joint Army to Resist Japanese Aggressors were sent in groups to Moscow for study by the Chinese Communist Party delegation to the Communist International. He said, "I was one of these comrades. Kang Sheng, who knew us very well, examined all of our records. In 1938 and 1939, he recommended several of us to the Soviet intelligence agency and we were sent back to northeast China. However, all these comrades were labeled 'special agents of the Soviet Union' during the Cultural Revolution. Whoever asserted that Kang Sheng could testify that he had assigned them there was persecuted even more cruelly."

Hu Yaobang said that he did not personally know about Kang Sheng's record. But during the Cultural Revolution, Kang did a lot of bad things, and aroused enormous popular indignation. He labeled large numbers of people renegades and completely unrepentant capitalist-roaders. He went so far as to place Chairman Zhu De and Vice-Chairman Ye Jianying in the category of those "who have made serious mistakes — the nature of which has not yet been determined." He also directed some students of Nankai University in Tianjin to smash the so-called "southern renegade group," in an attempt to oppose Premier Zhou.

I also took notes of the speeches regarding Kang Sheng delivered by Jin Ming, Wang Liusheng, Huang Huoqing, Ji Pengfei,[11] Wu

Qingtong,[12] Zhao Ziyang, Li Baohua,[13] Zhao Cangbi,[14] Li Chang, Ren Zhongyi, Jia Tingsan, Zhang Xiangshan, Luo Qingchang, Liu Jingping, and Zhang Dingcheng. According to their speeches, Kang Sheng made plenty of shocking remarks and some absolutely absurd ones as well. For example, while tackling the Anhui problem during the Cultural Revolution, Kang went so far as to tell those from Anhui Province that "Li Dazhao[15] was a renegade." He added that he had materials to that effect. What I quoted was only a portion of the speeches, as I did not have time to quote all of them.

CHAPTER 6

DISCUSSION OF THE CRITERION FOR TESTING TRUTH

Confrontation Over the Criterion for Testing Truth

The conference attendees included both the principal proponents of the discussion about the criterion for testing truth and the principal opponents.

After the *Guangming Daily* carried an article on the criterion for testing truth in May 1978, comprehensive discussion about the issue was held in all localities and departments across the country. Many conference participants had already participated in the discussion in their localities or departments, aired their views, and were already quite familiar with the issue. Shortly after the opening ceremony of the Work Conference on November 10, quite a few participants talked about those discussions in their group meetings. The discussions in these meetings held after the plenary session on November 25 were livelier than ever before. This was due to the following three reasons: (1) Major issues were resolved in the general meeting held on November 25, such as affirming the nature of the Tiananmen Incident and redressing framed, false, and wrong cases. Yet the discussion about the issue of the criterion for testing truth had not been fully resolved. Naturally participants realized the need to allow time to discuss this issue. (2) Wang Dongxing was criticized by name, so that the participants felt all the more free about taking the floor. (3) Before November 25, Li Xin, Wu Lengxi, Xiong Fu, Hu Sheng, and some other comrades had kept silent. Many participants strongly objected to this. For instance, after the *Guangming Daily* carried the article "Practice Is the Sole Criterion for Testing Truth," the participants had waited for these comrades who had supported the "Two Whatevers" to declare their positions. Other participants watched them closely. After November 25, however, suddenly all of these people came out to declare their stands one by one. Some gave oral statements, while others delivered written speeches.

Li Xin talked briefly about the issue of the criterion for testing truth. He spoke abstractly, remarking that his political awareness had not been high. As they deemed his comments unsatisfactory, these participants, when they questioned him, focused all the more on his attitude toward Kang Sheng under whom he had served, especially as he had taken part in drafting the "memorial speech" for Kang. After the downfall of the "Gang of Four," he revealed that Kang had exposed the problems in Jiang Qing's record, in an attempt to whitewash himself. Thus, participants focused on these areas and refrained from asking his views on the criterion for testing truth.

For his part, Wu Lengxi defended himself by saying that Hu Jiwei had misheard his view, and went on to explain his views under questioning. After reading the summary bulletins, members of all groups thought that his explanations simply proved that Hu Jiwei's telephone call was convincing.

The participants in the Central Work Conference resented the attitude of the journal *Red Flag* under Xiong Fu's leadership. Moreover, on November 22, two comrades with *Red Flag* put up a big character poster exposing Xiong Fu in their own unit. After the article on the criterion for testing truth was published, *People's Daily* and *Liberation Army Daily* immediately reprinted the article, but *Red Flag* always refused to carry the article on the criterion for testing truth. The participants in the Central Work Conference already harbored strong resentment against Xiong Fu. In the early period of the Central Work Conference, Xiong refused to carry an article written by Tan Zhenlin[1] in commemoration of Mao Zedong. Xiong had written a letter to the Party Central Committee, saying that since the guiding thinking of Tan's article was to stress that practice was the criterion for testing truth if *Red Flag* carried it, the magazine would become involved in this debate. He insisted on implementing the principle of not becoming involved. After his letter was submitted to the Party Central Committee, Deng Xiaoping wrote, "I think this article is very good. At least it is free from mistakes. I made some revisions. If *Red Flag* is unwilling to carry it, it can be sent to the *People's Daily*." Deng asked, "Why should *Red Flag* not become involved? It should become involved and can carry articles with different viewpoints. It seems to me that being uninvolved actually means being involved."

Hu Sheng said that he was unfamiliar with the editorial on the "two whatevers." On the issue of the criterion for testing truth, the participants did not know what view he had expressed and originally did not have too many criticisms of him. In the speech he delivered in the Northeast China Group on November 25, Hu Sheng appeared to have disagreed to saying that the criterion for testing truth was crucial to our ideological and political lines, and to the future and destiny of the Party and state. In a speech delivered at a symposium on the relationship between theory and practice, Zhou Yang[2] aired this view of Hu Sheng. The symposium was held July 17–24, 1978 and was jointly sponsored by the Philosophy Research Institute of the Chinese Academy of Social Sciences and the Editorial Board of *Philosophy Research*. After "Practice Is the Sole Criterion for Testing the Truth" was reprinted by *People's Daily*, Wu Lengxi immediately placed a telephone call to Hu Jiwei and criticized him, saying that reprinting the article was tantamount to "chopping down the flag." Many people had heard about this call a long time ago. Now at the Central Work Conference Wu failed to make a good speech, causing dissatisfaction among the members of all groups. All in all, the declaration of their positions by Li Xin and several other comrades touched off a wave of speeches by other participants in the Central Work Conference.

Why did these comrades remain silent before November 25 only to come out in unison to declare their stands soon after November 25? At the Central Work Conference some comrades agreed that during discussions of economic issues at the conference, they decided to speak out with the intention of shifting the orientation of the conference. I did not agree with this view. In my view, prior to November 25, they still anticipated that in declaring its stand, the Party Central Committee might not necessarily support the view that practice is the sole criterion for testing truth. However, at the third plenary session, held on the afternoon of November 25, particularly after the Political Bureau Standing Committee members formally declared their stands to the leaders of the Beijing Municipal Party Committee and the leaders of the Central Committee of the Communist Youth League of China, they concluded that they could not resist the pressure any longer and must declare their positions.

But they failed to change their stands and their speeches were full of loopholes. Nonetheless, this enabled the participants to gather more information and enhance their understanding.

From the very beginning the discussion about the criterion for testing truth was very political. It was a discussion about a philosophical question and was held to criticize the "two whatevers." At the Central Work Conference, this discussion had a characteristic different from the discussions at academic meetings and in newspapers and magazines. It seemed that this characteristic could be summarized as follows.

At the Central Work Conference, the time spent on discussing this issue was exceptionally long and concentrated. In over thirty days of group meetings, we touched on this issue directly or indirectly almost every day. Speeches on the issue were substantial and extensive. As the Central Work Conference was a high-level meeting within the Party, relevant matters could be exposed thoroughly and the participants could be straightforward and sharp, without being ambiguous or hiding something by expressing something else. All the major figures of the two contending parties were present at this high-level intra-Party meeting and could confront one another face to face. Those in the same group confronted one another, as did those not in the same group after reading the summary bulletins of other groups. I remember that while reading the summary bulletins of the Southwest China Group, I followed the dialogue between Hu Jiwei and Xiong Fu. Xiong defended himself for opposing the discussion about the issue of the criterion for testing truth, while Hu Jiwei cited facts and produced plenty of written materials to prove Xiong's dishonesty. Hu Jiwei was so completely logical that Xiong Fu was unable to rebut his statements. Thus the discussions were more profound, lively, and specific. Yang Xiguang, editor-in-chief of the *Guangming Daily*, was one of those presiding over the discussion about the criterion for testing truth. Well informed and with a profound understanding, he made many speeches in the Northwest China Group.

I had worked in the State Council Research Office together with Li Xin, Wu Lengxi, Hu Sheng, and Xiong Fu. I opposed the "Gang of Four" together with Wu, Hu, and Xiong, and along with them I was criticized and denounced by the movement to "criticize Deng Xiaoping". After the downfall of the "Gang of Four," I resolutely opposed the "two whatevers." I also made many critical comments and delivered many speeches in the Northwest China Group to confront these people who supported it.

Participants in the conference exposed Wang Dongxing and other top officials for supporting those who opposed discussion on the criterion for testing truth. They thereby clarified more thoroughly and profoundly the questions under discussion. It was awkward to indicate this clearly in discussions held in the academic community. In addition to the two contending parties, also present were the leading cadres from various localities across the country and various central departments, as well as many members of the Political Bureau of the Party Central Committee. All of them were not only fair referees, but also active speakers taking part in the discussion.

The Political Bureau Standing Committee members who were present at the conference, declared their stands and drew the proper political conclusions during the discussions.

Shen Baoxiang's[3] book *Discussing the Issue of the Criterion for Testing Truth* had been published recently. The author noted that the discussion at the Central Work Conference marked the phase in which an all-round victory was won in the decisive battle over the issue of the criterion for testing truth. I think that this accords with historical facts.

Three Joint Speeches That Yang Xiguang, Wang Huide, and I Delivered

Yang Xiguang, Wang Huide, and I delivered three joint speeches on the issue of the criterion for testing truth at the Central Work Conference.[4] Two speeches were joint ones by the three of us; one was a collaborative effort between Yang Xiguang and me. There was also a joint speech by Yang Xiguang and Wang Huide. Of course, Yang Xiguang, Wang Huide, and I made individual speeches and interposed remarks many times. I delivered nine individual speeches about the issue of the criterion for testing truth, in addition to the three joint speeches. Judging by the content of Shen Baoxiang's book, he seemed to know very little about what had happened at the

Central Work Conference and to know almost nothing about what had gone on in the Northwest China Group. Since I do not remember clearly the speeches given by others at the conference, I can only offer readers my own speeches, which I do remember clearly. Of course, because it would take up an enormous amount of space, I cannot give a detailed introduction to them. Instead, I have made a chronological list of my speeches on the criterion for testing truth with capsule summaries.

First Speech. On November 13, Yang Xiguang, Wang Huide, and I made a joint speech. I served as the principal speaker. We demanded an unequivocal affirmation of the Tiananmen Incident as a great revolutionary event, and expounded on the necessity of advancing democracy in China. In our speech we quoted Lenin's remark, "If full democracy is not practiced under victorious socialism, it is impossible to retain the victory it has won." We maintained that Lenin's remark was a general important tenet of Marxism and was fully in line with the reality in China. We also stated that another viewpoint should be made clear inside the Party, that is, after becoming a ruling party, our Party should still stand among the masses of the people and lead them in winning democracy. We held that in order to lead the masses in achieving democracy, it was imperative to declare explicitly the correct stand regarding the Tiananmen Incident. Giving full scope to democracy should serve as the norm for us to resolve the Tiananmen Incident.

Second Speech. On November 26 I made an individual speech in which I criticized Li Xin's speech at the Work Conference for his failure to expose Kang Sheng's mistakes. I also exposed and criticized him for his dishonesty in compiling and selecting Chairman Mao's works. In addition, I exposed and criticized Wu Lengxi, Xiong Fu, Zhang Yaoci, Zhang Pinghua, and some other comrades for their mistakes in the discussion about the criterion for testing truth.

Third Speech. On the same day, November 26, Yang Xiguang and I made a joint presentation, with Yang serving as the principal speaker. We criticized Comrade Wang Dongxing by name and Comrade Zhang Yaoci under Wang's direct leadership for their remarks and acts in opposing the affirmation of the Tiananmen Incident, clinging to the "two whatevers," and vilifying the article on practice serving as the criterion for testing truth. Yang cited many facts in our speech. On the morning of that day, Jiang Yizhen in the Northwest China Group gave the first speech at the conference that criticized "Vice-Chairman Wang" by name. Our speech echoed Jiang's speech. Jiang mainly cited Wang Dongxing's wrong attitude toward several cadres in the Ministry of Health. In our speech, Yang Xiguang focused on Wang's mistaken attitude and activities. We criticized Zhang Yaoci and also Wang's assistant because he was not in charge of publicity work and yet uttered a lot of nonsense concerning the issue of the criterion for testing truth. Zhang also attended the Central Working Conference in his capacity as the deputy director of the General Office of the Party Central Committee. We also criticized Xiong Fu for his written speech at the conference.

Fourth Speech. On November 28, I gave a speech exposing Li Xin for his erroneous attitude on the verification and checking of Kang Sheng's resumé after Kang's death.

Fifth Speech. On December 1, I gave another a speech in which I criticized some people for using the term "crime of vicious attack, " to punish people without a basis in the legal code. For instance, a person who had put up big-character posters criticizing Wu De was sentenced to prison for this "vicious attack."

Sixth Speech. On December 2, I elaborated my criticism of Li Xin for his mistakes in compiling *Selected Works of Mao Zedong*.

Seventh Speech. On December 4, Wang Huide delivered a speech, in which he exposed Li Xin and Wu Lengxi for obstructing him from writing articles to criticize Zhang Chunqiao's fallacy of "exercising all-round dictatorship." I followed up by presenting a lot of relevant supporting information.

Eighth Speech. Also on December 4, I criticized Li Xin, Wu Lengxi, Xiong Fu, and Hu Sheng for the contents of their speeches as reported in the summary bulletins. I strongly criticized the article "Study 'On Practice'" carried in *Red Flag*.

Ninth Speech. On December 7, I cited Mao Zedong's remark, "As a rule, the dust of Wu Lengxi and his like will not be gone until the iron broom of Chen Boda comes" to indicate that those insisting on the "two whatevers" did not personally necessarily act completely in accordance with everything that Mao said and directed.

Tenth Speech. On December 13, I criticized the Beijing Municipal Revolutionary Committee for making preparations with an eye toward issuing an order restricting the posting of big-character posters.

Eleventh Speech. On December 14, Yang Xiguang, Wang Huide, and I made our third joint speech. Wang was the principal speaker. We praised Hua Guofeng for assuming responsibility in regard to the "two whatevers" and on the issue of the criterion for testing truth. By doing so, he set an example for everyone to follow in making self-criticism on the basis of facts. We supported the speeches made by Comrades Ye Jianying and Deng Xiaoping at the closing session and emphatically expressed our delight at the support in the discussion of the criterion for testing truth. We also expressed our dissatisfaction with Wang Dongxing's written speech. We agreed with the speech Song Shilun delivered in the Central-South Group and particularly agreed with his remark that, "Li Xin and other comrades have been put in important positions, and Wu Lengxi, Hu Sheng, Xiong Fu, Zhang Yaoci, and other comrades are audacious. Comrade Wang Dongxing serves as the behind-the-scene boss for all of them." We pointed out that on the matter of "the discussion of the criterion for testing truth," Wang Dongxing not only was answerable for the problem of assuming leadership responsibility, but also had made mistakes in ideological and political lines. We noted that Wang had always taken a negative attitude toward the article "Practice Is the Sole Criterion for Testing Truth." In our joint speech we also cited instances in which Wang impeded publicity that correctly urged revolutionary cadres to act in accordance with the criterion for testing truth. We proposed that the Party Central Committee urge Wang to make a further profound self-criticism.

Apart from the three joint speeches I participated in, on December 14, Yang Xiguang and Wang Huide made a joint presentation criticizing the speech Hu Sheng delivered in the Northeast China Group.

CHAPTER 7

HU YAOBANG AT THE
CENTRAL WORK CONFERENCE

The Lively Northwest China Group

At the Central Work Conference, ordinary participants like me spent virtually all our time in our regional group meeting except for attending the four plenary sessions. I never asked to be excused except for going to Deng Xiaoping's home for business a couple of times. I went to the meeting hall of the Northwest China Group on time every day. At the meetings I earnestly listened to the others speak, took notes, observed what was going on, and thought deeply. I believe that a description of the meetings of the Northwest China Group will help readers gain an on-the-spot sense of the conference.

The first group meeting of the Northwest China Group was held on the afternoon of November 11, the day following the opening ceremony. Until November 19, only one meeting had been held, namely, on November 14, and no meetings were held on November 20 and 21. At the meeting on the morning of November 22, Wang Feng conveyed the essence of a meeting held on the afternoon and evening of November 21 for Political Bureau Standing Committee members to listen to reports from the group conveners. Wang Feng gave a lengthy and very detailed report on this meeting. It seemed that no group meeting had been held on November 21 to allow time for this report. All participants wanted to know the thinking of the Standing Committee members before delivering their speeches. Subsequently, after three days of group meetings, all group members attended the third plenary session to listen to Hua Guofeng deliver his speech. On November 23 and 24, our group members spent two afternoons discussing the views on revising the "Rules Governing the Work of Rural People's Communes," prepared by Li Dengying, Wang Huide, and Yang Xiguang, a task assigned some days previously by the Standing Committee. All group members spent a long time discussing the revisions article by article. After finishing this task, they then discussed the written views on the draft "Resolution on

105 of Rural People's Communes,"

105

Accelerating Agricultural Growth Rate" that Hu Yaobang, Wang Renzhong, and I had prepared. The group members found our material OK, and agreed that it could be submitted to the Party Central Committee without further revisions.

After the November plenary session, at the group meeting that was held on the morning of November 26, the group members expressed satisfaction with Hua Guofeng's speech at the plenary session. They also reached consensus on the arrangements according to which Jiang Yizhen would be the first to criticize Wang Dongxing by name on the morning of November 26, and Yang Xiguang and I would criticize Wang Dongxing by name again that afternoon. On November 28, Wang Feng conveyed the gist of a meeting for the Standing Committee members to listen to reports held on November 27. In the name of the whole group, the Northwest China Group made a 12-point proposal. Among other things, the group advocated the election of nine additional members to the Party Central Committee, three members to the Political Bureau, and one vice-chairman to the Party Central Committee who would serve concurrently as a Standing Committee member. The proposal was passed by a show of hands, and everbody affixed their signatures. On December 11, Wang Feng conveyed that the Political Bureau held a meeting to discuss the Northwest China Group's 12-point proposal and similar proposals made by other groups. Wang said that the Political Bureau agreed to the proposal. I presumed that the Political Bureau members must have held a meeting prior to this. The list of the new senior Party leaders to be elected could be regarded as decided via the link of the Political Bureau.

On December 12, the participants discussed the list of the candidates for membership in the Central Commission for Discipline Inspection. On the 13th, they discussed the "Decision of the Party Central Committee Concerning the Adjustment of Farm Product Prices." The Northwest China Group decided that Yao Yilin should provide an explanation. The closing ceremony was held on December 13; three Standing Committee members delivered speeches.

The Northwest China Group held a meeting on December 14 to discuss the speeches delivered at the closing ceremony and Wang Dongxing's written self-criticism speech, with a comprehensive summary bulletin that the Northwest China Group had written. At the meeting the bulletin was discussed, revised, and submitted to higher authorities with the four conveners signing. Also on the 14th, Hua Guofeng wrote on the comprehensive bulletin for the Northwest China Group the directive, "Please print and distribute this bulletin to all comrades attending the conference."

Of the 35 people in the Northwest China Group, 34 had been active in taking the floor. Ji Dengkui spoke only once at the group meeting, briefing us on the documents he was in charge of drafting. He did not make any other speeches. Furthermore, nobody knew why he was seldom present. However, at the conference he was criticized by name and he seemed to be absent when such criticisms were made. In speeches within the group nobody ever mentioned his self-criticism and there was no confrontation with him at the conference. People varied greatly in the number of speeches they gave. Two people delivered more than 10 speeches; eight people delivered seven to nine speeches; 15 people made four to six speeches; and nine people made three or fewer speeches. The majority gave six speeches. In addition, there were two declarations on which the whole group collectively agreed.

Some members of the group were engaged in office work, others in army work; some worked in departments, and still others did theoretical work or journalistic work. By attending such a conference, I learned a great deal. To my surprise, a few army participants who were members of our group were quite familiar with theoretical work. When we talked with one another, we shared a great deal of common ground. There was no member in our Northwest China Group who had supported the "two whatevers." This made our group different from the five other groups, especially from the Southwest China Group. In our group we just made critical comments about the members of other groups and it was thus rather easy for us to reach unanimity.

Four Speeches by Hu Yaobang at the Northwest China Group

When I said that Hu Yaobang was a very important figure at the Central Work Conference, I did not mean to compare him to Deng

Xiaoping, Ye Jianying, and other comrades of the Standing Committee, but I believe that without Hu Yaobang, the conference would not have been such a success. Yet, if I am asked to cite specific facts, I really have difficulty, because I was unaware of the many things he did. I hope other comrades will write recollections to supplement my record. When the conference was in session, he was as busy as a bee. He was a co-chair of the Northwest China Group, yet he requested "leave" many times when group meetings were held. So, the other three co-chairs presided over the meetings many times. Hu delivered only four speeches in meetings of the group. His remarks were not long, but the content was brilliant. Of course, he provided ideas that were vital to many of the Northwest China Group's actions. Our Northwest China Group had many ideas, such as the twelve-point proposal, that we adopted by a show of hands. After the closing ceremony we wrote a comprehensive bulletin signed by the four conveners. All this involved his ideas.

His position as a co-chair of the Northwest China Group was just one task that Hu Yaobang was assigned at the conference. He was also busy with lots of other tasks. It was in his capacity as head of the Organization Department of the Party Central Committee that he was invited to attend the Central Work Conference. He sharply pointed out the problem of the Central Group for the Examination of Special Cases, a problem with which he was particularly concerned as head of the Organization Department. He also served concurrently as a vice-president of the Party School of the Party Central Committee. But at the Central Work Conference, he did not work in his capacity as the leader of a certain unit. Since he held no title at the conference, he did not directly participate in the activities of the Standing Committee. Nobody knew what procedures he had gone through before participating in the organizing work for the conference and the liaisons between the Political Bureau Standing Committee members and all groups.

During the Work Conference, Hu Yaobang turned sixty-three; I was four months older than he. He was not afraid of hard work. Hu Deping[1] once told me that during the conference recreational activities were arranged in the evenings in the Jingxi Hotel, but Hu Yaobang did not go to a single dance. Although movies were shown many times in the evenings, Hu Yaobang watched only one, which was connected with his work. (Hu Deping also told me that Hu Yaobang had told him that he had had several talks with me during the conference.) But at the conference he did not show up many times, because he was busy in small discussions about how to move the conference forward.

Of course, I did know some things that others might not necessarily know. For example, I knew that Hu Yaobang had been authorized to find people to help draft Ye Jianying's speech. The text Hu drafted became the basic text for the speech Ye Jianying delivered at the closing ceremony. On November 13, after he returned home from a visit to a number of Southeast Asian countries, Deng Xiaoping asked me to find some people to draft the text for his speech at the Work Conference. Hu Yaobang contacted me to make relevant arrangements and was also involved finalizing the text of Deng's speech.

Hua Guofeng planned to write the text of the speech for delivery at the closing ceremony of the Third Plenum. He asked Hu and several others to make preparations. Hu Yaobang revealed this at a Political Bureau meeting on November 19, 1980. I had not known that Hu had played a part in the speech Hua Guofeng delivered at the closing ceremony of the Central Work Conference. Early in the conference Hua had not yet decided whether to issue a document on agriculture at the Central Work Conference. Hu Yaobang and others helped him make up his mind to draft such a document.

In his speech to the plenary session on November 10, 1978, Hua Guofeng cited the conference's three topics and then said, "The Political Bureau has decided that before discussing these topics, we should discuss one issue, that is, under the guidance of the general line and overall task for the new period, as of January next year, shifting the focus of the whole Party's work to the socialist modernization drive." He reported that the Political Bureau Standing Committee and the Political Bureau unanimously agreed that it was necessary to adapt to domestic and foreign developments, to end promptly and resolutely the nationwide mass movement to expose and criticize the "Gang of Four," and to shift the focus of the whole Party's work to the socialist modernization drive.

In the first two days of group discussions, almost all speakers, responding to Hua Guofeng's request, declared their stands on the issue of shifting the focus of work beginning in January 1979. According to my notes, Hu Yaobang made four individual speeches to our Northwest China Group. He also represented our Northwest Group in collective speeches.

Hu Yaobang gave his first speech to our Northwest China Group on November 13, 1978. In it, Hu said that the issue of shifting the focus of work as proposed by Hua Guofeng concerned work principles and work arrangements. He cited Mao Zedong's remark, "Hardly has one wave subsided when another rises." In other words, each task should be thoroughly completed as another wave rises. Then he said the "wave" of exposing and criticizing the "Gang of Four" had just reached its crest, and that this precisely is the time to put forward tasks for construction. Meanwhile, Hu noted that shifting the focus of work did not mean that the work of exposing and criticizing the "Gang of Four" had been completed. He also stressed that the cardinal issue of right and wrong must be resolved thoroughly. Many speakers expressed similar positions, approving the shift of the focus of work to the socialist modernization drive beginning the next year. But they also stressed that existing problems should be completely resolved.

Hu went on to detail the work remaining in exposing, criticizing, and investigating the "Gang of Four." In the first place, he noted that there were many topics to be covered in the criticism of the "Gang of Four" and that efforts should never be slackened. Secondly, he spoke of the organization work, pointing out that since the 11th Party Congress (1978), the struggle against the "Gang of Four" and the determination of the nature of the "Gang of Four" had been successful. He said the range of attacks had been handled well and the range of public education on the issues was quite extensive. Hu said there was no need to jump to conclusions regarding determination of the nature of the 170 people at the central level who had been adjudged members of the "Gang of Four." Those people had already been dismissed and punished according to law. He added, "We can determine the final disposition of their cases in two or three years. This will not impede the shift in the focus of our work."

Hu Yaobang also referred to the issue of rehabilitating cadres who had been criticized earlier. Of the 17 million full-time cadres in the nation, 17 percent, or more than two million, had been "examined" (i.e., criticized in various movements). Also examined were two million part-time cadres who were also engaged part-time in production at grass-roots-level units at lower levels. As for people who had previously been wrongly framed, it was imperative, in the spirit of objectivity, to correct all mistakes and reverse the wrong verdicts. Otherwise, it would be impossible to eliminate the factors detrimental to stability. As head of the Organization Department of the Party Central Committee, Hu said that this task must be mostly completed before 1979, the thirtieth anniversary of the founding of New China and that some matters could be "dismissed altogether." Hu specifically mentioned the cases of the "renegade group of sixty-one members, the "south renegade group," Peng Dehuai, Tao Zhu, Wang Heshou, Kang Sheng, and others.

Chen Yun delivered his speech to the Central Work Conference one day earlier than Hu Yaobang's speech. At the time, Hu's formal position was much lower than Chen's, yet his speech was substantial and concrete in content. However, many of his remarks were deleted in the conference summary bulletins, so members of other groups knew little about the content of his speech. If I had not taken notes, I would have been unable to recall so much of his speech. Hu pointed sharply to the case of Kang Sheng. He noted that Kang Sheng was a chief culprit during the Cultural Revolution, committing many errors that brought great tragedy. The International Liaison Department, the Organization Department, and the Party School had submitted many materials to him. He expressed his view that the "Gang of Four" should be renamed the "Gang of Five," with Kang Sheng as the leader of the "Gang of Five."

Hu did not "take issues out of context." He raised a fundamental question. Hu said, "It is now time to summarize the lessons from the Cultural Revolution." He urged the participants to reflect on why Lin Biao and the "Gang of Four" were able to be in power for as long as ten years. What was the fundamental lesson, he

111

asked. He said that Kang Sheng refused to make self-criticism, so that Mao Zedong had to apologize for him. He maintained that inner Party life had then been abnormal and pointed to the long-lasting phenomenon in which "there is a party within party and there are laws beyond existing laws." Then Hu cited Deng Xiaoping's remark that inside the Party there should be a large number of cadres who dare to think deeply about problems, dare to speak, and dare to tackle problems. He advocated the exposure of contradictions in real life. Hu next gave a detailed introduction to the massive organization that then existed, the Central Group for the Examination of Special Cases. He also referred to the question of which group for the examination of special cases was in charge of what category of people. I will not now go into these details. On November 16 Hu delivered his second speech on the issue of agriculture.

On the morning of November 26 Hu Yaobang delivered his third speech, a declaration of his stand on Hua Guofeng's November 25 speech at the Central Work Conference. Hu spelled out four points: First, he expressed his delight at Hua Guofeng's pledge to solve a host of problems left over from the Cultural Revolution, such as formally affirming the Tiananmen Incident and redressing a number of major framed, false, and wrong cases. Second, it was imperative to keep up the practice of criticism and self-criticism prevailing at the Central Work Conference. Third, it was necessary to continue to clarify the cardinal issue of right and wrong, assess the Cultural Revolution, and appraise Chairman Mao in an all-round manner. Although some people felt otherwise, this was a matter that could not be avoided. He said that in his view, the Party Central Committee should make careful and thorough preparations before these two issues were addressed. In the meantime, it was imperative not to repeat the lessons of the previous few years. People should not rush to point out the shortcomings and mistakes in the Cultural Revolution, for whoever noted that Chairman Mao had some shortcomings would be refuted in a simplistic way and given political labels, thus arousing people's resentment. Fourth, it was necessary to respect the theory of practice, that it was impermissible to accept the "theory of genius" and the "theory of flunkies," and it was imperative to use practice to observe and test everything.

It should be said that in his speeches Hu Yaobang "stood high and saw far." How wonderful he was to have been able to make such a speech at that time! After listening to his speech, I appreciated his wisdom.

Hu's fourth speech just briefly mentioned a specific example. He said that according to leading officials of the Beijing Municipal Prison, the prison still held 100 people who had been thrown in for opposing the "Gang of Four." He expressed the hope that relevant departments would investigate these cases.

CHAPTER 8

PERSONNEL AND INSTITUTIONAL ADJUSTMENTS

The Issue of Personnel of the Party Central Committee

After the November 25 plenary session, the issue of selecting personnel for the Party Central Committee, including the Political Bureau, became a key topic. One after another, participants spoke on this issue at group meetings. This issue had not been included in the original topics for the Central Work Conference. As the conference proceeded, participants all came to realize that this was a key question that must be settled correctly. After the conference had been in session for 20 days, breakthroughs were made on the original agenda. The "two whatevers" had been further denounced, the question of the criterion for testing truth had been discussed at a higher level, and the basic ideological and political lines had been resolved. Everything depended on people's effort. Future tasks would require a better group of central leaders. The top leadership of the Party Central Committee was considering this matter. The personnel arrangement was, of course, not the business of all groups. But discussions about it in groups could play a role expressing various perspectives and advancing consensus.

Consequently, in all the groups quite a few members discussed who should be elected into the Party Central Committee, into the Political Bureau, and into the Political Bureau Standing Committee. The participants then accepted the spirit of "admission but no exclusion" at the "top level," i.e., one could express opinions on who could be elected into the Party Central Committee but should not express views on who should be excluded. So far as the content of the speeches was concerned, whoever had knowledge of someone who deserved to be elected to the Party Central Committee should, in his speech at a group meeting, express his own views or support the views of others.

The most comprehensive speeches in all the groups were those in which the participants expressed support for Chen Yun's election to the Political Bureau of the Party Central Committee and concurrent service as a Vice-Chairman of the Party Central Committee. All agreed that inside the Party Chen Yun enjoyed seniority and high prestige, that he had a high level of political consciousness and great ability, and that he therefore should serve as Vice-Chairman of the Party Central Committee. They also emphatically stated that he should be placed ahead of Wang Dongxing in the list of names. Concerning personnel changes at this time, since the participants approved the principle of discussing "admission but not exclusion," they only proposed that Chen Yun be elected to the Standing Committee, and did not suggest that Wang Dongxing be removed from the Standing Committee. As a result, the number of Standing Committee members increased from five to six. The number did not matter, and the participants all knew that Wang would temporarily remain on the Standing Committee. They all knew that it was better to avoid disputation than it was to challenge the understanding that we should discuss "admission but no exclusion."

On the issue of personnel for the Party Central Committee, I put in many good words on behalf of Hu Qiaomu at the Northwest China Group meetings. One participant in the Central Work Conference was Li Xin, who had previously served as Kang Sheng's secretary and had always worked by Kang's side during the Cultural Revolution. Li had led several younger people in processing and compiling Mao Zedong's works, and he had always kept Mao's manuscripts and records of Mao's speeches. When in charge of the routine work of the Party Central Committee in 1975, Deng Xiaoping assigned Hu Qiaomu to lead the processing and compilation of the fifth volume of the *Selected Works of Mao Zedong*. The work proceeded as follows: First, several people — Wu Lengxi, Xioang Fu, and Li Xin — prepared the manuscripts to be included in the fifth volume of the *Selected Works of Mao Zedong*. Then Hu Qiaomu, Wu Lengxi, Hu Sheng, Xiong Fu, Yu Guangyuan, and Li Xin compiled and made corrections sentence-by-sentence and paragraph-by-paragraph. In the late period of the Cultural Revolution, Hu Jiwei was liberated. Under the pretext of having him taking part in compiling the fifth volume of the *Selected Works of Mao Zedong*, Hu Qiaomu had Hu Jiwei transferred to the State Council Political Research Office. Yet after being transferred to the State Council Political Research Office, he also did work in other areas.

With Hu Qiaomu in charge, the articles to be included in the fifth volume of the *Selected Works of Mao Zedong* were compiled one by one before being submitted to Deng Xiaoping to be finalized. While finalizing some articles, Deng asked all of us to come to him. He and Hu Qiaomu finished some short articles. As a result, in the work to process and compile the fifth volume of the *Selected Works of Mao Zedong*, Li Xin was demoted as the de facto leader to one of several leaders. He was disgruntled about this, but he had no alternative except to accept the change. Shortly afterward, the movement to "criticize Deng Xiaoping and strike back at the right-deviationist tendency of 'reversing the verdicts'" unfolded, offering Li Xin an opportunity to regain his power to preside over the processing and compilation of the fifth volume of the *Selected Works of Mao Zedong*. Li then criticized Hu Qiaomu for revising and distorting Mao Zedong's works at a meeting to "criticize Deng Xiaoping" held by the State Council Political Research Office. At the time I noted that Li Xin harbored evil intentions. Li Xin achieved his purpose after the movement to "criticize Deng Xiaoping" was launched and the "Gang of Four" was smashed. He brought Wu Lengxi, Hu Sheng, Xiong Fu, and others to the General office of the Committee for Compiling and Publishing Chairman Mao Zedong's Works and wielded the power to compile the rest of Chairman Mao's works.

After the downfall of the "Gang of Four," a letter written by Hu Qiaomu to Jiang Qing, requesting permission to attend the memorial services for Mao Zedong, was found in her office. Hua Guofeng then took charge of the work at the central level, namely, the work of the Party Central Committee and that of the State Council. In line with the organizational system, Hu Qiaomu should not have written Jiang Qing to request permission to attend Mao Zedong's memorial service. But Jiang was Mao's widow, so it was not totally unreasonable for Hu to write her. Nevertheless, Li Xin pounced upon this issue, and used it to allege that Hu wrote a "letter of loyalty to Jiang Qing."

When a Central Work Conference was convened in March 1977, Li Xin was the most capable assistant to Wang Dongxing and a key member of the small group of people on whom Wang relied. I did

117

not know whether or not Wu Lengxi, Hu Sheng, and Xiong Fu had attended that conference. Hu Qiaomu and I were not invited to attend. At the 1977 Work Conference, Li Xin made a speech in which he attacked Hu. Yet when the Central Work Conference for 1978 was convened, Li Xin's slander of Hu Qiaomu had already long been known and the conclusion reached that it was unwarranted. I did not mention this at the 1978 Work Conference, so that those who had not known of the matter would remain unaware of it. Therefore, the good words I put in for Hu focused on his work compiling the *Selected Works of Mao Zedong*. Li Xin continued to be Wang Dongxing's capable assistant and a member of Wang's inner circle. He held several posts simultaneously, such as a deputy director of the General Office of the Party Central Committee and as a deputy director of the General Office of the Committee for Compiling and Publishing Chairman Mao Zedong's Works. Hence he still played a considerable role in the Party.

As the Central Work Conference proceeded in late November, with all the groups discussing the issue of the personnel for the Party Central Committee, the members of some groups nominated Hu Qiaomu as a candidate for the Party Central Committee. But several acquaintances of mine in other groups asked me whether Hu had mistakes before and after the movement to "criticize Deng Xiaoping." In talks with me, some members of the Northwest China Group expressed doubts about Hu's election to the Party Central Committee and even expressed opposition to his election. On the one hand, I thought it was necessary for me to expose Li Xin; but, on the other hand, I felt it was necessary for me to put in more impartial words for Hu, in the hope of creating public support for his election to the Party Central Committee.

So, the day after the November 25 plenary session, I exposed Li Xin's role in the 1976 movement to "criticize Deng Xiaoping." I mentioned that as part of his "criticism of Deng Xiaoping" Li had claimed that Deng had placed Hu Qiaomu in an important position. This way I criticized Li Xin for his cruel role. While "criticizing Deng Xiaoping," Li Xin did everything possible to belittle Hu Qiaomu, saying, "It seems to me that he does not have any Marxist thought at all." Furthermore, Li said Deng had placed Hu Qiaomu in charge of "revising and distorting" Chairman Mao works. I thought that perhaps the editing had been a little excessive when Mao Zedong's talks and speeches were processed into written texts under Hu Qiaomu's leadership in 1976. (I shared responsibility for this because I, too, had taken part in reading and revising the manuscripts. But I did not mention this at the Work Conference). Since Hu Qiaomu processed Mao's manuscripts while Mao Zedong was still alive, the finished manuscripts were subject to examination and finalization by Mao himself. Hence, there was no revision or distortion to speak of.

I also cited as an example the processing of the article "On Ten Major Relationships." Previously, following the editing by Li Xin and others, the manuscript had one sentence reading: "Everything in the world has its occurrence, development, and extinction." I told Hu Qiaomu, " This sentence is correct only in a narrow sense. In a broader sense, this sentence is not correct." Hu accepted my view and made a revision, which was submitted to Deng Xiaoping for examination and final approval. Deng expressed his approval, as did Mao Zedong. When the movement to "criticize Deng Xiaoping" was under way, Li Xin also cited this as a revision and distortion by Hu Qiaomu. In the end, one article in the fifth volume of the *Selected Works of Mao Zedong* published under Li Xin's leadership still retained that wrong sentence.

In my speech to the Northwest China Group, I said, "I do not know who on earth has no Marxist Thought." When the movement to "criticize Deng Xiaoping" was under way, I had noticed that Li Xin harbored evil intentions. After the downfall of the "Gang of Four," Li continued to make all kinds of charges against Hu Qiaomu and seized Hu's position. Later, he requested higher authorities to remove Hu from his post. I said at the conference, "We should formally rehabilitate Hu Qiaomu. Should there be any document against Hu, it should be declared null and void." In my speech on December 2 I again criticized Li Xin. Fang Yi, who was in the same group as I, expanded upon my remarks, saying that in causing Hu Qiaomu to suffer that way, Li Xin was not only dishonest, but also indulged in schemes and conspiracy.

119

The Cases of the Central Group
for the Examination of Special Cases
and of Several Other Organizations

At the time of the Work Conference, Wang Dongxing was still in charge of several central institutions such as the Central Group for the Examination of Special Cases, the Central Guards Bureau, the guards unit, and the General Office of the Committee for Compiling and Publishing Chairman Mao Zedong's Works. As participants at the Central Work Conference began to talk about personnel, they also needed to deal with the role of certain institutions closely related to personnel issues. Thus the question of how to deal with these institutions was placed on the agenda.

The Central Group for the Examination of Special Cases came first. This institution was vital to redressing framed, wrong, and false cases. The organizational form of such a group had probably come into being a long time ago. Conference participants were concerned with the groups set up during the Cultural Revolution to persecute veteran cadres. Major cases were created one by one during the Cultural Revolution. The emergence of a major case was followed by the establishment of a special ad hoc group for the examination of the case. With so many groups of this type established, several offices were set up above them to coordinate their activities, such as the No. 1 Office, the No. 2 Office, and the No. 3 Office. Meanwhile, as a single case involved many people and a major case involved many minor cases, a number of subgroups were set up below one major group for the examination of special cases. Each group had one leader and a number of members. General offices were established respectively under the leadership of these groups. I do not know how many groups of this type were established during the Cultural Revolution, but there must have been many. The groups became massive institutions.

The groups had the authority and responsibility to collect materials and air views on the nature of the cases they undertook to investigate, namely, the targets under examination, and to recommend how to deal with them. Although they did not have decision-making authority, the materials they provided and the views they aired were considered authoritative, and they held absolute power over the life and death of the people involved in various special cases. Therefore, the participants at our Work Conference believed that the problems in these groups were extremely serious. Since their work was highly confidential, it was almost impossible for outsiders to know about their inside information. Later, as the cases of the "May 16th Clique," the Lin Biao incident and the "Gang of Four" arose, special groups were established to investigate them. After the downfall of the "Gang of Four," everyone felt very uneasy that the people who had been in the groups that previously persecuted veteran comrades were now in charge of investigating the still pending cases of Lin Biao and the "Gang of Four." All groups for the investigation of special cases were led directly by Wang Dongxing, who had the final say.

The participants in the Central Work Conference believed that if the problems of these groups were not resolved, it would be impossible to redress effectively framed, wrong and false cases and deal with Lin Biao and the "Gang of Four." Hu Yaobang, the head of the Organization Department of the Party Central Committee, was very annoyed with the role played by these groups. While these groups existed, it would be impossible for the Organization Department to process these cases and rehabilitate cadres. The groups retained large amounts of materials and files, which were beyond the control of the Organization Department. In the meantime, the power to resolve these cases was wielded by the groups under Wang Dongxing, not by the Organization Department of the Party Central Committee.

On the third day of the group meetings of the conference, Hu Yaobang talked at length concerning what he had learned about such groups. He pointed out that the circumstances then were quite abnormal. There "was a party within a party and laws beyond existing laws." He said that two groups were then investigating Peng Zhen, Luo Ruiqing, Lu Dingyi, and Yang Shangkun; two groups were examining *"gong jian fa"*;[1] one group was lookng into the case of "Sixty-one people"; another group was making inquiries about the "Palace of the King of Hell of the General Political Department"[2] and still another group was investigating the "February Adverse Current." After the Lin Biao incident occurred and the "Gang of

Four" was smashed, two groups of those who had undertaken to persecute veteran cadres were examining the case of the "Gang of Four"; six of these groups were examining the case of Kang Sheng; and another three were looking into the case of Xie Fuzhi. Hu Yaobang indicated that he was uncomfortable with people who had persecuted veteran cadres examining the case of the "Gang of Four." I did not hear very clearly the remarks he made, especially the figures he cited, so I am not certain that what I wrote down was consistent with the facts.

In short, with respect to the groups for the investigation of special cases, there were participants who discussed it from the very beginning of the Central Work Conference. After the third plenary session on November 25, all the groups concentrated on discussing it.

At the time I did not remember who had given me the excerpts from Wang Dongxing's two directives to the "No. 1 Office" of the Central Group for the Examination of Special Cases, that is, to the staffers of the "No. 1 Office," a group that examined special cases involving veteran Party and government cadres. In any case, the documents that contained the two directives he gave to the "No. 1 Office" fell into my hands. But I did not have an opportunity to give a speech on the matter. Excerpts of the material were later kept in my home. Wang gave his first directive on January 8, 1976, and his second directive on April 21. We could tell from the two directives that the staffers of the groups wavered in persecuting veteran cadres toward the end of the Cultural Revolution, but that Wang Dongxing encouraged them to be more severe.

In the first directive Wang said, "The Party Central Committee has discussed and determined the nature of the cases of Tao Zhu and Lu Dingyi. Peng Zhen, Yang Shangkun, and Bo Yibo are attempting to have their verdicts reversed. We should ignore them. The group for the examination of special cases should now study well, summarize its work on special cases, take class struggle as the key link, learn how to correctly handle the problem of contradictions within the people, and study the No. 23, No. 24, No. 25, and No. 26 documents issued by the Party Central Committee in 1975. We must uphold the principle of seeking truth from facts. Yes, some people have stayed out of work and yet they still have erred. It is wrong to presume that people we have treated leniently are free from all mistakes. The Party Central Committee decided in the past to examine them. What are you afraid of? You should not fear retaliation. What do you fear under the leadership of the Party Central Committee? The fact that some people are attempting to have their verdicts reversed does not mean that they are opposing your group for the examination of special cases. Rather they are attempting to reverse the verdicts made by the Ninth and Tenth Party Congresses, and are opposing the lines of those congresses. The No. 1 Office has resisted the tendency toward reversing the verdicts in accordance with the directive of the Party Central Committee. We should affirm the cases that should be affirmed and we should deal with people leniently. But we should not be ambiguous in writing the conclusions. We should write what is true. You should study hard the works of Marx, Lenin, and Chairman Mao. You should not engage in eclecticism, which means revisionism. It was good and necessary for veteran comrades to be attacked during the Cultural Revolution. The range of the attacks was a bit too wide, but the attacks were 70 percent correct and 30 percent not so correct."

In the second directive Wang said, "We should now concentrate on criticizing Deng Xiaoping and striking back at the tendency toward reversing the verdict. We must not be lenient toward our enemies. As to whether Lu Dingyi should be released, we should choose the right moment. Now we should reconsider some cases and investigate those spreading rumors. Why is Deng Xiaoping attempting to reverse verdicts? It is because his son attempted to kill himself by jumping out of a building at Peking University. Such being the case, how can he not feel hate? The wives of some people under examination died. How can people like Bo Yibo not feel hate?"

Liu Zhen from the Xinjiang Military Area Command and Chen Heqiao from the Second Artillery Forces, both in our Northwest China Group, delivered a joint speech about the case of the Central Group for the Examination of Special Cases on December 15. I do not remember the discussion. What I do remember is that the navy found out about the "Investigation Targets Registration Form of the No. 2 Office of the Central Group for the Examination of Special Cases." Comrades Liu and Chen gave our group the material, which was carried in the summary bulletin. The document cited ten such groups:

1. The Group for the Examination of the Special Case of Luo Ruiqing. Group members included Wu Faxian,[3] Ye Qun,[4] and Li Zuopeng.[5] The material appeared to be a document issued before the downfall of the Lin Biao Clique. The targets under examination in the special case included Luo Ruiqing and his wife Hao Zhiping.

2. The Group for the Examination of the Special Case of Peng Dehuai. Group members included Xie Fuzhi and Wu Faxian. The targets under examination included, apart from Peng Dehuai and his wife, Huang Kecheng,[6] Tan Zheng,[7] and a friend of mine, Li Rui[8].

3. The Group for the Examination of the Special Case of Rao Shushi. Group members included Jiang Qing, Xie Fuzhi, and Ye Qun. The targets under examination included Rao Shushi[9] and Pan Hannian.[10]

4. The Group for the Examination of the Special Case of Xie Fang. I had no information about Xie Fang and know nothing about him even today. The targets under examination included Lu Zhengcao.

5. The Group for the Examination of the Special Case of He Long. The targets under examination included—apart from He Long—Huang Xinting, Guo Linxiang, and Chen Heqiao of our Northwest China Group.

6. The Group for the Examination of the Special Case of Radio.

7. The Group for the Examination of the Special Case of "April 3rd."

8. The Group for the Examination of the Special Case of Wang Quanxiang. I had no idea about what the No. 6, No. 7 and No. 8 groups were examining. Judging from the fact that the targets under examination by the Group for the Examination of the Special Case of "April 3rd" included Ma Mingfang,[11] Zhang Ziyi,[12] and Yang Zhihua,[13] the group seemed to be connected to Xinjiang.

9. The Group for the Examination of the Special Case of Ye Xiangzhen (a daughter of Ye Jianying). Among the group members were Wu Faxian, Qiu Huizuo,[14] Ye Qun, and Wang Dongxing. As far as I know, the targets under examination included Liu Shikun,[15] as well as Ye Xiangzhen.

10. The Group for the Examination of the Special Case of Liu Zhijian.[16]

The name list was quite complete. But I only wrote down the persons I knew and the persons I cared about. Having heard this, I really learned a great deal.

In addition to the problem of the groups for the examination of the special cases, there was also the problem of the Central Guards Bureau and the 8341 Unit. The participants agreed that these institutions must be reorganized. Wang Dongxing was a Vice-Chairman of the Party Central Committee. Yet he not only concurrently held the post of the director of the General Office of the Party Central Committee, but also served as the director of the Central Guards Bureau and as commander of the 8341 Unit. He wielded power over the security of the Party Central Committee. He played an important role in smashing the "Gang of Four," but many comrades were uneasy about how he might use his position. Moreover, the number of security troops was too huge. The participants argued that this problem also needed to be solved.

There was also another institution, the General office of the Committee for Compiling and Publishing Chairman Mao Zedong's Works. This office was then headed by Li Xin, a deputy director of the General Office of the Party Central Committee and an assistant to Wang Dongxing. Of course, this institution needed to be reorganized and its leadership reshuffled.

The "12-Point Proposal" Made by the Northwest China Group and Other Similar Proposals

On December 7, while discussing the issue of personnel, the Northwest China Group, speaking for all its members, made a 12-point proposal to the Party Central Committee. One of the twelve points was the above-mentioned proposal to elect new members of the Party Central Committee, new members of the Political Bureau, and a new member of the Political Bureau Standing Committee. The proposal addressed other issues as well. I still have the text of the 12-point proposal, which reads as follows:

> 1. Comrade Wang Dongxing made positive contributions in guarding Chairman Mao and smashing the "Gang of Four." Nevertheless, his attitude toward the "two whatevers" has caused

many comrades to have misgivings about him. We believe that insisting on the "two whatevers" and persisting in completely and accurately understanding Marxism and the Mao Zedong Thought system are not just ideological differences, but create a political issue of paramount importance to the destiny and future of our Party and state. How does Comrade Wang Dongxing view the "two whatevers"? We hope that he can explain his views at the conference. What attitude does Comrade Wang Dongxing take toward the criterion for testing truth and the failure of Red Flag magazine to be involved in the discussion? Did Comrade Wang Dongxing support the mistaken remarks and acts of Comrades Wu Lengxi, Xiong Fu, Hu Sheng, Li Xin, and Zhang Yaoci on related issues? What attitude does Comrade Wang Dongxing take toward their remarks and acts? He should explain.

2. How did Comrade Wang Dongxing treat Premier Zhou Enlai and Chairman Zhu De? We hope that he will make explanations at the conference.

3. Chairman Mao praised Comrade Deng Xiaoping many times, saying, "It is hard to come by a person of such extraordinary ability." But Comrade Wang Dongxing said he [Deng Xiaoping] has a deep-rooted hatred for the Cultural Revolution. We cannot agree to this assertion.

4. In order that Comrade Wang Dongxing can concentrate on major state affairs, we propose that he should not concurrently serve as the director of the General Office of the Party Central Committee, still less as the director of the Central Guards Bureau.

5. Over the past two years Comrade Wang Dongxing, who is in charge of publicity work, has erected many barriers to exposing and criticizing Lian Biao and the "Gang of Four." The comrades doing publicity work have many criticisms about these constraints, and their views have been reflected in the conference summary bulletins. We hope Comrade Wang Dongxing will explain these questions.

6. The General Office of the Party Central Committee, the General Office of the Committee for Compiling and Publishing Chairman Mao Zedong's Works, the Central Guards Bureau, and other units need to be reorganized and should expose, criticize, and investigate the "Gang of Four" in a comprehensive manner. In terms of the organization system, the 8341 Unit should be handed over to the Beijing Garrison and make business contacts only with the Central Guards Bureau. Its authorized size of one division is too large, so it should be turned back into a regiment.

7. Various central groups for the examination of special cases should hand over their materials and staffers to the Organization

Department. They may not burn or otherwise destroy any documents, including fragments of writing.

8. We propose that Comrade Chen Xilian should not concurrently serve as the Commander of the Beijing Military Area Command.

9. We propose that Comrade Ji Dengkui should no longer serve as the executive Vice-Premier.

10. We warmly support the election of Comrades Chen Yun, Deng Yingchao, Hu Yaobang, and Wang Zhen as members of the Politiburo. We propose that Comrade Chen Yun should be elected a member of the Standing Committee of the Political Bureau and a vice-chairman of the Party Central Committee, and should be placed before Comrade Wang Dongxing in rank and position on the name list. We agree that Comrades Xi Zhongxun, Wang Renzhong, Zhou Hui, Song Renqiong, Han Guang, Hu Qiaomu, and Chen Zaidao should be elected members of the Party Central Committee.

11. To reduce the burden of the Political Bureau Standing Committee, we propose that the Secretariat of the Party Central Committee be restored.

12. It is necessary to reshuffle the General office of the Committee for Compiling and Publishing Chairman Mao Zedong's Works. Comrade Hu Qiaomu should take charge of compiling the Selected Works of Mao Zedong. All the works, manuscripts, and objects left by the Chairman should be handed over to the General office of the Committee for Compiling and Publishing Chairman Mao Zedong's Works.

Thirty people endorsed these twelve points, and the proposal incorporating the points was adopted by a show of hands. I remember very clearly that Hu Yaobang was absent when the 12-point proposal was adopted. This is probably because one of the twelve points was a proposal to elect him to the Political Bureau and he felt it would be awkward for him to approve the proposal by raising his hand. However, I do not remember whether the thirty people who approved the 12-point proposal included Wang Zhen and Song Renqiong, both of whom were in our Northwest China Group. We also proposed that both be elected to either the Political Bureau or the Party Central Committee. I do not remember either whether Ji Dengkui was present on the occasion or whether he raised his hand because one of the twelve points was a proposal that he should no longer serve as the executive Vice-Premier. Perhaps he was there.

I thought that voting for such a proposal was just the innovation of our Northwest China Group. Only when I read the summary bulletins on the following day did I learn that the Northeast China Group had made a similar 10-point proposal. Another proposal similar to ours was made in the Southwest China Group. I do not remember whether the three other groups — the North China Group, the Central-South China Group, and the East China Group — made similar proposals. I imagine that they also made similar proposals. This was, in effect, a vote. The first seven of the 12 points raised by our group were directed at Wang Dongxing. The last point was also, in fact, directed at him. Altogether, there were eight points directed at him.

The point of proposing that the Secretariat of the Party Central Committee should be restored was included in a speech I delivered at a group meeting. This proposal was not written into the communiqué of the Third Plenum. The Secretariat of the Party Central Committee was not established until over a year later, in February 1980. I also raised the last point, the proposal that Comrade Hu Qiaomu should again take charge of compiling the *Selected Works of Mao Zedong,* and this was included with the approval of other members of our group.

CHAPTER 9

DENG XIAOPING AND THE DRAFTING OF THE "DECLARATION" FOR THE NEW PERIOD

Deng Xiaoping's Comments on Drafting the Text of His Speech for the Closing Session

By the end of November, many questions had been raised and many participants had delivered speeches on key questions. They had finally raised the issue of personnel and organization of the Party Central Committee and some groups made written proposals as well. It was time for the Central Work Conference to come to an end. Of course the central leaders would speak at the closing session. Three plenary sessions had been held. Except for the second plenary session at which Ji Dengkui made a presentation, only Hua Guofeng had spoken at the two other plenary sessions. Before and after the Central Work Conference opened, Ye Jianying and Deng Xiaoping began preparing the speeches they would deliver at the conference and found people to draft the texts of their speeches. I only learned about this a long time later and I did not know it while the Central Work Conference was in session.

Naturally Hua Guofeng would speak at the closing session. In addition to Hua's speech, the participants all presumed not only that Deng Xiaoping and Ye Jianying would speak, but that it would be impossible for them not to speak. At a meeting of Political Bureau Standing Committee members to listen to reports from co-chairmen, Hua asked Ye and Deng to address the closing session. When this news reached the Northwest China Group, all comrades of our group thought, "Iit should be." Nobody mentioned whether Li Xiannian, a Standing Committee member, would speak. Participants did not know what Wang Dongxing, who had received so much criticism, might say at the closing session, but they speculated. In the end, three people spoke at the closing session on December 13, 1978: Hua Guofeng, Deng Xiaoping, and Ye Jianying. Li Xiannian did not speak and Wang Dongxing submitted a written speech that was essentially a self-criticism.

As for the process of drafting the speech that Deng Xiaoping delivered at the closing session, I can write about my own experiences since Deng asked me to help guide the people to draft his speech and clearly told me what he wanted to say and how he wanted to say it. I was there when the text was written and personally approved by Deng, and I participated in the drafting. When Han Gang, an editor of the *Hundred Year Tide* magazine, came to my home to ask me to write an article, I told him that when Deng Xiaoping asked me to organize people to turn his ideas into a text, Deng gave me three pages of the outline he personally wrote. I showed Han this manuscript. Han said that neither he nor the Party history researchers had known of the existence of this outline and that it was therefore a "new discovery" for them. For two decades I have carefully preserved these three pages. I originally kept them as a souvenir and I did not want to use them to prove anything. Of course Deng Xiaoping knew better than anyone about the efforts to draft his speech, and Hu Yaobang knew more about it than I. For instance, I learned much later that Deng had originally assigned Hu Qiaomu to draft his speech, but did not use Hu's draft. When Deng and Hu were alive, it was not necessary for me to recall how this speech was drafted. But now I am the person who had more direct access to this matter and knows more about it than anyone else still alive. I feel a responsibility to record what I know.

When the conference was more than half over, Hu Yaobang sought me out to discuss drafting Deng Xiaoping's speech for the closing session. On December 2, Deng asked Hu and me to come to his home to discuss the text of his speech. Deng himself wrote an outline for the speech, covering seven issues:

1. Emancipating our minds and using our heads.
2. Carrying forward democracy and strengthening the legal system.
3. Looking to the past to help people look to the future.
4. Overcoming bureaucracy and overstaffing.
5. Allowing some regions, enterprises and people to become better off sooner than others.
6. Strengthening the responsibility system and making several decisions.

7. Tackling new problems.

At the beginning of his outline, Deng added the issue of "assessing the conference." So, there were really eight issues altogether.

It was precisely in accordance with this outline that Deng Xiaoping talked with us about drafting his text. I have long thought that I did not possess any other relevant materials, aside from this outline and the formal text of Deng's speech. While going through my own "musty" books and papers recently, I unexpectedly discovered some notes from the talk Deng held with us about drafting his speech and the notes of our talks about revising Deng's speech. This enabled me to provide more details on these discussions. This taught me not to neglect "musty" books and papers because sometimes they can help solve major problems.

Deng said, "After considering the matter, I do not want to prepare a long text." The first issue was the assessment of the conference. He said, "The present conference has been very wonderful. We have not held one like it since 1957. We held conferences like this before 1957,for instance, during the Yan'an period. This practice must be continued. This reflects the vitality inside the party and a very good style of Party work. It helps promote stability and unity, and prevents the ossification of our minds. This is really gratifying."

The second issue was emancipating our minds and using our heads. He told us that in writing about this issue, it was necessary to "put some stress on the importance of theory." He said, "The debate [referring to the debate about the criterion for testing truth] is excellent. The more I view it, the better it appears. The more I view it, the more I regard it as a political issue, one crucial to the future and destiny of our country." He noted that to solve new problems, the whole Party and the people of the entire country must open their minds and use their brains.

The third issue was carrying forward democracy and strengthening the legal system. Deng noted, "During the current period we must do more to promote democracy. Since centralism has been practiced for so many years, the problem now is the lack of democracy. Now people dare not speak up and still have lingering fears. To develop the economy, it is imperative to practice democratic elections, democratic management, and democratic supervision. In factories, workers should exercise supervision, and in rural areas commune members should exercise supervision." He also said, "At present we should focus on opposing empty politics and indulging in empty talk. The problem now is that correct decisions are not implemented to the letter. We lack specific measures to ensure implementation, and often the implementation of such decisions is delayed for one year. We must stress the transfer of power to lower levels, the use of all measures possible, and the stimulation of local initiative. We must utilize every inch of land, planting one tree on a small piece of land, raising aquatic products on every water surface available, and planting grass on every pasture."

Speaking of the contradiction between the decision-making authority and the state's plans, Deng pointed out that the contradiction could be adjusted only by applying the law of value and adjusting the balance between supply and demand. Otherwise, it is impossible for anyone to enjoy decision-making authority. He said, "We must rely on quality because quality goods can sell well throughout the country. We should not be afraid of chaos caused by reliance on the market. We should accept a certain degree of regulation by the market.... In terms of economic democracy, the emphasis has been placed on politics only. But for economic democracy, we must also turn to laws, such as Civil Law, Criminal Law, and various specific laws. We should have a law on planting trees. Localities can also pass legislation."

The fourth issue was looking to the future. Deng said, "At the present conference we have looked to the past aiming to solve some problems and help us look to the future. We should not prescribe a single solution for diverse problems. In solving problems inherited from the past, we should be quick, resolute, and nimble, and we should not spend too much time. It is impossible to achieve complete satisfaction.... Stability and unity are of prime importance. We should not get entangled with the problems caused by Chairman Mao during the Cultural Revolution. We should not touch upon the Cultural Revolution. Instead we should let time clarify it. We can put aside this problem for some time before dealing with it again. In doing so, we will not incur any loss at all."

The fifth issue was overcoming bureaucracy. He criticized the phenomenon of overstaffing and sluggishness, as well as that of several "too manys," such as too many meetings. Deng Xiaoping pointed out: "We must master the management, training, and selection of officials and use people of great ability. We must reform regulations, rules, and systems. Efficient enterprises must be managed with advanced methods. To judge whether a Party committee exercises effective leadership, we should see whether an enterprise under its leadership is managed efficiently, whether it is profitable, and whether it pays the workers good wages. This is true for cities and rural areas and for all trades and industries."

The sixth issue was allowing some regions, enterprises and people to become better off sooner than others. Deng said, "This is a major policy. We should permit some people to achieve prosperity sooner than others, with the percentage of rural people who are prosperous first reaching five percent, rising to 10 percent, and increasing further to 20 percent. The percentage of urban people who are prosperous can stay at 20 percent.... Only this way shall we have a market, which itself will enable us to open up new industries. We must oppose egalitarianism. Whoever fares well will set a good example for his or her close neighbors to follow."

The seventh issue was strengthening the responsibility system. Having criticized the phenomenon of nobody assuming responsibility, Deng Xiaoping said, "We should make several kinds of decisions, decisions about: (a) which project to select; (b) where imports will go; (c) where the project will be located; (d) who will be in charge of the process from negotiations to management. We may make six or seven kinds of decisions and pass out forms for the decision-makers. These matters should be handled simultaneously so as not to cause a delay. What is the use of severely criticizing the State Planning Commission for failing to handle these matters? If criticism needs to be made, it should be directed at individuals. Domestic enterprises should specifically assign people to assume responsibility. They should set up special bodies to make decisions and invite experts to help them. For example, Rong Yiren[1] can serve as an expert."

The eighth issue was formulating new measures and studying new problems. Deng Xiaoping stressed the need to set standards for evaluating personnel.

Since Deng had such a detailed outline and gave us such specific directions, we, the drafters of his speech, found it easy to draft his speech. After coming back from his home, Hu Yaobang and I asked Lin Jianqing and others with the State Council Research Office to draft Deng's text promptly, and to complete the draft within two or three days.

The first draft was immediately sent to Deng Xiaoping for examination. In the course of modifying the draft, he got us together and talked with us several times. He gave his recommendations for revisions word-by-word and sentence-by-sentence. I still have two records of his talks on revision. One record is incomplete. I have not found my notes for the first part.

In talking with us about revisions, Deng emphasized the need to create conditions for people to dare to think and act. He asked, "What can help people dare to think and act? This problem must be solved from systems, with the fundamental one being the democratic system. We may not take strong measures against our comrades without a good reason. For new initiatives we should take an attitude of support and encouragement. Especially in academic research and in the ideological field we need more democratic discussions. Drawing arbitrary conclusions will never do. We must earnestly follow the principle of 'letting one hundred flowers bloom and letting one hundred schools of thought contend.' What if the principle is violated? Here again is the issue of trusting the masses and cadres."

Deng once again spoke about the question of opening our minds and using our brains. He said, "So long as we can allow our brains to work freely at the sight of an open field unplanted with trees or of a small pond unused for aquatic production, the members of a production team will lay awake at night, thinking about what they might do. If we open our minds, think how much wealth shall we be able to increase! For what should we use our heads? For the four modernizations!"

Deng Xiaoping also called for the establishment and perfection of Party rules and regulations. He said, "Our Party must have a fine style of work. Our Party's work style should be none other than the 'three work styles,'² which are intended to check violations of law and discipline. Now the Party's rules and regulations seem to be more important than state laws. We should emphasize economic democracy, which involves the problem of delegating power to lower levels and democratic supervision. We stress economic democracy. But if elections are not effective, power is not delegated to lower levels and Party Committees intervene at will, there will be no democracy and no people of ability will be trained. We must conscientiously implement the Party Constitution, which has defined the rights and obligations of Party members. Without democracy there will be no legal system. Now we do not have a whole range of laws to go by. So, we must formulate all types of laws, step-by-step. At the beginning it does not matter if laws are broadly outlined and incomplete. We can gradually perfect what is imperfect. We do not now have a special law on planting trees and reforestation or special economic laws. So, we can start by formulating ordinary laws. We should not require that laws be completely revised in a short while. We should formulate specific laws, and various localities should formulate their own rules and regulations. In short, we cannot do without laws."

Speaking of looking to the future, Deng Xiaoping said, "We should not require that those bearing responsibility have a perfect past. Past problems are very complicated. If they fail to make adequate self-criticism, let them reflect on their errors so that they will correct their mistakes in their actual work. But we should be stricter with new mistakes that are made in the future."

As for new problems, he said, "Numerous new problems and new contradictions are now cropping up, especially in the area of the superstructure. These involve problems of rules and systems, the use of people, and standards for selecting people. Developing productive forces for socialism and the people should serve as the prime standard. Otherwise, what does being strong politically mean? We should still extensively use economic means to manage the economy and should not wait for the superstructure. We should start from a factory or a specialized company. In rural areas we should start from a people's commune. There are barriers to reform. Veteran cadres favor reform as a whole, but oppose specific reform measures. We must take the overall situation into consideration and subordinate personal interests to collective interests. We must reason things out. In short, we must have explicit principles and proper methods. We cannot do without good methods."

Deng also talked about the problem of delegating power to lower levels and giving responsibility to individuals. He said, "We have a problem in assigning responsibility to individuals. The practice of a collective or a Party committee taking responsibility amounts to nobody taking responsibility. When we make a severe criticism, we should not be without a target. Since responsibility is assigned to individuals, individuals should have appropriate powers. Without power there can be no responsibility. The fundamental criterion for judging leadership should be the rise in labor productivity and whether technology is constantly upgraded. Relying on physical labor will not do."

Speaking about letting some people achieve prosperity sooner than others, Deng said, "The average monthly wage of 80 yuan per worker is not enough and should be increased to 100 yuan. Cities should stimulate the countryside and big cities should spur on small ones. We should make a success in the urban service sector. We can accomplish a great deal in this regard." He also referred to the problem of urban planning, citing Singapore as an example. "Even the island state of Singapore has satellite towns. Why don't we have such towns? Plans for Xishan and Shijingshan in Beijing should be drawn up. In Singapore, whoever has 1,500 Singaporean dollars is entitled to buy an apartment. A five-room apartment with a floor space of about 70 square meters costs a worker six months' wages and can be bought on installments. In Japan, in the units giving fairly high bonuses, bonuses are equivalent to six months of a worker's wages and are enough to buy a car. Rent in Singapore amounts to 15 percent of a worker's monthly wages, and in Europe, one third." He also said that the countries with a great number of small producers have problems and that the influence of past customs in small-scale production could be mentioned in the text of his speech.

In conclusion, he said that a shorter text of his speech would serve the purpose, a lengthy speech or article was not good, and that shorter and neater sentences would be more forceful. He also expressed the hope that the revision of the text of his speech would be completed soon and if it could be done within two days, so much the better.

Deng met with us again after the text of his speech was further revised. He confirmed that he would refer to four questions instead of the original eight. Meanwhile, he urged us to refer at the beginning or in the middle of the speech, to the issue of the shift in the focus of work. He said this was a major principle that did not require many words, but was a major overall premise of the speech. In my notes I wrote the phrase "truly reflect the new period and the shift in the focus of work."

In his talk with us, Deng criticized the cult of placing individuals above the Party Central Committee. "This is a very important matter and is more important than the 'two whatevers.' In essence, it involves problems in the superstructure. Bureaucracy is part of the content. The overconcentration of powers really departs from democratic centralism and the role of the organization. The essence of the problem is the concentration of power divorced from democracy. This kind of problem exists in organizations at all levels. The leaders of all organizations, including the secretaries of Party branches, all have too much power. This is not good. Our system does not encourage people to dare to think or act or to support them when they do. Ideological encouragement and material encouragement are both inadequate. The reason for ossification lies in the fact that those performing well and those performing poorly get the same treatment. Moreover, those performing poorly get everyone's vote because they do not offend others and everyone thinks that they are acceptable. This is true in the government system as well as in the Party system. Consequently, strange phenomena have cropped up."

Deng particularly stressed the necessity of adding a paragraph on the so-called problem of investigating rumors. He said that this was a manifestation of weakness and neurasthenia. He added that retaliation was a very bad practice and must be fought against and

137

stopped. He also proposed adding to the speech the content of "to each according to his work."

> Those, including leading cadres, who perform better should earn more and become prosperous sooner than others. Initiative will not be stimulated without economic incentives. It will not do merely to stress the display of proper character. As far as the relatively small number of advanced people is concerned, it will not matter too much if we stress the display of character. But when it comes to the masses, that approach can only be used for a short time. It will not work in the long run. We must manage the economy by economic means.... In short, this problem should be expounded in connection with rewards, punishments, and economic interests. Rewards, including material rewards, should be granted to specific people and specific workshops. With a system of responsibility, rewards, and penalties, we should promote those who should be promoted and demote those who should be demoted. We should demote those unqualified for their jobs. We should train experts and let them continue without interruption once they start work. Serving socialism and bringing happiness to the people constitute the political norm.

Deng Xiaoping also stressed the need to formulate necessary laws, citing the names of six laws. He added: "We should study international law. Without a good knowledge of foreign laws and more international exchanges, we will fall farther behind in the future."

In his talk he once again referred to the question of looking to the future:

> We have too many problems to solve. So, we cannot solve every detail and must concentrate on the big picture.
>
> Moreover, a short passage should be written on the issue of stability and unity. We can solve the problems left over from the past in a positive way and don't have to investigate the details. Proceeding from our overall tasks, we can be relatively lenient with people who have made mistakes in the past, particularly those who made political errors. But they should help us clarify past problems and consider how to improve in the future. Summarizing experience takes time. People who made mistakes in the past should not be compelled to make self-criticism right away. This is also the Party's workstyle. So long as we make clear

the basic questions of right and wrong, it is impossible and unnecessary to clarify minor questions of right and wrong one by one. It is inappropriate to talk too much about some matters.... Some people who indulged in beating, smashing, and looting, who advocated factionalism, those who toadied and curried favor, and who just want to serve their time cannot be placed in important positions. We must guard against and educate those seeking factional interests and indulging in beating, smashing and looting. We should not blindly trust them.

As regards the new problems brought by reforms, Deng noted:

Reforming the superstructure and reforming the relations of production can both create many new problems affecting vast numbers of people. It is difficult to lay off some workers and find new jobs for some, to decide which people should study more and which should switch to another trade or line of work. Some people waiting for new job arrangements who receive their wages as before are still dissatisfied. These reforms will involve the immediate interests of a large number of people. We must trust and rely on the masses, and create conditions to enable each benefit from his appropriate role. By trusting the masses, we shall gain their understanding.... The shock will be fairly serious. The new contradictions will not be simpler than the existing problems, but rather will be more complicated. We can solve this problem by following the mass line, trusting the masses, and teaching them to take the overall situation into consideration. With the development of production, there will be many new social pressures. Even if such demands are not numerous next year, they will certainly arise in large numbers the following year. In short, with the development of productive forces, the problem can be solved effectively.

During our talk Deng read the text in greater detail and made more specific comments. The comrades drafting his speech made revisions again in line with his views. I don't remember the date, but one day, after listening to a speechwriter read through the text, Deng said, "All right. Take it as the final text as it stands now." Our drafting was then completed.

There is one thing that I need to explain here. On the day after the text was finalized, Deng Xiaoping asked me to come to his home. When he saw me, he said, "Yu Guangyuan, it is really absurd that the

Beijing municipal authorities want to open a case to investigate people who wrote their views on the 'Xidan democracy wall.' In my speech, when I speak of the problem of 'creating files' on people to criticize, I will depart from my speech text to interpose a few remarks." He assigned me to draft some remarks on my own and cite some instances. After the "Gang of Four" was smashed, especially after the "two whatevers" principle was concocted, some leaders and some departments were "investigated" many times, and the records of a few isolated leaders and people who had criticized "ultra-Left" mistakes were "placed on file to be examined." In the comments he gave me for drafting the text of his speech, Deng expressed extremely great resentment about this practice. He said that investigating such "rumors" would cause tension and was, in fact, an expression of weakness and anxiety. Retaliation was a very bad practice and must be halted.

The "Xidan democracy wall" was a venue for the masses to express their views on their own after the Cultural Revolution and was then quite influential. The leadership and the rank and file held different views on the "Xidan democracy wall." Deng Xiaoping expressed his affirmation of it; Ye Jianying also approved of it. In the speech he delivered at the closing ceremony, Ye said unequivocally that the Central Work Conference was a good example of giving full play to inner Part democracy and the "Xidan democracy wall" was a good example of giving full play to democracy outside the Party.

When Deng talked with me alone, Ye Jianying had not yet delivered his speech. Of course, I had no way of knowing what he would say. I also did not know whether Deng and Ye had exchanged opinions. But I knew about the "Xidan democracy wall" and I wanted very much to go there to have a look. However, I had heard that some of the people who went there had been roughed up. I was worried that a man of my age could not endure that, so I had not gone there yet. I heard that Hu Qiaomu went there at night to read big character posters by flashlight. It was quite easy to fulfill the task Deng assigned me. I soon finished drafting a 1,000-character paragraph and gave it to him. Nevertheless, in the end, he did not use these comments in the speech he delivered at the closing session.

The following are the main points I want to emphasize in reference to the overall drafting of Deng's speech text. The content of his speech was his own, the train of thought was his own, and most of the expressions that left a profound impression on people were his own, too. Deng read the text written by the drafters very carefully. While examining the draft, he constantly deepened and amplified his ideas before approving a final version of the text. He decided upon the topics himself, although there were no topic headings in the document distributed to the participants because a unified style was followed.

I also want to say, first, that Hu Yaobang and I were present on all occasions when drafting assignments were made, when the text was revised, and when it was put into final form at Deng's home. There was no one else present apart from the writers of the text. Hu also made some comments. Second, my role was to select the people to write the text in line with Deng Xiaoping's and Hu Yaobang's ideas, to pass Deng's ideas on to them, to discuss the framework of the text with them, and to set deadlines for completing the text. I did not voice any ideas of my own worth mentioning.

People like me who specialized in writing documents were duty-bound to help the leaders, who were busy with their work, to do some writing. Even if I had done a little more work than I did, I could not credit myself with "merits." In any case, Deng already had very clear ideas and I did not have to do much.

Deng Xiaoping's Speech at the Closing Session

Deng Xiaoping's speech was a document of great historical significance. People have said and written so much about this speech that it seems unnecessary to write more about it. It seems wrong, however, if I do not write something since I took part in drafting and polishing the documents, and also listened to Deng deliver his speech at the closing session. I feel I should record my own impressions and understanding at the time, as well as what I learned and understood about it from subsequent study.

First of all, I remember that the nineteen-character headline for the speech was chosen by Deng Xiaoping himself: "*jie fang s ixiang, kai dong nao jin, shi shi qiu shi, tuan ji yi zhi xiang qian kang* "[emancipate

141

the minds, use our heads, seek truth from facts, and unite as one in looking to the future].   These nineteen characters were not on the three-page speech outline Deng originally gave me. Nor were these nineteen characters in the draft written by Lin Jianqing and others, which I read before passing it on to Deng Xiaoping.

On the first part of the three pages of the original outline, Deng had written a headline of eight characters *"jie fang si xiang, kai dong ji qi* [emancipate the mind and put the machinery in motion]." Below this he had written, "The whole Party and the people of the whole country should use their heads." In another sentence he wrote, "Seek truth from facts." The headline of the third part of the outline was, "Examining the past will help people look to the future." Deng added another sentence, "Stability and unity are of prime importance." Ideas and expressions such as "emancipate the mind," "use our heads," "seek truth from facts," "unity," and "look to the future" were already in the outline. But they had not been synthesized into the nineteen characters, which were written into the final text later and which appeared in two places: first in the lead-in at the beginning of the text, then in the first part of the text. Exactly the same nineteen characters thus appeared in two places. As I recall, in the course of preparing the final version of the text and in discussing the lead-in, Deng Xiaoping asked if this sentence could be used as the headline for his speech.   Both Hu Yaobang and I answered "Very good," noting that it summarized the three most important points for the rest of the speech, although giving the headline went against the conventional pattern for speeches. We also discussed the possibility of omitting four characters, *"kai dong ji qi"* [put the machinery in motion], from the headline, cutting the 19 characters down to 15.

I do not remember clearly what the final text was like.[1] I only found that in the published version there were no headlines in the speeches of Hua Guofeng, Ye Jianying, and Deng Xiaoping. Probably for the sake of unity of style, there was no headline for Deng's speech. As to when the headline was later added again, I really have no idea. All this is waiting to be "discovered" in written materials. Obviously,

[1] Editor's note: The phrase, "put the machinery in motion," was omitted in the final printed version.

archaeology is a branch of learning, so is the "study of present material evidence." People's memories are of great value. But only written materials allow people to remember things more accurately and to correct the mistakes from their memories. Some written materials were in times past not regarded as of great use. When it comes to studying problems, they were found to be of great use. The three pages of the outline that I have kept for twenty years are of great use today.

Let us return to the content of Deng Xiaoping's speech. The headline of the first part was finally set as "Emancipating the Mind Is a Vital Political Task." Deng pointed out immediately why he attached special importance to the fundamental issue of emancipating the mind. After writing the nineteen characters, this part of his speech said explicitly, "The primary task is to emancipate our minds." He noted, "Only then can we, guided as we should be by Marxism-Leninism and Mao Zedong Thought, find correct solutions to the emerging as well as inherited problems; fruitfully reform those aspects of the relations of production and of the superstructure that do not correspond with the rapid development of productive forces; and chart the specific course and formulate specific policies, methods and measures needed to achieve the four modernizations under our actual conditions." Here Deng Xiaoping highlighted the overall guideline for China's reforms, enabling the reform of the relations of production to meet the need posed by the rapid development of productive forces. To turn this into reality, the prime point is to emancipate the mind. I think that it is entirely appropriate that in his report to the Fifteenth Party Congress, Comrade Jiang Zemin described this speech as a "declaration for charting a new course in the new period and creating the new theory of building socialism with Chinese characteristics."

Meanwhile, I thought it was very good to refer to emancipating the mind together with seeking truth from facts, because it emphasized the emancipation of the mind, while not departing from the basis of materialism. This also left me with a very profound impression.

While elaborating on the emancipation of the mind, Deng affirmed that practice serves as the sole criterion for testing truth. The debate of over six months and the confrontation at the Central Work Conference required that Deng Xiaoping make the concluding remarks. Speaking of this issue, he pointed out that the debate "was, in fact, also a debate about whether people's minds need to be emancipated," thus elevating the significance of emancipating the mind to a very high level. He said, "When everything has to be done by the book, when thinking turns rigid and blind faith is the fashion, it is impossible for a party or a nation to make progress. Its life will cease and that party or nation will perish.... In this sense, the debate about the criterion for testing truth is really a debate about the ideological line, about politics, about the future and destiny of our Party and nation."

The second part of Deng's speech was on democracy. Reference to democracy is generally abstract and not very deep. But Deng Xiaoping's speech was different. The subheading "Democracy Is a Major Condition for Emancipating the Mind" summarized this section of his speech. Previously, democracy had seldom been referred to this way. Here Deng again spotlighted the importance of "emancipating the mind." In this section he had written about the April 1976 Tiananmen Incident, which I thought highly appropriate. At the Central Work Conference many participants advocated reversing the verdicts on the Tiananmen Incident to uphold justice, for only then could the enthusiasm of the masses for socialism be greatly stimulated. In keeping with the remarks he had made while finalizing his speech at his home, Deng said, "The masses should be encouraged to offer criticism. There is nothing to worry about even if a few malcontents take advantage of democracy to make trouble. We should deal with such situations appropriately and have faith that the overwhelming majority of the people are able to use their own judgment. One thing a revolutionary party does need to worry about is its inability to hear the voice of the people. The thing to be feared most is silence." He was particularly dissatisfied with conditions that caused people to remain silent, and with some people and organizations who "attack and try to silence people who make critical comments, especially pointed ones, by ferreting out their political backgrounds, tracing political rumors to them and opening 'special case' files on them." Hu Yaobang and I readily agreed with these words.

This section also contained remarks that Deng had made on the issue of economic democracy. He disapproved of the over-concentration of powers in China's economic managerial system. He advocated boldly delegating powers to lower levels and giving full scope to the initiative to all four actors — the state, local authorities, enterprises, and individual laborers. He maintained that it was necessary, under unified leadership, to expand the decision-making authority of local authorities, especially in enterprises and production teams in the countryside. He said that with the decision-making authority in their hands, workshop directors, production team leaders, and workers and farmers would take responsibility, get their brains moving, and use their heads. He also spoke about the material interests of the masses. At the Central Work Conference many comrades also talked about this, but Deng Xiaoping's speech on this issue was the most comprehensive and profound.

The subheading of the third section of Deng's speech was "Solving Old Problems Will Help People Look to the Future." The three pages of the outline he gave me originally contained one sentence, "Examining the past will help people look to the future." The range of his remarks on this topic in our discussion was broader than in our final draft. In the earlier drafts, Deng talked about the fundamental attitude with which we should view problems left over from the past. We must pay great attention to history, face it squarely, never forget the past, and never forget the precious experience provided by the past for us and important lessons left us by the past. We should especially never forget the bitter lessons of the Great Cultural Revolution. Studying history is also of significance in understanding the laws governing historical development. We should never forget the past because forgetting the past means failing to grasp the future. In later drafts of Deng's speech text, the range of comments on this issue was narrowed deliberately. The final text primarily addressed handling inherited problems and referred only to some people's merits and demerits and to redressing framed, wrong and false cases. The narrower range of the discussion of history would allow this speech to focus on current urgent problems, to reduce the talk on contentious issues, to show Deng Xiaoping's generosity toward past errors, and to promote unity as one looked to the future.

We particularly appreciated Deng's use of the expression of "looking to the future," which guided us as we considered the direction of our advance. In his final speech, he said, "Our principle is that every wrong should be corrected. All wrongs committed in the past should be corrected." He also stressed that "Settlement must be prompt and effective, without leaving any loose ends, and should be based on facts. We must thoroughly resolve the problems left over from the past. It is not good for them to be left unsolved. It is not good that the comrades who have made mistakes refuse to make self-criticism, or that we do not deal with their cases properly." But taking into consideration realistic possibilities as well as means conducive to solving problems, he noted, "We cannot possibly settle all cases at once ... we cannot possibly achieve, and we should not expect, a perfect settlement of every case. We should keep in mind the big issues and solve them in broad outline; to go into every detail is neither possible nor necessary."

Deng Xiaoping reiterated *ex tempore* such remarks as "We should settle cases in broad outline rather than go into every detail." If people got too entangled with some of the details, they may not focus on the major aspect of their problems and think through their problems. Later, some people misunderstood or deliberately used this remark to distort it into the notion that We should not study historical problems "carefully and earnestly." Those studying history should try their best to restore the original features of things, should not be careless and make caricatures. Still less should they cover up or distort history, as later generations will not be able to know historical truth or to gain profound historical experience and lessons. This is particularly true for the history of the Cultural Revolution. We could not adopt such an irresponsible approach toward the history before and after the Third Plenum of the Eleventh Party Central Committee. Deng was creative and wise to say we should "settle cases in broad outline rather than go into every detail."

I also liked the fourth section of his speech, "Study the New Situation and Tackle New Problems." Deng noted, "In order to look forward, we must study the new situation and tackle new problems in good time. In three fields especially, new situations and new problems demand attention: methods of management, the structure of management, and economic policy." As for the question of what to learn, he said, "Basically, we should study Marxism-Leninism and Mao Zedong Thought. At present, most of our cadres need also to apply themselves to three subjects: economics, science and technology, and management." He said, "We must place particular stress on strengthening the responsibility system. By allotting rewards and penalties fairly, we should create an atmosphere of friendly emulation in which people vie with one another to become advanced elements, working hard and aiming high.

"By allowing some regions and enterprises and some workers and peasants to earn more and become better off before others, in accordance with their hard work and greater contributions to society . . . this will inevitably be an impressive example to their 'neighbors,' and people in other regions and units will want to learn from them. This will help the whole national economy to advance wave upon wave."

The trumpet call to initiate reforms sounded at the Third Plenum found expression in Deng's speech. His ideas were first contained in those three pages of the outline. Then, in the three days when the text of his speech was being revised into final form, he further supplemented his original outline, making the content much richer. It was not true that the drafters of his speech and those contributing to the process of preparing the final version of the text did not play any role. But the brilliant opinions found in his speech can properly be credited to Deng himself. Some new ideas and new views at the Third Plenum were not contained in his speech at the Central Work Conference. But I marveled at how he could ponder matters so profoundly and so substantially, and in such great detail.

In our joint speech delivered on December 14, Wang Huide, Yang Xiguang, and I spoke of our own understanding of some points we had chosen from his speech. What I have written today is more than the speech we gave that day. Even so, I still have referred to only part of his speech and I cannot possibly refer to his speech in its entirety. Meanwhile, I also want to add one point. In delivering his

147

speech, Deng Xiaoping had to take into consideration the likely degree of acceptance by many participants at the time; some remarks made then perhaps would not have been made that way today.

CHAPTER 10

YE JIANYING'S ENDURING CONTRIBUTION

The Drafting of the Speech by Ye Jianying

Ye Jianying was part of the collective leadership at the Central Work Conference from beginning to end. He was a Vice-Chairman of the Party Central Committee elected in the First Plenum of the 11th Party Central Committee and one of the five members of the Political Bureau Standing Committee. The five Standing Committee members were the Party Central Committee chairman, Hua Guofeng, and the vice-chairmen—Ye Jianying, Deng Xiaoping, Li Xiannian, and Wang Dongxing. Ye was the second in position in the name list of the Standing Committee members. As one of the decision-makers, Ye played a significant role in the historical action to smash the "Gang of Four" in 1976 and was personally involved on October 6, 1976. Many people know that he performed a deed of great merit in smashing the "Gang of Four." Many details were contained in a recently shown TV documentary series about Ye Jianying's life. But only a few people know the contributions Ye made at the Central Work Conference and at the Third Plenum of the 11th Party Central Committee. Few people have mentioned this in recent years. At the time when activities were conducted to mark the twentieth anniversary of the convocation of the Third Plenum, I, as a witness to history and a researcher, felt obligated to record the historical facts. The words "Ye Jianying's Enduring Merits" should be written on an important page in the history of the Party and the People's Republic of China.

I was fairly well informed on the Central Work Conference. I learned about the preparations for drafting Ye Jianying's speech from Hu Yaobang who told me that very early Ye had asked him to find people to draft the speech he would deliver at the conference. When the conference drew to a close, he was still considering how to revise his speech even as his secretary took up his pen. I also heard that he intended to focus his speech on democracy and the legal system. Ye was the chairman of the Standing Committee of the National People's Congress, and I believed he was the most suitable person to speak on

149

this issue. At the end of November, I wrote a long letter to Comrade Ye Jianying. He had been my superior before Liberation (1949) when I worked with the *Liberation Daily* in Beiping, so I was worried about disturbing him.   I made a three-point proposal about further promoting democracy, strengthening the legal system and improving the work of the National People's Congress. I also criticized, from the viewpoint of the science of law, a national conference on people's judicial work that was held in May of 1978 for incorrectly "labeling as active counterrevolutionaries those viciously attacking Chairman Hua and the Party Central Committee headed by Chairman Hua" and citing "those people as the focus of crackdown." I pointed out that before the Cultural Revolution there had been no charge of "vicious attack" in either China's criminal legislature or the criminal courts. I maintained that such provision was detrimental to the Chinese legal system. After I mailed my letter, I received a phone call from his secretary, who said that Ye Jianying had praised me.

I phoned Ye's secretary, asking him to tell Ye that Wang Huide, Yang Xiguang, and I had quoted Lenin in our November 13 speech, which was carried in the Northwest China Group's summary bulletin. "If full democracy is not practiced under victorious socialism, it will be impossible for socialism to retain the victory it has won and guide mankind to the elimination of the state." Ye later quoted this sentence in his speech. It was Wang Huide who proposed including this sentence in our speech with Yang Xiguang. As it was inconvenient to refer to books in the Jingxi Hotel, I was afraid that the remark was not quoted accurately. Wang said, "You don't have to worry because I remember it clearly. There is no mistake." To write this article, I referred to *The Complete Works of Lenin* on my bookshelf, but I could not find the sentence. When the meeting to discuss theoretical principles for 1979 was in session, I wrote an article titled "The Issue of the Elimination of the State after Victory Is Won in the Proletarian Revolution," in which I quoted 109 paragraphs of Lenin's remarks. One paragraph read, "The development of proletarian democracy and the elimination of the state are the same thing." In preparing that article I had also been unable to track down Lenin's remark. Finally, the only things I could do was call the Central Compilation and Translation Bureau for help. Staffers there told me that the remark was contained in a long article written by Lenin in August or September of 1916, "On Marxism Distorted beyond Recognition and the 'Imperialist Economy.' " Wang Huide was worthy of his post as the Director of the Central Compilation and Translation Bureau. When we delivered our joint speech, thanks to Wang, almost every word in the Lenin quotation was exactly the same as that in the original remark. Readers can refer to page 168 in Volume 28 of the new edition of *The Complete Works of Lenin*. The full text is as follows:

> "Without democracy, there cannot possibly be socialism, which contains two meanings: (1) If the proletariat does not make preparations for the socialist revolution through the struggle to win democracy, it will not be able to achieve this revolution; (2) If full democracy is not practiced under victorious socialism, it will be impossible for socialism to retain the victory it has won and to guide mankind to the elimination of the state."

Ye's speech also quoted another remark by Lenin, "In addition to publicizing scientific socialism, the Russian socialist democrats should publicize simultaneously democracy."

Ye Jianying's Speech at the Closing Session

It had been some twenty years since I listened to Comrade Ye Jianying speak. I had always cherished the memory of how, when I rode with him in his military vehicle from Guilin to Chongqing in 1939, he had told us stories about the Long March, and of how he guided the work of the Beiping Liberation Daily with which we worked when he served as the Party member of the Beiping Military Mediation Department in 1946.[1] I was truly delighted to hear his voice this time.

Like Deng Xiaoping, Ye highly appraised the current Central Work Conference, saying: "It is really a very good beginning that such full democracy has been practiced at the current conference, which has taken the lead in this regard. We must persist in it and carry it forward permanently." Indeed, at the Central Work Conference, there were no limits set on the time length of the speeches, the number of the speeches to be made, or the range of the speeches. Consequently, every participant was really able to speak without reservation. Of course, it was not possible for all central conferences to last 36 days like this Central Work Conference. That was a specific phenomenon that occurred under those concrete historical conditions. However, everyone hoped that the spirit of giving full scope to democracy displayed at the conference could be upheld permanently, as stated by Ye Jianying in his speech.

Ye referred to three issues. The first was the issue of leadership. This was the issue with which the participants were particularly concerned as the conference drew to its end. By the end of 1978, Liu Shaoqi, Zhu De, Zhou Enlai, and Mao Zedong had died in succession. Liu had been persecuted to death and the others died of illness. Zhu De, who was eleven years older than Ye Jianying, Zhou Enlai, who was one year younger than Ye, and Mao Zedong, who was four years older than Ye, all died in 1976. Ye Jianying, who was eighty-one at the time, said with emotion,"We veteran cadres and comrades have spent more than half a century working for China's revolutionary cause, fighting in the north and south. Now we are advanced in age. The law governing natural development cannot be violated."

Of course, the participants all urgently hoped that Deng Xiaoping, who was seven years younger than Ye, would come out to preside over the work of the Party Central Committee. If we say that it was at the Zunyi Meeting held in 1935 that the leadership position of Mao Zedong in the Party Central Committee was actually established, it was at the Central Work Conference held in 1978 and the Third Plenum that Deng Xiaoping's leadership status in our Party Central Committee was established. Furthermore, the status Deng achieved was more solid than that Mao achieved at the Zunyi Meeting. After the Zunyi Meeting Mao Zedong's status was solidified by the 1938 Sixth Plenum of the Sixth Party Central Committee, the Yan'an Rectification Movement, and the Seventh Plenum of the Sixth Party Central Committee. Yet Deng did not go through a similar process. The status that Deng achieved was due to his own moral integrity, his ability, and the love that vast number of cadres and people felt for him. Yet the support of Ye Jianying, who was of age and eminent virtue, was also a critical factor. Meanwhile, the support among conference participants for selecting Hu Yaobang as the general secretary had begun to wane. In his speech Ye Jianying made remarks highlighting the importance of taking great care in training successors to the revolutionary cause. Listening to his speech at the closing session, all of us could understand his intention.

The second issue Ye addressed was carrying forward democracy and strengthening the legal system. He referred to this issue both in the introduction and the second section of his speech. While praising the conference, he said, "At this conference, all of us have spoken without reservation, held adequate discussions, and made criticisms. Some comrades who have made mistakes have also made self-criticisms to varying degrees. This is the sign of our Party's vitality." In the section titled "Carry forward Democracy and Strengthen the Legal System," he said, " To realize socialist modernization, we must earnestly practice democratic centralism." Then he repeated three times the phrase "only by giving full scope to democracy." He said, "Only by giving full scope to democracy, will we be able to arouse, to the maximum extent, the initiative of the vast number of cadres and masses, draw on collective wisdom and absorb all useful ideas, and build socialism by pooling the wisdom and efforts of the masses. Only by giving full scope to democracy, will we be able to open all channels for people of ability, find in good time outstanding people of ability inside our Party, and ensure the right of the vast number of cadres and masses to supervise and criticize the leadership. Only in this way will we be able to promptly ferret out and expose conspirators, careerists and double-dealers like Lin Biao and the 'Gang of Four,' in order to consolidate our state power and provide an effective guarantee for our socialist modernization." In conclusion he said, "Here it is appropriate to quote Lenin's remark, "If full democracy is not practiced under victorious socialism, it will be impossible for socialism to retain the victory it has won and guide mankind to the elimination of the state.'" Lenin's remark was really very apt.

Ye criticized Lin Biao and the "Gang of Four" for creating the illusion that practicing democracy was tantamount to restoring capitalism. Ye said, "This strange theory and absurd argument they spread on the question of democracy have twisted the thinking of some of our comrades. Consequently, on hearing the word 'democracy,' these comrades become quite nervous.... Lin Biao and the 'Gang of Four' passed feudalism off as socialism, asserting that they used socialism in opposition to capitalism. Any view different from theirs they labeled "bourgeois" and "capitalist." Consequently, our thinking was distorted and we were unable to distinguish what feudalism is, what capitalism is, and what genuine socialism is. China remained a feudal society for more than 2,000 years. Capitalism never fully developed in China. Our socialism began to be built on the basis of a semifeudal and semicolonial society. Therefore, one of the major tasks to emancipate our minds is to pay great attention to overcoming the influence of the remnants of feudal ideas. Lenin said, 'We must not only publicize the ideas of scientific socialism, but also the ideas of democracy.' We must break the ideological superstition created by feudal superstition and emancipate our minds from these fetters."

Ye Jianying's remarks went to the very essence of things and were profound. I was very excited listening to him. When studying his teachings again 20 years later, I still feel they are very apt and significant.

Then Ye made further comments, noting that to promote democracy, leading cadres must act in the spirit of modestly soliciting the opinions of the masses and daring to make self-criticism. He criticized some comrades for "talking loudly every day about making criticism and self-criticism and behaving with modesty and prudence. But when it comes to receiving slightly critical comments, they will immediately make a long face. They can only criticize others, but never criticize themselves. They are just like a tiger whose backside nobody dares to touch." He also made several remarks on the inner-Party democracy that was fully practiced in our Central Work Conference and on democracy in society that was reflected beyond the conference. These remarks were later deleted from the final text distributed to participants. Yet they also left a profound impression on the participants. On December 15, after Ye's speech, the Northwest China Group particpants, while discussing their reactions to the closing session speeches by Standing Committee members, expressed their support for Ye Jianying's remarks. This was shown by the joint speech that Wang Huide, Yu Guangyuan, and Yang

Xiguang delivered, and in the comprehensive bulletin written in the name of all members of the Northwest China Group.

The third issue Ye referred to was "studying diligently and emancipating the mind." He said, "Studying diligently and emancipating the mind are two interrelated aspects. The more effectively we study the wider range of knowledge we have, the more effectively we can emancipate our minds. In pursuing the socialist modernization drive, we not only want to greatly develop social productive forces, but also to make a profound social revolution from the economic foundation to the superstructure. Are our comrades fully prepared ideologically for such a revolution?"

He thought that many people were inadequately prepared. "Some comrades still fear wolves ahead and tigers behind, stick to convention, stay in the old rut, do not emancipate their minds and dare not to take a single step forward. What are they afraid of? Are they afraid of being criticized for 'restoring capitalism,' of having someone seize upon their vulnerable points and label them, or of losing their official posts? So far as fear is concerned, why is it that they are not afraid that handicraft production practices left over from 2,000 years ago might continue to exist or that China is poor and backward or that the Chinese people do not permit such a state of affair?"

What a great speech Ye Jianying made! Having worked inside the Party, I had seldom read a Party document that dealt so thoroughly with the issue of democracy. Most people could not see Ye, whereas I personally listened to him speaking of the issue. Moreover, I have relevant written materials in my hand. For this reason, I wanted to quote his remarks as fully as possible, and having done so, I feel there is really very little I need to add.

There was a division of labor between Ye Jianying's speech and Deng Xiaoping's. Ye did not address all aspects of Party work comprehensively, but instead spoke in earnest of three key issues. I wondered why the book Since the Third Plenum[2] compiled in 1982 by the Party Literature Research Center of the Party Central Committee—either the Selected Important Documents of the Party or the Collection of Important Documents of the Party—did not contain Ye's speech. Ye made tremendous contributions to the struggle to smash the "Gang of Four." After the downfall of the "Gang of Four," the Party Central Committee issued a circular to the whole Party on his contributions to this great historical action. After the 11th Party Congress, even when the Central Work Conference and the Third Plenum were in session, he was the first in the name list of the four vice-chairmen of the Party Central Committee. Before the Central Work Conference was held, it was he who proposed holding a meeting to discuss theoretical guidelines. When the Central Work Conference closed, in addition to Hua Guofeng, both he and Deng Xiaoping spoke and his speech was very important. I really can see no reason for not including Ye's speech in the book Since the Third Plenum.

CHAPTER 11

THE CLOSING SESSION AND THE END OF THE CENTRAL WORK CONFERENCE

The Speech by Hua Guofeng at the Closing Session

Hua Guofeng was the last leader to address the closing session. He gave a summary of the conference, which had already lasted 36 days. The text of Hua's speech was not demarcated into four distinct sections, but the actual content fell into four parts. The first part dealt with the the conference's successes; the second focused on the "two whatevers" and the "debate about the issue of the criterion for testing truth;" the third part covered the issue of party unity and improving the leadership; the fourth part related the background for convening the Third Plenum.

In the first section of his speech, Hua, like Deng Xiaoping and Ye Jianying, gave a very positive assessment of the conference. Speaking in the name of the Political Bureau as well as all comrades attending the conference, he said that the participants unanimously agreed that the conference had given full scope to democracy and was a complete success. Then he summarized the conference's four major results. First, all participants agreed that as of January of 1979, the focus of the Party's work should be shifted from the large-scale movement to expose and criticize the "Gang of Four" to the modernization drive. Second, pending historical issues were resolved. The conference had thoroughly affirmed the correctness of the April 1976 Tiananmen Incident and solved major problems left over from the Cultural Revolution and several other relatively important problems. It had formulated the policies and principles to solve these problems. Third, the participants had discussed and revised two documents concerning agriculture and had decided in principle on the national economic development plans for 1979 and 1980. Fourth, the participants had deliberated on personnel issues of the Party Central Committee.

In the second section of his speech he dealt with three points. The first point involved the "two whatevers." Hua made the following explanations. He recalled that his speech at the March 1977 Central Work Conference grew out of complicated circumstances — the "Gang of Four" had been smashed and the international Communist movement had accumulated positive and negative experiences in safeguarding the banner of revolution. Hua Guofeng stressed that in the struggle against the "Gang of Four," our whole Party, especially the senior cadres of the Party, needed to make special efforts to resolutely safeguard the great banner of Chairman Mao. Guided by this thinking, he stated, "We must uphold whatever policy decisions the Chairman made and must stop whatever words and actions damage Chairman Mao's image." He said, "My intention then was that in the great struggle to mobilize the masses wholeheartedly to expose and criticize the "Gang of Four," Chairman Mao's great image should never be damaged." This was an important matter he had pondered when the "Gang of Four" had just been smashed. Later, he found that he had made the first remark too absolute. He acknowledged that the second remark deserved attention, but Hua did not then make clear how to proceed. He had not given these two remarks thorough consideration. He acknowledged that it now seemed that it would be better not to mention the "two whatevers."

Then Hua added, "On February 7, 1977, the People's Daily, Red Flag, and the Liberation Army Daily jointly issued the editorial "Study Documents Carefully and Grasp the Key Link." The theme of the editorial was to mobilize the whole Party, the whole army, and people of all ethnic groups to expose and criticize the 'Gang of Four' in a thoroughgoing way." Nevertheless, guided by his thinking at the time, the editorial also referred to the "two whatevers": "We must resolutely uphold whatever policy decisions Chairman Mao made; and we must unswervingly follow whatever instructions Chairman Mao gave." In Hua's view, "The wording of the "two whatevers" became too absolute and inappropriate. He said, "Although the wording related to the 'two whatevers' in the above two places was not exactly the same, they have fettered people's minds to varying degrees, and are detrimental to implementing the Party's policies on the basis of facts and detrimental to enlivening the thinking inside the Party." Hua said that although his speech and that editorial had been discussed, perused, and approved by the members of the Political Bureau, he should assume the major responsibility. On this question, he should make self-criticism and also welcomed the criticism of other comrades. Most participants were basically satisfied with his self-criticism on the question of the "two whatevers."

Of course, it did not require high political awareness to notice that Hua's speech did not tell the whole truth about how the "two whatevers" were first put forward; nor did he completely say what was really on his mind. Instead he uttered quite a few remarks in self-defense. Furthermore, much of his narration of facts and thinking was illogical and even ran counter to the process of the time, such as explaining earlier events as if they had been guided by his thinking later. Hua did not make a single remark about how he had obstructed the return of Deng Xiaoping and a large number of other veteran cadres. However, the participants agreed that in fact it was not feasible for him to speak in defense of himself and to relate what had really been on his mind at the time. It was really not easy for a principal leader of the Party Central Committee to address a conference to such an extent as conceding that the wording of the "two whatevers" was inappropriate and that he himself should make self-criticism. This is what won the approval of the conference participants.

The second point in this section of Hua Guofeng's speech dealt with the issue of the criterion for testing truth. He said, "On May 11, 1978, the Guangming Daily carried the article "Practice Is the Sole Criterion for Testing Truth." On May 12, the People's Daily and the Liberation Army Daily reprinted the article. As I had just returned from a visit to the Democratic People's Republic of Korea, I had so many urgent matters to handle that I did not have time to read the article." He said that he did not know there had been different views on the article until other Political Bureau Standing Committee members told him in June and July what they had heard. When the Standing Committee members met, they discussed this question and agreed that the theme of the article was good, but they did not devote any time to studying it.

Considering that the meeting to discuss guidelines convened by the State Council was a complete success, Marshal Ye Jianying proposed calling the comrades engaged in theoretical research to come together to a meeting to discuss guidelines. At the meeting the participants could air different views freely and unify their understanding on the basis of fully democratic discussions in order to settle the criterion for testing truth. The Political Bureau Standing Committee members all approved this. Hua said that he planned to settle the question in a meeting when all Standing Committee members could be in Beijing to hold a meeting. As Comrade Deng Xiaoping was then abroad, there was no time to hold this meeting before the Central Work Conference.

On the afternoon of November 25, after the speeches were delivered at the plenary session of the Central Work Conference, a member of the Political Bureau Standing Committee met with the leaders of the Beijing Municipal Party Committee and the Central Committee of the Communist Youth League, and listened to their reports on the opinions of the masses concerning the reevaluation of the 1976 Tiananmen Incident and the big character posters on the Beijing streets. Referring to this question, he said, "It is necessary to solve some specific problems on the basis of facts and in accordance with the principle that practice is the sole criterion for testing truth. Now newspapers are discussing the question of the criterion for testing truth in a lively manner and thinking creatively. It is inappropriate to say that those articles are spearheaded at Chairman Mao because then people would find it hard to speak out. But referring to the problems, it is necessary to consider appropriateness and the consequences as well. In referring to some matters, Chairman Mao cannot be mentioned and it is inappropriate to mention him because this practice would weaken unity. Newspapers must be very cautious. Once one step is taken over the limit, truth will be turned into falsity." He added that "this is the view of all members of the Political Bureau Standing Committee." This paragraph showed that he had accepted the view of the participants on the evening of November 25 and that the Political Bureau Standing Committee members, including himself, favored the declaration on the issue of the criterion for testing truth.

Hua's comments were not as clear-cut on the issue of the "two whatevers." The remarks he made here expressed the position collectively taken by the members of the Political Bureau Standing Committee on the evening of November 25, which only mentioned the assessment of the debate over the issue of the criterion for testing truth rather than dealing with the debate directly. Furthermore, it was Deng Xiaoping who had made the remarks Hua mentioned. At a minimum, Hua Guofeng should have made some comments of his own on the issue and discussed his own views as the Central Work Conference drew to a close. That was why after Hua's speech, Wang Huide, Yang Xiguang, and I delivered our own commentary. We shared the view that he had not straightened out his thinking and that his problem could not be considered completely solved.

In this section of Hua's speech he also elaborated on the third point in association with the criterion for testing truth. He said, "At the conference many comrades cited circumstances related to the issue that 'Practice is the sole criterion for testing truth.' They raised many relevant questions and made quite a few critical comments about certain comrades, thus creating a climate favorable for holding the meeting to discuss theoretical principles. As the current Central Work Conference has many topics and yet a limited time, we cannot spend lots of time resolving these issues. In the view of comrades on the Political Bureau, in accordance with Marshal Ye's proposal, following the Third Plenum of the 11th Central Committee, it will be better to convene a special meeting to discuss theoretical guidelines in an effort to resolve this issue effectively. The Central Committee is convinced that this issue can certainly be resolved effectively, in accordance with the spirit of the current Central Work Conference and the Third Plenum of the 11th Central Committee. The Central Committee hopes that the comrades working on the theoretical front and with the publicity departments will further unite on the basis of distinguishing right from wrong and unifying our thinking. We hope they will follow closely the strategic arrangements of the Party Central Committee and play an even greater role in shifting the focus of the Party's work to the socialist modernization drive and making a success in publicity and theoretical work."

When Hua commented on these remarks, Wang Huide, Yang Xiguang, and I always felt something was not quite right, yet we lacked enough time to make a judgment. We read through his speech twice before finally realizing that in this section Hua used the word "resolve" three times: (1) "We cannot spend lots of time resolving the issues in this regard"; (2) "it is better ... to convene a special meeting to discuss theoretical guidelines in an effort to resolve this issue effectively"; (3) "this issue can certainly be resolved effectively." This meant that the issue had not been resolved effectively at the current conference in accordance with the spirit of the current Central Work Conference and the Third Plenum of the 11th Central Committee. This meant that resolving the issue effectively still required correct ideological guidance.

We felt that such an assessment of the Central Work Conference achievements on this issue was far too low. Hua should have stated that this issue had been resolved at the current Central Work Conference. At the time Hua Guofeng made this remark, he had already read the text of the speech to be delivered by Deng Xiaoping at the plenary session and had listened to Deng's speech. But he did not acknowledge that Deng declared this issue resolved, making it unnecessary to convene a special meeting to discuss theoretical guidelines. If there was still a problem that needed to be resolved at a meeting on theoretical guidelines, it was the problem of a tiny number of comrades who originally opposed using practice as the criterion for testing truth and who did not fully accept the conclusions of the Work Conference.

Hua then added, "The Party Central Committee hopes that comrades working on the theoretical front and with the publicity departments will, on the basis of distinguishing right from wrong and unifying our thinking, further unite, follow closely the strategic arrangements of the Party Central Committee, and play an even greater role in shifting the focus of the Party's work to the socialist modernization drive, making a success in publicity and theoretical work." In terms of principle, these remarks are unassailable because unity undoubtedly needed to be stressed and, more importantly, he added the premise that right must be distinguished from wrong. The critical issue was who was right and who was wrong, yet he did not offer any explanation on this issue. So, we felt his speech fell short of what he should have said at the close of the Central Work Conference.

In the last section of his remarks, Hua referred to the issue of collective leadership, expressing the hope that when all regions and units in the future asked the Party Central Committee for instructions or sent reports, it was acceptable for the first line of their documents to contain the phrase "Party Central Committee" instead of "Chairman Hua and the Party Central Committee." Hua hoped that when issuing documents to subordinates, the Party and government departments at the central level would act in accordance with this practice. He said that it was not necessary to mention him as the wise leader and that it was better to cite him as a comrade. Hua hoped more literary and art works would praise the revolutionaries of the older generation and the heroic deeds of workers, peasants, and soldiers, instead of publicizing himself as an individual. These strictures against the cult of personality were well received.

In the fourth section, Hua said that the Third Plenum of the 11th Central Committee would be held following the Central Work Conference. He cited the topics for the plenum: (1) shift of the focus of the Party's work; (2) examination and adoption of documents on agriculture and two-year planning arrangements; (3) personnel, with the candidates for new posts being those proposed at the Central Work Conference, and organization, including the establishment of the Central Commission for Discipline Inspection. Such is the rough outline of Hua's speech. The participants in the conference were by and large satisfied with his speech.

Wang Dongxing's Written Speech

Only three of the five Standing Committee members spoke at the closing session of the Central Work Conference, namely, Hua Guofeng, Ye Jianying, and Deng Xiaoping. Wang Dongxing delivered a written speech, implying his admission that he had committed errors, in word and deed, both during the Cultural Revolution and after the downfall of the "Gang of Four." I do not have in hand the formal document containing his written speech, probably because it was announced that his text would be recalled, but I did make extracts of his speech and present them here.

Wang wrote,"At the conference comrades have made many good criticisms of my mistakes. This reflects their concern and desire to help. I hereby express my sincere acceptance of these views. I really did commit errors in word and deed during the Cultural Revolution and after the downfall of the 'Gang of Four.' Comrades have made many criticisms concerning the No. 1, No. 2, and No. 3 offices of the Central Group for the Examination of Special Cases. I think these comments are all very good. I committed mistakes in the work I was in charge of. After the downfall of the 'Gang of Four,' I did not pay due attention to the work to redress some framed, false, and wrong cases, and I did not act promptly and failed to do the work well. Consequently, the cases that should have been redressed failed to be redressed promptly. I should assume principal responsibility for this problem. The materials processed jointly by the No. 1. No. 2, and No. 3 offices of the Central Group for the Examination of Special Cases and the Special Group for the Examination of the 'May 16th' Special Case will all be handed over to the Organization Department of the Party Central Committee, in accordance with the decision of the Party Central Committee.

"After the downfall of the 'Gang of Four,' when I took charge of publicity work, a number of mistakes were made. On February 7, 1977, the People's Daily, Red Flag, and the Liberation Army Daily jointly issued the editorial 'Study Documents Carefully and Grasp the Key Link.' The editorial cited the problem of the 'two whatevers' and then I agreed to this wording. I read through this article before submitting it to the Party Central Committee for examination and approval. Reviewing the editorial later, I found the wording inappropriate and detrimental to implementing the Party's policy on the basis of facts. As regards the debate about the issue of whether practice is the sole criterion for testing truth, the members of the Political Bureau Standing Committee clarified the issue while talking with the leaders of the Beijing Municipal Party Committee and the Central Committee of the Communist Youth League of China. I fully agree with the view of the Standing Committee members. After finding that there were different views and opinions concerning the article on the issue of the criterion for testing truth, I did not organize and lead the debate effectively in time. I failed to unify thinking and understanding through discussions. I assume leadership responsibility for my failures.

"The masses have made many criticisms regarding an underground project and an aboveground construction project at Zhongnanhai. At this conference comrades have also criticized this. I think the criticism is good. Although the projects were approved by the Party Central Committee, while organizing and arranging construction I did not carefully consider the danger of undertaking too many projects, at excessive costs, thus causing a bad political impact. I should assume principal responsibility for this problem. I have submitted a report to the Party Central Committee for approval, so as to promptly halt the undertaking of all projects at Zhongnanhai and move the construction teams out to undertake the construction of apartments in Beijing.

"I have also committed various kinds of shortcomings or mistakes in the departments I lead or in other aspects of work I am in charge of. I should take responsibility for those mistakes attributed to me personally as well as for those departments and certain individuals under my leadership. The comrades' criticism of me reflects their concern and desire to help. I am deeply convinced that the posts I hold exceed my ability, and I am unworthy of these posts. For this, I sincerely request that the Party Central Committee should remove me from these posts. After the Party Central Committee makes a decision, I will earnestly hand over all my posts to the comrades concerned.

"In the future I must read more books in a real and earnest way and read the works of Marx, Lenin, and Chairman Mao, so as to enhance my ideological and political awareness and draw on experience and lessons. In particular, I must see to it that I will be modest and prudent and safeguard the unity inside the Party. Under the leadership of the Party Central Committee, I am determined to contribute my bit to the socialist four modernizations."

Additional Remarks on the Stands and Viewpoints of the Five Standing Committee Members of the Central Work Conference

In the preceding sections I have given a detailed introduction to the positions, views, status, and roles of the five members of the Political Bureau Standing Committee at the Central Work Conference. After relating the course of the conference's development and my own understanding of the conference's essence, here I would like to summarize my own personal understanding by making a few more remarks.

Let me speak of Hua Guofeng first. Hua presided over the conference from the very beginning to the very end. On the issue of construction, he was active, took the initiative, and was ready to talk more. We can see that he really hoped that the participants would focus their discussion on those three topics proposed at the opening session and that he also tried to guide the participants to hold such discussions. I thought that he was ideologically prepared to accept the views of the vast majority of participants that were different from views he previously expressed: the Tiananmen Incident; the importance of redressing many major framed, false, and wrong cases; the criticism of the "two whatevers"; and practice as the criterion for testing truth. There were two points that could prove this: one was that at the closing session he no longer mentioned the "two whatevers" or quoted the "supreme instructions" because that practice would certainly infuriate or cause loathing among the participants. The other was that Hua took the initiative to approve the delivery of a speech on the Tiananmen Incident at an enlarged meeting of the Standing Committee of the Beijing Municipal Party Committee, a speech that was totally different in content from the speech he had made at a March 1977 work conference. On the whole, Hua was passive on these issues, but he was not stubbornly resistant. Although he could not possibly change himself thoroughly, he always considered the participants' views, took them into account, and even accepted many of their views. His attitude played a positive role in ensuring that the conference proceeded relatively smoothly.

Now let me speak of Ye Jianying. Knowing that he was of venerable age and eminent virtue, he did not talk much. Yet he was clear and definite about the orientation of the conference. He energetically supported the debate about whether practice was the sole criterion for testing truth and affirmed that it was the sole criterion for testing truth. Hua Guofeng was also very clear on this, as were many other veteran comrades. Quite a few senior army officers knew well that Ye had advocated holding the meeting to discuss theoretical guidelines and that he had made it clear that he maintained that it was necessary to distribute to the whole country the article on the issue of the criterion for testing truth. Ye supported Deng Xiaoping's views on the current conference. He also trusted Hu Yaobang and asked Hu to find people to draft the text of the speech he would deliver at the conference. The views expressed in his speech on giving full scope to democracy were brilliant. Ye personally spent a long time preparing his speech. In my view, it was inappropriate that the book Since the Third Plenum does not contain Ye Jianying's speech. I maintain that Marshal Ye's role at the conference and the Third Plenum were critical and his merits enduring.

What of Deng Xiaoping? It was only one year and four months since he had been reinstated for the second time after being "overthrown" during the Cultural Revolution. Deng's moral integrity, ability, and his prestige in the whole Party made him the soul of the conference. He had the support of the entire country, including a large number of veteran comrades who had been persecuted during the Cultural Revolution but were now liberated and again in leading positions. Deng gave suggestions and instructions concerning convening the conference and its basic orientation, the setting of the conference's objectives, every major development at the conference, the solution of major problems, and decisions that should be made at the Third Plenum. His speech "Emancipate the Mind, Seek Truth from Facts, and Unite as One in Looking to the Future," delivered at the Central Work Conference, was described by the report delivered to the 15th Party Congress as the declaration for the policy of reform and opening. It was the most important contribution he made to the Central Work Conference. The Third Plenum of the 11th Party Central Committee did not issue a thematic report. So, Deng's speech at the Central Work Conference functioned in reality as such a report for the Third Plenum. The report was of far-reaching significance. Even today, we still urgently need to emphasize the spirit of emancipating the mind and seeking truth from facts. Just as the status of Mao Zedong inside the Party was established in fact at the central conference held in Zunyi,

Guizhou Province in 1935, so Deng Xiaoping's status inside the Party was established at this Central Work Conference.

I should also write a few words about Li Xiannian. He did not speak at the plenary sessions of the Central Work Conference; nor did he pass on instructions to various group meetings, but his role at the Central Work Conference should not be neglected. One of the three topics set early in the meeting was discussion of his speech at the State Council meeting to discuss principles. From beginning to end he participated in the collective leadership of the Standing Committee members over the conference, and actively took the floor at the meetings when the Standing Committee members listened to reports from the conveners of all groups. He also paid great attention to the documents concerning agriculture and called a forum attended by thirteen people.

Finally, let me speak of Wang Dongxing. I want to say a few words in his favor. He also always participated in the Standing Committee members' collective leadership of this conference at which he was criticized, and criticized by name at that. Regardless of what was really on his mind, he still submitted a written text of his self-criticism speech to the conference, which was printed and distributed in the Third Plenum held later. It was improper to say that he simply made no contribution at all to the success of the conference.

At the Third Plenum Comrade Chen Yun was elected a member of the Political Bureau Standing Committee, bringing the number of members to six.

Ending the Central Work Conference

The "closing" and "ending" of the Central Work Conference was not the same thing. The conference did not end until two days of group meetings were held after the closing plenary session. The closing date was December 13, 1978; the ending date was December 15. It was unusual for a central work conference to hold two days of meetings after the closing plenary session.

Why? In my view, there were three reasons why group meetings continued after the closing plenary session. The first was to continue to give full scope to democracy. Three Standing Committee members of the Political Bureau of the Party Central Committee spoke and also listened to the opinions of the participants in the conference. Only when all participants were satisfied could the conference be described as winding up successfully. The second reason was that apart from the fact that the three Standing Committee members addressed the conference, the text of Wang Dongxing's written self-criticism speech was distributed at the closing session. The participants also wanted to comment on the written self-criticism. The third was that at the closing session, Hua Guofeng, after announcing the convocation of the Third Plenum of the 11th Party Central Committee, said,"The Political Bureau holds that the guidelines from the current Central Work Conference should be transmitted to lower levels together with those of the Third Plenum. The specific methods to pass on the guidelines will be determinded at the closing of the Third Plenum. Those comrades who will attend the Third Plenum may, on the basis of the speeches of vice-chairmen Ye and Deng and the three speeches I have delivered at the current conference, relay the essence of this conference. It may be relayed to the Standing Committee members of the Party Committees of various provinces, municipalities, and autonomous regions, and the Party Committees of various military area commands, as well as to the Standing Committee members of the Party Committees of all Party, government, and army departments at the central level or to the members of leading party groups."

Those comrades who attended the Central Work Conference but would not attend the Third Plenum also needed, before departure, to study and digest the speeches delivered at the closing session and exchange views with the comrades in the same groups they were in.

Speeches delivered in various groups were much the same, but with minor differences. Here, as far as I can remember, let me talk about what happened in the Northwest China Group on December 14 and 15.

On December 14, the members of the Northwest China Group, vying to be heard, took the floor one after another. Wang Huide, Yang Xiguang, and I also had an opportunity to deliver a joint speech, with Wang as the principal speaker. The speeches of the three Standing Committee members had been very substantive. In particular, Deng Xiaoping's speech had covered a wide range of topics. We could only select a few paragraphs we especially favored to express our resolute support. The main content of our joint speech was to express our strong dissatisfaction with Wang Dongxing's written speech. The point of our speech was first to express our agreement with Wang's declaration that "the posts I hold exceed my ability, and I am unworthy of these posts. For this, I sincerely request that the Party Central Committee should remove me from these posts. After the Party Central Committee makes a decision, I will earnestly hand over all my posts to the comrades concerned." Meanwhile, we pointed out that whether or not this declaration was sincere would depend on how Wang would behave in the future. Then we expressed our dissatisfaction with his self-criticism. We quoted Comrade Song Shilun's remarks to the Central-South Group in which he exposed the mistakes that Comrade Wang Dongxing had made from the Cultural Revolution to the current Central Work Conference. Song emphatically pointed out the mistakes he had made after taking up the post of Vice-Chairman of the Party Central Committee, such as insisting on the "two whatevers" and suppressing people with correct opinions. On behalf of Yang Xiguang and me, while delivering the speech, Wang Huide also cited quite a few facts which the participants had not known previously or which had not been revealed in the group meetings, about how Wang Dongxing had opposed the debate about the criterion for testing truth. These facts included how Wang used absolutely untenable reasons to suppress the resumption of the publication of the first issue of Chinese Youth, ordering the magazine to halt distribution, to the strong opposition of many people. We proposed that Wang Dongxing should make an initial self-criticism at the Third Plenum of the 11th Central Committee. As may be seen in the summary bulletins, speeches by other members of the Northwest China Group as well as by comrades in the other groups reflected roughly the same points of view.

At the group meeting held on the last day of the conference, our Northwest China Group unanimously adopted the "Comprehensive Bulletin on the Speeches Delivered in Discussions Held by the Northwest China Group on the Morning of December 14." This bulletin differed substantially from the summary bulletins containing personal speeches in that it was a little bit like the "12-Point

Proposal." It expressed the collective opinion of the whole Northwest China Group. This bulletin also contained 12 points as follows:

1. We support the speeches made by Hua Guofeng, Ye Jianying, and Deng Xiaoping at the closing session. We pledge to implement the guidelines in their speeches to the letter.

2. We praise Hua Guofeng for his remarks on the "two whatevers" and the issue of the criterion for testing truth and his attitude toward assuming full responsibility. We maintain that he has set a good example for us to follow in seeking truth from facts. We also say that this is also a sign of the vitality of our Party.

3. We praise Hua Guofeng for his remarks supporting collective leadership and opposing publicizing individuals. We hold that it is imperative to thoroughly change the abnormal state in which in the past one or two persons could decide many matters, while all others could only follow orders.

4. We hold that the views of Ye Jianying and Deng Xiaoping on promoting democracy and strengthening the legal system are of overriding importance. We fully agree with Ye Jianying's statement that the current Central Work Conference reflects democracy inside our Party. We maintain that this spirit of democracy should be promoted.

5. We are extremely dissatisfied with Wang Dongxing's written speech. We are of the view that with regard to the debate about the criterion for testing truth, it is not only that he should accept leadership responsibility as he said, but also accept responsibility for a mistake in the ideological line. His attitude toward Comrade Deng Xiaoping is not only a personal relationship, but also a matter pertaining to the overall situation.

6. It is appropriate that Wang Dongxing should request that the Party Central Committee should relieve him of all the posts he concurrently occupies. Meanwhile, we hope that he will make an appropriate self-criticism at the Third Plenum of the 11th Central Committee.

7. Comrade Wang Dongxing exerted himself in capturing the "Gang of Four," but he should not take this as his personal capital.

8. We support Deng Xiaoping in pointing out, "We must be strict in promoting cadres in the future."

9. We propose that the mistakes made by Wang Dongxing and several other members of the Political Bureau be conveyed to the cadres at the division chief level throughout the country.

10. We support the announcement revoking the twelve documents issued in 1975 and 1976. We maintain that all kinds of

171

documents issued by the Party Central Committee during the Cultural Revolution need to be screened, and some revoked.

11. It is strictly forbidden to use electronic bugs on cadres, to check their letters, to follow and scout their personal relations, to search their residences, to place them under isolated examination, or to employ fascist means to force a confession from them.

12. The state should give all-around assistance to a number of poor areas including northwest China and southwest China.

The 12-point proposal was signed by the chairmen of the Northwest China Group, namely, Wang Feng, Huo Shilian, Hu Yaobang, and Xiao Hua. After reading the bulletin, Hua Guofeng wrote the inscription, "Print and distribute the bulletin to the participants in the conference." This practice of giving full scope to democracy continued throughout the conference.

CHAPTER 12

CHARACTERISTICS OF THE
CENTRAL WORK CONFERENCE

Emphasis on Scientific Thinking

The conference was over. The participants in the Central Work Conference who were not members of the 11th Central Committee, except the nine proposed for election to the Party Central Committee and a small group of staff members, all returned to their regions or departments ready to transmit the guidelines of the Central Work Conference and to do their respective work better. At the closing session of the conference it was announced that the guidelines of both the Central Work Conference and the approaching Third Plenum should be relayed together. Yet the comrades returning home could already relay the essence of the Central Work Conference.

My work unit was the State Council Research Office, a very small unit, whose routine work had always been handled by other comrades. I concurrently served as a Vice-President of the Chinese Academy of Social Sciences. There I was in charge of long-range plans for various branches of learning. My task was to help set principles, and I enjoyed a great degree of flexibility. So I was unlike the leaders of other units, who, having been away, had a great deal of important work to attend to when they got back. After the Central Work Conference was over, Hu Jiwei, Zeng Tao, I, and some others stayed on in the Jingxi Hotel because we were told that we might be required for further work after the conference. However, I was not assigned any work in these five days, so that I was able to live there comfortably, observing and pondering during that period.

It did not occur to me immediately after the conference that I should also make a summary of my own perceptions of the conference. I am now using this opportunity to make up the work. So, I decided, after writing the chapter "Ending of the Conference," to write something about my own thoughts on the essence of the conference.

First, I want to say that the conference was convened under the guidance of scientific thinking. Of all the major meetings held by the Party Central Committee that I was familiar with, there were not many for which full preparations were made in Marxist theory, and in which theories were linked fully to the realities of existing problems. The Seventh Congress of the Party in 1945 was such a meeting. Prior to the congress, on the one hand, criticisms were made of dogmatism toward Marxism. The history of different lines during the agrarian revolutionary war was summarized. At the same time, China's national conditions were studied, and creative theory and viewpoints were presented for the new democratic revolution and the new democratic society. Since that congress in 1945, perhaps the current Central Work Conference was the next meeting to meet these criteria.

The debate at this conference about whether "practice is the sole criterion for testing truth" was in accord with objective scientific thinking. So far as the principle is concerned, seeking truth from facts and grounding everything in reality constitute the common ground for this conference and the Seventh Party Congress. The Seventh Party Congress was convened on the basis of scientifically summarizing the Party's history during the period from 1927 to1937. At that congress the political, ideological, and organizational mistakes made by the leading body of the Party were criticized and corrected, particularly the mistake of the "Left" deviaionist Wang Ming line that had dominated the entire Party during that period. Only this way did it become possible to formulate the correct line and principle for the Seventh Party Congress and to strive for the ultimate victory in the new democratic revolution.

After the downfall of the "Gang of Four," the problem was that some people inside the Party regarded Mao Zedong as a deity and his "directives" and "policy decisions" as sacred. In his last years Mao was too old and weak to work and think in a normal way. Yet after his death, some maintained that his "directives" and "policy decisions" must always be implemented unswervingly, setting forth the "two whatevers" principle. On the one hand, these people directly protected many erroneous viewpoints advanced during the Cultural Revolution and impeded the effort to right wrongs. On the other hand, they also hindered the Party and people from summarizing historical lessons and from pursuing a new line that could build China into a new modern socialist country during the years after the downfall of the "Gang of Four." If we had still kept to the wrong course of the Cultural Revolution, even after the demise of the "Gang of Four," we might have caused our Party and state to perish. Compared to the Seventh Party Congress, after the downfall of the "Gang of Four," our Party found itself in different times, facing different conditions and different tasks. But we cannot depart from scientific thinking. In guiding revolution or construction we require people to study it. After the downfall of the "Gang of Four," I made three comments: The reason why religion is religion is that it needs people to worship; The reason why laws are laws is that they require people to abide by them; The reason why science is science is that it requires people to study it, understand it, and respect and apply it in their own activities. Since Marxism is a science, people should never worship and obey it.

Even with regard to Marxism as a science, our attitude should not be one of worship and obedience. The "two whatevers" that cropped up after the downfall of the "Gang of Four" required people to worship and obey remarks made and things done in the name of Marxism. During the Cultural Revolution, Kang Sheng, Zhang Chunqiao, Yao Wenyuan, and their ilk created such anti-Marxist fallacies as "continuing the revolution under the dictatorship of the proletariat," "exercising all-round dictatorship over the bourgeoisie," "to each according to his work produces new bourgeois elements," and "criticizing the theory of unique importance of productive forces."

After 1976 and after the downfall of the "Gang of Four," China's theoretical community criticized these fallacies in the economic and political spheres. Of course, these fallacies waved the banner of Marxism and Leninism. This did not pose a problem for the theoretical community, which could easily lay bare these distortions. Nevertheless, Mao Zedong himself had affirmed some of these fallacies, and others were repeating Mao's views. For example, in October 1974 Mao said, "Our country now practices the commodity system and an unfair wage system including an eight-grade wage system, etc. This can only be reduced under the dictatorship of the proletariat. So, if people like Lin Biao were to come to power, it would be very easy for them to restore the capitalist system."

In criticizing these fallacies, although we tried to avoid criticizing Mao Zedong as much as possible, we still encountered the accusation that "You turn your spearhead at Chairman Mao." Furthermore, several major cases, including the 1976 Tiananmen Incident, were not easy to redress because of Mao's approval and his remarks. It seemed that if the problem were not elevated to the height of philosophy, it could not be solved. Therefore, in the spring and summer of 1978, Chinese theoreticians in the philosophical sphere published the article "Practice Is the Sole Criterion for Testing Truth." Discussions about this article were held first in the academic community and spread later to the leading circles of the Party, government, and army. They were first held in Beijing and later spread to other provinces and municipalities. The discussions elicited a lively response. Since some people quickly subjected the article to severe criticism, a more thorough theoretical elaboration and debate was necessary.

In August or September 1978, before the Central Work Conference was held—I did not write the specific time down in my notebook—Deng Xiaoping brought several of us working in the Chinese Academy of Social Sciences together for a talk. He was greatly concerned with the work to criticize the fallacy of the "Gang of Four" regarding the issue of to each according to his work. He asked us whether the issue of to each according to his work was expounded adequately. Deng said that a major issue was the tenet of to each according to his work, which was common knowledge in Marxism. He also said, "Common knowledge should not become a problem." He encouraged the theoreticians to speak out. "You yourselves are not aware that the speeches of theoreticians carry authority." He added, "Your Chinese Academy of Social Sciences is a theoretical institution and should not make concessions on theoretical questions. I advise you not to accommodate yourselves theoretically because accommodating yourselves will lead to the loss of the principle." Deng asked the theoretical community to stand still higher, taking heed of methods that would be conducive to solving problems and achieving unity. He noted that, of course, facts and principles must be made clear, but that it was imperative to consider on what occasions they must be clarified.

On the day when Deng spoke with us, he expressed the hope that a way might be found to resolve the debate, and asked us to consider how to achieve this. He said he hoped the debate would not "crop up at the Central Work Conference." Instead he hoped that in the theoretical community the two sides of the debate should promote mutual understanding. Shortly after the Central Work Conference opened, however, debate "cropped up" as expected and turned into a very significant discussion. Thereupon, Deng called Hu Yaobang and me together and pointed to the importance of expounding theoretical questions. He said, "The debate about the criterion for testing truth is very good. The more I consider it, the better it appears, and the more I consider it, the more I regard it as a political issue." Later, in his speech at the closing session, he reiterated, "Judging from the tenor of the debate, the more I consider it, the more important I think it is." His remark indicated that even Deng Xiaoping himself went through a process of deepening his understanding. The participants in the conference all shared such a perception.

I could sense the spirit of scientific inquiry from the very beginning of the conference. Prior to the conference, Ye Jianying and Deng Xiaoping had stressed the importance of this spirit. Moreover, preparations had been made in the sphere of theoretical work during the two years following the downfall of the "Gang of Four." I agreed with Hu Yaobang who said one month earlier, "The scale of ideological and theoretical work during the past two years, its contribution to intellectual debates, and to raising the theoretical level of the whole Party during this time have exceeded any other period since the founding of New China. We can say that the theoretical work in these two years has been the best and most successful since the Yan'an Rectification Movement." Not only comrades specializing in theoretical work, but also those engaged in practical work showed great interest in theory. Many participants in the Central Work Conference stressed the importance of scientific thinking as well as the scientific spirit and attitude.

Giving Full Scope to Democracy

The Central Work Conference gave full scope to democracy. All the participants in the conference were keenly and thoroughly aware of this, and it was a source of great satisfaction. Those in attendance dared to think and to speak, and boldly crossed into areas previously considered "forbidden zones." By speaking about previously taboo subjects, participants in the conference were exercising their democratic rights. Originally, democracy was not something people waited for; nor was it something bestowed by higher authorities. At the conference the participants did not make unfounded criticism, they did not attach labels to others, and they did not restrict others' freedom of expression. Moreover, no limits were set on the length or number of speeches or on the range of topics that could be addressed. The conference organizers did not explicitly announce the absence of limits, but this reality was accepted as a matter of course. Of course, this reflected the level and the conscientiousness of the participants as well as the fact that the conference organizers never attempted to restrain the wide scope for democracy. If one or two members of the Standing Committee had made remarks prejudicial to permitting full scope to democracy, if the participants had kept silent and not dared to demand the correction of a mistake, things would have been quite different. But this did not happen.

An incident occurred at the conference. At a meeting for the conveners of various groups to report the speeches of their respective groups to the Standing Committee members, Comrade Wang Dongxing made a speech, saying, "We must take the overall situation into consideration. We should not be disturbed. We shall practice democracy, and democratic views should be unified under the leadership. The whole Party should unite. We should not say or do things detrimental to unity." The report was given on the eve of the second plenary session held on November 25, but I did not record the specific time in my notebook. Wang's remarks were not literally wrong, but such remarks implied criticism of some of the speeches delivered at group meetings and also conveyed an implied warning. Since the participants in the Central Work Conference were all experienced senior Party cadres, it is hard to imagine that they failed to discern the warning implied in these comments. Therefore, after

Wang's remarks were transmitted to the various groups, strong dissatisfaction was voiced from many quarters. When the conveners made a report to the Standing Committee members on the evening of November 27, all groups expressed the opinion that the remarks on democracy and concentration under the leadership made by Vice-Chairman Wang at the previous meeting were inconsistent with the evaluation of the conference made by Chairman Hua at the November 25 plenary session. Wang's comments on the need for leadership could be seen as a constraint on free expression of opinion. The wording, "We should not say or do things detrimental to unity" was also no good. The conference was designed to clarify questions. Wang Dongxing was present at the meetings reporting on the speeches in the group sessions when the conveners transmitted the critical comments that had been directed at Wang's speech. He did not say anything in response to the criticisms directed at him. Thereafter, none of the participants felt constrained by Wang Dongxing's remarks.

Giving full scope to democracy at the Central Work Conference meant permission to criticize and expose comrades who had made remarks and done things that had had a bad impact on life during the Cultural Revolution and the two years after the downfall of the "Gang of Four." One expression of this spirit was found in the criticism of people by name, including a vice-chairman of the Party Central Committee and a member of the Political Bureau Standing Committee. Participants were very satisfied with this practice, which was specifically praised at a meeting by the Political Bureau Standing Committee. Although critics sometimes spoke rather sharply, there was no attempt to apply pressure or stop others from stating their positions and engaging in refutation. The practice of making critical speeches while their intended targets were present was meant to elicit different views.

Speaking from the floor was a major aspect of giving full scope to democracy. One after another, the participants stepped up to the podium and almost all voiced their own views. Another major aspect was participating in drafting and revising documents. The conference organizers informed participants about matters on which the conference was prepared to make decisions, in the hope that they would fully air their opinions, which would in turn guide the revision of previously prepared document drafts. The process of drafting the two documents on agriculture was a good example of how democracy was fully implemented.

The Central Work Conference did not have the right to adopt resolutions for the Party Central Committee or elect members of the Party Central Committee and the Political Bureau. Although the participants could not vote and lacked the right to elect Party leaders, they did have the right to recommend and propose, and they made full use of this right.

In practicing democracy, it is imperative to emphasize equality. At group meetings of the Central Work Conference, Political Bureau members did not speak in the name of the Political Bureau, but took the floor in the same capacity as other participants. They were on an equal plane with other participants and not treated as higher-level leaders. Their speeches were not especially "serious and cautious," and other participants did not treat them with special consideration. The five members of the Political Bureau Standing Committee were not assigned to the six groups. Yet they also voiced their opinions, sometimes at meetings of the Standing Committee and sometimes at the meetings where reports from the various groups were presented. They also expressed their own viewpoints, most of which were transmitted to the different groups. The members of these groups could also comment on their viewpoints. At the meetings for reporting group discussions, the Standing Committee members used their respective democratic rights to voice their own views. There were two aspects to their speeches. First, each of them voiced their own viewpoints; second, on behalf of the Standing Committee, they provided guidance for group discussions. The first of these supported the objective of giving full scope to democracy.

It goes without saying that democracy has many dimensions. Giving full scope to people's initiative and creativity can be regarded as an essential part. At the conference the participants all felt that their initiative was not subject to any constraints. Of course, they were constrained by the prevailing intellectual and social climate. For instance, they had to pay attention to "holding high the banner of Mao Zedong Thought." They had to consider whether "holding high" meant repeating Mao Zedong's remarks over and over again or whether it meant treating matters in real life on the basis of facts. However, nobody was willing to question whether the concept of "holding high" itself was correct.

Nobody knew when the practice of inserting a few sentences on practicing democracy into a document on national work became "standard operating procedure," but it often was just an empty formula. An empty formula may have had its own rationale, but could not give people any fresh insights or ideological enlightenment and education. Consequently, it could not stimulate people's enthusiasm for democracy. Things could be quite different, however, if there were thoughtful opinions, fresh language, and contents linked to reality. At this Central Work Conference, Ye Jianying's and Deng Xiaoping's remarks on democracy produced a profound impression on the participants as well as on those who read the speeches. Ye Jianying's speech at the closing session made special reference to the need to give full scope to democracy, instead of simply commenting generally on the need to practice democracy. Ye pointed out, "In creating the absurd argument that practicing democracy seemingly amounted to practicing capitalism, the 'Gang of Four' passed off feudalism as socialism. Therefore, an important task of ours is to pay great attention to overcoming feudalism." He also noted that leading cadres should not mention democracy every day, and should not make a long face at hearing slightly pointed criticisms. These speeches touched the heart of the matter and were not merely conventional formulas. Ye also urged that the democratic spirit displayed at the Central Work Conference be upheld permanently. His remarks on democracy were very sincere. Reading them today, I think that they still have profound significance for educating people.

Deng Xiaoping had a new wording for granting the "right of initiative" to the cadres at lower levels. Giving full scope to democracy meant granting everyone the "right to take initiatives." Some people may question whether or not the two speeches played a role in the conference since they were delivered at the closing session. I want to emphasize that they had revealed their thinking on democracy many times long before the closing session. Deng used the expression "the right to take initiatives" at a November meeting of the Political Bureau Standing Committee when members listened to reports from the various groups. After being transmitted to various groups, his remark stimulated the participants' enthusiasm for giving full scope to democracy.

Lenin had a brilliant opinion on democracy: Practicing democracy requires certain conditions. Legally speaking, different people may enjoy the same democratic right. But how can a person who must spend all of his time and energy securing the minimum means for his survival have time to participate in social and political activities and lead a democratic life? Some people want to call meetings but they do not have an auditorium and cannot afford to rent one. So, their activities are necessarily restricted. In a capitalist country, everyone knows that it requires large amounts of money to campaign for an elected position. Without a huge amount of money, nobody can launch a campaign for a high political position like the presidency, no matter how popular he is. While attending the Central Work Conference, we stayed in a good place—the Jingxi Hotel—and had many good meeting rooms and enjoyed good food, accommodations, and services. All this constituted a good material basis for making the conference a success. As cadres of the Party and government, we participants were basically guaranteed time to take part in political activities.

Participants at the conference were given ample time to voice their opinions. At the beginning of the conference Hua Guofeng said that the conference was set to last over 20 days, opening on November 10 and closing around the end of November. The Third Plenum of the 11th Central Committee was originally set to open on December 7. Later, the conference was extended repeatedly, as necesary, to 36 days. Hence the time allotted for the conference was ample.

For the Conference participants, the compilation of summary bulletins was an important condition for fully promoting democracy. Without such bulletins, we participants could only have conducted activities within our own groups and attended the plenary sessions. We would have been unable to know what was going in other groups, and it would have been impossible for us to hold discussions beyond the range of our own group. I attended, or attended as a non-voting member, many central conferences, with bulletins issued at most conferences. Frankly speaking, the bulletins issued at some conferences contained nothing but empty talk or a conventional formula providing nothing of interest. One reason was that some people became accustomed to expressing themselves in conventional formulas. Another reason was that interesting views aired by many people were deleted. Consequently, the members of a group only knew what had gone on in their own group, and had almost no knowledge of what had transpired in other groups. The bulletins distributed in this Work Conference were different, however, because the participants could learn a lot about what had gone on in other groups. They thus took part in discussions about questions raised by other groups and made comments on the speeches of comrades in other groups. I was quite satisfied with the bulletins compiled at the conference. I delivered many speeches at the conference. I had texts for some speeches and gave some impromptu speeches as well. I did not systematically compare my speeches to the excerpts of my speeches carried in the bulletins. My impression was that the excerpts were quite good and that nothing of importance had been omitted. Furthermore, bulletins came out promptly. I could also find materials of interest to me in the bulletins of other groups such as the speeches of comrades who had resisted the debate about the criterion for testing truth by clinging to the "two whatevers." I could also make comments and discuss them via the bulletins. The conference summary bulletins were essential reading at the Central Work Conference. The comrades who compiled the bulletins must have been working very hard. They were the unsung heroes at the conference for they did very important work. But I knew none of them. Nor did I know which comrades led the work of compiling the bulletins.

The content of the bulletins distributed in the first few days of the conference were not quite the same as those distributed later. In the first few days the bulletins seemed to focus on problems. Hu Yaobang's speech to the Northwest China Group on November 13 was quite long, but the portions carried in the bulletin were quite short. At first I thought that Hu Yaobang had deliberately cut his speech. Recently, from a heap of musty papers, I found the record of the speech Hu made in the Northwest China Group. The record contained a comment by Deng Xiaoping, "Inside the Party we should have a number of the cadres who dare to speak their minds and to tackle problems." He also said, "In the bulletins there should be no deletion of key issues." Hu Yaobang once said at a Political Bureau Standing Committee meeting that our group reported Xu Xiangqian had expressed dissatisfaction with the fact that the speeches were not carried in the bulletins until six days later. Apparently the compilers of the bulletins complied, for they were much better after Xu Xiangqian, Hu Yaobang, and others made criticisms. What I found most satisfying was that after Jiang Yizhen, Yang Xiguang, and I jointly criticized Wang Dongxing by name, the bulletin, which came out very soon thereafter, reported our speech fully. Probably, the guidelines for compiling the bulletins had been codified by then, and deletions and delay of publication had been proscribed. Nevertheless, when criticisms were made later on of the mistakes some Political Bureau members elected at the First Plenum of the 11th Central Committee had made during the Cultural Revolution, Wang Dongxing, at a meeting of the Standing Committee, again proposed that "the bulletins involving the mistakes of Political Bureau members should come out at a later date." His proposal was rejected.

Of course, not all participants were satisfied with the bulletins. After reading the bulletins, various people had differing perceptions of how their own speeches and the speeches of other persons had been reported. I myself was satisfied, but that was not true of everyone. In one issue of the bulletins I found that a speaker had made a critical comment on the bulletin, and that this comment was itself carried in the bulletin. I thought that was a good sign.

The bulletins distributed at the conference were quite voluminous. As I knew, the Northwest China Group had published over 70 issues of the bulletins, and other groups published roughly the same number of issues. These bulletins provided precious data for studying the Central Work Conference. The department for studying Party history must have kept all the materials. However, some people at a meeting reported back to the conference had noted that the characterization of many people's position conveyed in the bulletins did not necessarily accord with the facts. Some people asked if verbal comments should be verified, but the Standing Committee expressed the view that this was not necessary. I agreed with the Standing Committee. First, the characterizations were largely accurate. Also, the Party Central Committee would not immediately act upon the cases of these people in accordance with comments recorded in the bulletins. Instead it would first make earnest and realistic investigations to obtain all kinds of material evidence and eyewitness reports. So, this was a highly scientific process. The information presented at the conference would be taken only as clues or expressions of opinion. Thus, it was neither necessary nor possible for us to spend time verifying the information carried in the bulletins. In short, I am firmly convinced that the compilation of bulletins at the conference served as a valuable tool for giving full scope to democracy.

Participants came to attend the conference as a whole, not just meetings of a particular group. They had the right to know what went on in other groups and the right to let others listen to their own speeches. Restricting the publication of the bulletins would have amounted to restricting the rights of the participants.

Initiation of Reforms

I would like to note that the depth and scope of discussions at the Central Work Conference concerning economic reforms were inadequate compared to the discussions on political and ideological reforms. The conference marked the end of the initial phase of the primary stage of socialism in China, which was characterized by economic stagnation, political disturbances, cultural atrophy, poverty, and distress. It also marked the beginning of the reform phase of the primary stage of socialism in China.

The following points illustrate the inadequacy of discussions about economic reforms at the Work Conference. First, in terms of principle and theory, no profound and systematic elaboration was made with regard to the concept and necessity of reforms because awareness of issues concerning reform was still lacking. Second, as for actual economic work, concern was shown primarily with reform in the managerial system. In the spheres of ownership and distribution, participants barely touched on the reforms and then only within a narrow range, and they failed to face the problems squarely. As a matter of course, nobody then dared to think about the abandonment of a planned economy and the creation of a market economy. At that time it was still considered daring to express, in word or deed, positive views about a commodity economy or to approve of the law of value.

Deng Xiaoping had thought most extensively and deeply about reforms and he took the lead in initiating them. At the Work Conference Deng made remarks that are now universally known. He also made many comments at meetings of the Standing Committee dedicated to listening to reports from various conveners. He made additional comments in the talks with us in the course of preparing his speech for the closing session of the conference, as well as on other occasions. His oral comments were freer and more open than his written texts. His exposure of the drawbacks of China's existing economic structure and his ideas about how to carry out reforms were so explicit and sharp that I felt that he was then considerably more advanced in his thinking than other comrades.

While preparing his closing speech, he told us, "Our system discourages people from daring to think, say, and act, not only in the political sphere, but also in the economic sphere and other spheres. There is inadequate ideological and material encouragement. We should do our best to encourage people to dare to make innovations.... At present those doing a good job are treated the same as those doing a poor job. What is worse, those doing a better job are often attacked. Mediocrities can even win all the votes because they do not offend others and everyone finds them acceptable. This is true both in our government and Party systems. So, a strange phenomenon has cropped up." He made these remarks while asking us to consider why thinking became "ossified."

On this same occasion he said that enterprises should institute a responsibility system with rewards and punishments to promote the worthy and demote the unworthy. Persons unqualified for their jobs should be demoted. Enterprises should be strict with their workers and staff, and criticize and penalize those performing poorly. Then Deng added, "Moreover, we should not only criticize and punish people. Instead we should pay greater attention to rewards. Material rewards should be given to specific people, specific collectives, and individuals. This will have a greater effect than criticism and punishment." He also cited Singapore and Japan as examples, saying, "In Japan some factories give workers bonuses equivalent to six months of their wages, which are enough to buy a new car, and three months' wages are enough to buy a used car." He also said that the organization of production there was very good.

In China, factories often held various kinds of competition. In this connection, he said that the word "competition" should be considered. China's excessive formalism is manifested in such spheres as assessing work, hosting lavish dinners, paying formal visits, and making false reports. Deng praised the market. He expressed dissatisfaction with practices popular under a planned economy such as holding formal competitions. He said that good competition should be judged by its result in the market.

At the Work Conference, time and again Deng stressed the need to manage the economy by economic means. He believed that those doing a better job should earn more. He believed this should apply to leading cadres as well as to workers and staff. In addition to ideological incentives, they should also earn more and become prosperous sooner than others. He said, "Initiative cannot be aroused without economic means. It will not do to stress the display of character only. As far as the relatively small number of advanced people is concerned, it will not matter too much if we stress moral character. But when it comes to the masses, that approach can only be used for a short time; it will not work in the long run. We must manage the economy by economic means."

Deng Xiaoping encouraged, "Allowing some enterprises, regions, and people's commune members to achieve prosperity sooner than others." He talked about this a great deal. I can't recall whether he had expressed this view prior to the Work Conference. At the Central Work Conference, when he talked with Hu Yaobang and me on December 2, this was not the first time that he expressed this viewpoint. At a Political Bureau Standing Committee meeting where conveners' reports were presented, he said that he would cite this issue as one of the "two major policies."

The first policy was to "enable some regions to perform better and become more prosperous." He also calculated that if five percent of China's counties and five percent of the residents in China become relatively prosperous, China would have 100 such counties and 40 million such residents. The combined area of such counties and the number of residents would be equivalent to a country of considerable size. If 10 percent of China's counties and 10 percent of the residents in China become prosperous, the area of these counties and the number of such residents would equal a large country. He listed the 19 areas that he supposed would likely achieve prosperity sooner. The first on his list was Shenzhen, in Guangdong Province. Obviously, he had taken notice of this place at a very early date. In his view, a major factor in Shenzhen's quest to become prosperous sooner than other cities was its capacity to conduct foreign trade. Deng took into consideration individuals as well as regions. Individuals were, of course, linked to regions. He said, "The regions performing better and achieving prosperity sooner can increase wages and fringe benefits. This is a major policy as well.... We should try to encourage five percent of the farmers to enjoy fairly high purchasing power and some workers in cities to have such power, too. We should make up our minds in this regard. It will be even better if we encourage eight percent of the farmers to have such purchasing power." He cited some individual villages as examples. He said that a production team in the Beijing area achieved prosperity by quarrying and that fruit trees could produce the desired economic returns within seven or eight years. He also said that it was necessary to permit some enterprises, regions, and people's commune members to become better off sooner. Deng said both "become better off sooner" and "become prosperous sooner." The text of his concluding speech contained the phrase "become better off sooner." I find in my notebook that he made the remark "become prosperous sooner" on various occasions. I remember that Deng also said, "We should enable the people to become better off and to be as prosperous as possible." He expressed opposition to egalitarianism, noting that this was a major policy and that whoever performed better should be better off than his close neighbors.

The second policy he spelled out was "delegating power to lower levels." He emphasized the necessity of enabling all agricultural production teams to "operate on the basis of facts, emancipate their minds, and do what is appropriate to their conditions." Decision-making authority should be granted to them, so that they could operate according to laws governing production. Whether a production team fared well should be judged by whether or not its members increased their incomes. Moreover, at an early meeting for Standing Committee members to listen to reports from the conveners, he said that it was necessary to grant powers to the local authorities. In particular, the central authorities should never interfere in planting crops because the local authorities knew local conditions better than the central authorities, and that counties should enjoy greater decision-making authority and the "right to launch initiatives." He maintained that excessive criticisms of the "three freedoms" had been made so that what was legitimate was criticized as erroneous, resulting in rigid controls over urban and rural areas. In short, in an effort to promote prosperity, farmers must be granted authority with respect to planting crops.

At the Standing Committee meeting Deng also said, "When the necessary conditions prevail in any given province or autonomous region, it can seek loans from other countries. Yet they must pay back debts plus interest. After provisions are formulated, there should be no interference." He favored granting decision-making authority to lower levels so that under a unified plan, authorities at lower levels would enjoy a great deal of room in which to maneuver.

At a Standing Committee meeting where reports were presented, Deng said, "Now a production brigade equals a village. All production teams should be managed as economic organizations and should generally shift to economic management. We should manage enterprises by economic means and enable authorities at lower levels to enjoy some powers so as to enliven them. Enterprises can refuse to do what they are told by authorities at higher levels and instead they should do whatever is needed by production teams and people's communes." He also stressed that transferring powers to lower levels constituted a "major policy."

In sum, although one cannot claim that the Work Conference focused on discussing the theory and principles of reform, it did evince a strong spirit toward that end.

Promotion of Development

Even during the ten years of the Cultural Revolution, there were five-year plans and annual plans, the slogan of "grasping revolution and promoting production" was repeated, and nobody ever said that economic work should not be done. Yet the actual state of economic development was appalling. A constant refrain was that economic accounting should not be performed, only political accounting, and that it was imperative to "take class struggle as the key link." It was a "felony" to criticize political affairs from the viewpoint of economic rationale. Consequently, economic work really could not proceed, and the initiative of many economic workers was dampened.

On February 10, 1974, Jiang Qing gave a speech at the headquarters of the Fourth Machine-Building Ministry that was in charge of the electronic industry. There, for no reason at all, she created the so-called "snail incident." In the course of negotiations on importing a production line for making color TV tubes, the American business negotiators, as a gesture of goodwill, presented a snail-shaped handicraft article to their Chinese colleagues. Jiang Qing interpreted this gesture as a deliberate American insult insinuating China's slow economic development. Consequently, protests were lodged against the Americans, delaying for several years the importation of a production line for making color TV tubes. In the field of education, Zhang Tiesheng, a mediocre student who handed in a blank examination paper, was designated a "blank examination hero."

It was obvious that compared to the Cultural Revolution period when "socialist grass is preferred," the Work Conference promoted economic construction. It was not simply by comparing it to the Cultural Revolution that I came to realize the Central Work Conference was energetically promoting development. The conference proposal that the focus of the Party's work should be shifted to the socialist modernization drive starting in January clearly indicated that the conference served to advance China's economic construction. Everyone at the conference agreed with this, and opposed the long-term continuation of political movements. The three topics that Hua Guofeng, with the approval of the Central Committee, announced at the opening session, all involved economic construction. Later, breakthroughs were made in these topics and participants spent lots of time enthusiastically discussing these topics. The prevailing view throughout the conference was that while doing all kinds of work, it was imperative to emphasize economic construction, and that authorities at all levels should do everything in their power to promote industrial and agricultural production to improve the people's lives.

Reform served economic construction and was intended to achieve the desired results in construction. Opening to the outside world also served economic construction. Success in handling the problems left from the Cultural Revolution was also meant to serve construction. At a Political Bureau Standing Committee meeting devoted to conveners' reports from the various groups, both Deng Xiaoping and Li Xiannian expressed their hope for 20 years of stability and unity that could promote economic construction.

It should be acknowledged that Hua Guofeng, too, was very zealous in this regard. My contacts with him convinced me that he was a pragmatic man. In his opening speech at the conference, he departed from his text and interjected many remarks on economic construction. He said that after the downfall of the "Gang of Four," Japan, France, West Germany, and Italy vied with one another in signing long-term trade agreements with China. The amount of trade that Japan wanted to have with China was considerable, and Japan wished to increase bilateral trade substantially. This, he said, could help encourage China's development. We could observe from his many speeches that he was greatly concerned with managing China's economy and improving its technological standards.

While the Central Work Conference was in session, Deng Xiaoping referred several times to using every inch of land, planting trees on every idle plot, and breeding aquatic products on every water surface available. He also stressed the need to expand the use of methane gas, to encourage people to plant grass, and to pursue diverse activities in rural areas. He called for special attention to be

191

paid to experts and the training of experts. Deng maintained that the college of agriculture should move back to Beijing as soon as possible. He urged greater efforts to enroll more university students and to run all types of secondary technical schools and schools that trained skilled workers effectively. Deng Xiaoping reminded the conferees not to forget that solving problems left over from the Cultural Revolution required success in economic construction.

Comrade Li Xiannian, another Standing Committee member, who had been in charge of economic work for a long time, referred to construction at almost every meeting when chairmen of the group meetings reported to the Standing Committee. At the Central Work Conference, comrades from the government departments and from the ministries and commissions in charge of economic work and cultural work also showed special concern with economic and cultural construction. So did comrades from all provinces, municipalities, and autonomous regions; they gave many lengthy speeches on construction. The atmosphere of the conference was permeated with the desire to promote economic construction. Yet the conference concluded without contributing much in the way of specific plans for carrying out reforms in the economy.

Generosity and Unity

A large majority of the participants in the Work Conference had served as senior cadres before the Cultural Revolution, in which, to varying degrees, they were persecuted. After the downfall of the "Gang of Four," they did not immediately regain the full right to speak. At the Work Conference, however, they could speak fully and forcefully. They deemed it necessary to criticize the theory and line supporting the Cultural Revolution that had brought such calamity to our country and people and to draw lessons from it. Inside and outside the Work Conference, however, there were also some comrades who were in power during the Cultural Revolution. Some of them performed a deed of great merit by joining the struggle to smash the "Gang of Four." After the downfall of the "Gang of Four," some of them drew a distinct line between themselves and the "Gang of Four," citing their later opposition to the "Gang." Others had committed serious errors in word and deed during the Cultural

Revolution and even after the downfall of the "Gang of Four." They even erected obstacles to correcting the mistakes made during the Cultural Revolution and redressing framed, false, and wrong cases. All participants had many critical comments lodged against them while exposing the mistakes made during the Cultural Revolution. Some of them were members of the Eleventh Party Central Committee, others were members of the Political Bureau, and one of them was a vice-chairman of the Party Central Committee. In exposing and criticizing them, the other participants presented facts and reasoned things out, and did not soften their comments because of their high positions. The Work Conference participants upheld just one principle: Present the facts and speak strictly according to facts. The participants shared the view that they should not be ambiguous about this, and they were not. Nevertheless, the participants were generous toward those comrades who had made mistakes.

On November 25, all groups listed many major cases and requested that the Party Central Committee handle them. They also demanded the redress of many framed, false, and wrong cases that had not yet been tackled. This involved several members of the Political Bureau of the 11th Central Committee. While listening to reports from the various groups, Deng Xiaoping said, "The problems cited by all the participants should be solved. The Tiananmen Incident [1976] will be resolved. The case of the 61 comrades should be redressed, too, and also the cases of Yang Shangkun and Tao Zhu. But we cannot solve all of the problems cited." This was a sober estimation by Deng and he made this clear, so as to prepare people in case not all problems could be solved. He did not list which problems could be solved at the conference, and yet the participants knew definitely what they were. At the opening session of the Work Conference, however, Hua Guofeng affirmed all previous line struggles including the ninth line struggle, namely, the struggle against Liu Shaoqi's "counterrevolutionary revisionist line." This wording was written into the political report to the Eleventh Party Congress. Yet, the conference participants knew that Liu Shaoqi had not committed the mistake of pursuing a "counterrevolutionary revisionist line." It was not expected that this problem would be solved at the Central Work Conference or even at the Third Plenum scheduled soon after the conference. Participants realized that full investigation and discussion of such a case would take longer. While holding discussions, therefore, members of all the groups took note that there never had been a "bourgeois headquarters" headed by Liu Shaoqi.

Deng Xiaoping also said that the participants at the conference criticized Chen Xilian, Wu De, and Ji Dengkui, but did not go too far. He thought that the matter would pass after each of the three men found an opportunity to talk about their mistakes and they did not need to make self-criticism to satisfy everyone. He did not favor placing their mistakes on the agenda of the Third Plenum because, if that were done, the matter of punishment would arise. At the meeting of group leaders held on the evening of November 27 after the third plenary session, Deng said that foreign critics had asked what he thought about Wu De. He answered that Wu had made mistakes, and yet in judging a person, one should view his performance over a long time, not just over a short period of time.

The question of criticizing some comrades was mentioned at a subsequent meeting of the Standing Committee. Deng Xiaoping said, "I think we can wind up the matter. It will be OK if the comrades criticized have made basically appropriate self-criticisms. Can we make sure that everyone is satisfied? It is both necessary and correct for all the participants to expose and criticize. But the comrades who have made mistakes should not be criticized without their knowledge. We can continue exposing the mistakes made by anyone. As for the case of Chen Xilian, I said in Liaoning that it would be all right if he made a self-criticism on an appropriate occasion, for instance, when the Party Central Committee held a work conference. If comrades who have made mistakes have admitted their mistakes, namely, have made self-criticisms, whether deep or superficial, we should let them pass."

Then he mentioned Wu De, saying, "There will be no major impact if Comrade Wu De [who had cracked down on demonstrators at the 1976 Tiananmen Incident] is transferred from Beijing while remaining a member of the Political Bureau." At the conference, he asked Lin Hujia, a leader of the North China Group, who attended the Standing Committee meeting, "Did you applaud Wu De when he made a self-criticism?" Lin replied yes. Deng said, "You can go on criticizing him. We should still seek stability and unity. I have also advised Ji Dengkui to make a self-criticism. We should let him pass after he does. We also have Yang Chengwu[1] and Wu Zhong. Wu Zhong will not pass without criticizing himself. Will Yang Chengwu pass without making a self-criticism? We should make self-criticisms and deal with cases properly. The Political Bureau should also be mindful of stability. The Standing Committee members have unified their views that at the current conference those comrades making mistakes do not have to repeat their self-criticism. The above points should be made clear to all the comrades attending the conference."

Deng raised the issue of how to respond when comrades who have returned to work in the regions or departments are criticized by others. Deng said, simply say that they have already made self-criticisms and their cases are closed. He said that the principle in dealing with the cases should be leniency, and that those comrades making mistakes should make self-criticisms. He acknowledged that it is impossible to satisfy everyone completely. He said, "In short, these matters can be regarded as finished at the Work Conference, and will not be submitted to the plenum. Once they are submitted to the plenum, discussions will be held and it will be impossible for us to clarify them."

As noted above, the criticism of the "two whatevers" was a major issue discussed at the Work Conference. But when Deng talked with Hu Yaobang and me about how to prepare his closing speech, he specifically noted that he no longer wanted to mention the problem of the "two whatevers. " Consequently this topic was not included in his speech. This could also be regarded as an expression of his spirit of generosity and concern for unity.

Guidance to Cadres

Now I would like to turn to the question of the nature of the Political Bureau Standing Committee leadership. The collective leadership principle was strictly observed at the conference. The arrangements for the conference were decided jointly by discussion among the five Standing Committee members. While the conference was in session, the Standing Committee members heard and studied together the reports from the conveners of all groups. The five Standing Committee members also attended the three plenary sessions together. If you were not well informed and if you just read the written materials, you could not know the sequence of the speeches made by Hua Guofeng, Ye Jianying, and Deng Xiaoping at the closing session, because each said that he agreed with the content of the speeches that the other two had delivered. This showed that each of them had read the texts of the speeches of the other two prior to giving his own. In his speech, Hua said that the members of the Political Bureau had discussed some decisions and that all members of the Political Bureau had been invited to attend the conference. It would have been very convenient to hold a meeting of the Political Bureau during the Work Conference, but I never heard that such a meeting took place. Although several Political Bureau members took part in our Northwest China Group, I did not hear anyone mention such a meeting. But I did hear of some activities of the Political Bureau Standing Committee. The leadership role of the Standing Committee was manifested chiefly in the speeches of the three Standing Committee members at several plenary sessions and in their meeting with group leaders. Of course, there were other kinds of activities.

In the previous chapters I introduced the speeches delivered at the three general meetings. I listened directly to the three speeches while looking at the texts of the speeches that had been printed and distributed. I wrote in my notebook that Hua Guofeng departed from his text once. In his speech Ye Jianying made some brief remarks that were deleted in the final text printed for distribution. I also remember those remarks. The remarks the Standing Committee members made while listening to the reports from various conveners were not carried in the summary bulletins. I took notes of their remarks, however, some in detail, some in a few characters, and others in several lines on one or two pages of paper. I recall that these were all important materials. The meetings held by the Standing Committee members were useful in guiding the group discussions to progress gradually in a thoroughgoing way, and enabling such discussions to implement the intentions of the Standing Committee members. Yet participants were far from passive and they felt that they spoke entirely according to their own will.

In accordance with the usual practice for such conferences, there was no secretary general for the conference. (Some people said — not then, but later — that Wang Dongxing was the secretary-general). But in the materials on the conference the three characters "mishu zhang" (secretary-general) never appeared. Throughout the conference, there was no secretary-general who showed up to pass on information to the participants. Did this show that there was not a secretary-general at all for the conference? I did not know that then and still do not know today. I just knew that it was Hua Guofeng who declared the conference open, who announced all the changes in the planned length of the conference, the repeated extension of the conference, and the discussion topics at meetings with group conveners before they were transmitted to all groups. Yet this arrangement did not exert a great binding force over the various groups. The groups and even individuals were able to act according to their own will. On the whole, however, this arrangement played a certain guiding role.

At the meetings with the group conveners, the Standing Committee members could hear what was not reported in the bulletins. Then the five Standing Committee members would express their respective opinions. Judging from the reports I heard and the materials I read, the Standing Committee members had their respective foci but their views were complementary and there were no debates about different views. If at the conference the Standing Committee members voiced views that were politically highly aware, creative, and enlightening, those views were transmitted to all the groups and served to enlighten and guide all of the participants. The speeches of Standing Committee members stimulated the conference to probe more deeply as it proceeded.

How many reports did the Standing Committee members listen to and how many meetings did they hold with group conveners? Although I cannot remember them all, as far as I do remember, there were seven such meetings. I learned this from Hu Yaobang's speech at a Political Bureau meeting on November 19, 1980. Shortly before the closing of the Central Work Conference, Hu asked Comrade Hua Guofeng, "Should the texts of your eight speeches be printed and distributed to the whole Party?" Hu said, "I asked Comrade Hua Guofeng the question twice. He answered that he had already spoken of the matter and made a self-criticism. How about closing the case?" What did the eight speeches refer to? They could not be the five speeches of Hua Guofeng, Ye Jianying, and Deng Xiaoping because the texts of the five speeches were already printed and distributed to the comrades attending the conference. Besides, they were fewer than eight. They did not seem to be the remarks the Standing Committee members made while listening to reports. I remain in the dark even today.

However, extrapolating from what I know, in the thirty-six days during which the Work Conference was in session, the Standing Committee members must have held meetings by themselves. It would have been impossible for them to hold meetings only to listen to reports from the conveners. Many issues could only be discussed among the five Standing Committee members. It would have been inconvenient to discuss some matters in the presence of the group conveners because it was inappropriate for them to debate in the presence of these persons. The five men would also have needed to discuss jointly some matters such as the matter of personnel on the Party Central Committee. How many such meetings were held? I really have no idea. In any case, other participants also had no knowledge of activities among the Standing Committee members. However, all meetings they held with conveners were open to all participants. The transparency of the thinking of the Standing Committee members at the conference was rare and had been lacking in all previous central conferences.

Apart from attending the conference, the Standing Committee members also participated in some other collective activities. For example, on the evening of November 25, during the conference, they held talks with the leaders of the Beijing Municipal Party Committee and the Communist Youth League. It seemed that each word and sentence in the talks was evaluated jointly. There should be a written text for the declaration from the meetings, but I do not know whether or not the text has been kept and placed on file. That meeting occurred outside the conference, but it had an impact on the conference.

The written record of Deng Xiaoping's comments from his two meetings with foreign guests was also distributed to the participants, and also played a significant guiding role. At a Standing Committee meeting with the group conveners, it was discussed whether the talk that Deng Xiaoping had with Japanese guests should be distributed to the participants.

One or two Standing Committee members also held individual meetings during the conference. For example, Li Xiannian called a meeting of thirteen people to discuss the issue of agriculture. (I do not know whether it was the "Agricultural Forum" as mentioned in the The Doctrine of Heaven—Zhou Hui and the Lushan Mountain Meeting.[2]) Li Xiannian's meeting should be considered part of the conference for it played a role in formulating the documents regarding agriculture. Comrade Li Xiannian himself also mentioned this at a meeting with group conveners.

CHAPTER 13

THE FIVE-DAY THIRD PLENUM
OF THE 11TH CENTRAL COMMITTEE

Participants in the Third Plenum

On December 15, the Central Work Conference ended, and three days later the Third Plenum of the 11th Central Committee convened. After the Work conference ended, most of the participants who were not members of the Party Central Committee left the Jingxi Hotel. Zeng Tao, Hu Jiwei, and I, along with a few others, remained.

December 15 was a Friday. I went home over the weekend to rest for two days. Before returning to my home, I had learned about the agenda for the Third Plenum. On December 18, the participants in the Third Plenum would read documents and listen to the speeches that the three central leaders, Hua Guofeng, Ye Jianying, and Deng Xiaoping, had given at the closing session of the Central Work Conference. Of course, it was explained in the agenda that those who had attended the Work Conference did not have to read the documents again. Therefore, those persons who had already heard and discussed the speeches on December 14 and 15 were relieved of attending the session on December 18.

After I returned to the Jingxi Hotel on Monday, December 18, the first thing I did was study the name list of the participants in the Third Plenum and those attending the plenum as non-voting members of the Central Committee. From the list I noted that six of the 333 full and alternate members of the Party Central Committee elected at the 11th Party Congress had passed away, namely, Guo Moruo, Luo Ruiqing, Peng Shaohui, Wang Zheng, Lin Liming, and Xie Zhengrong. I knew the first four, but not the latter two. In accordance with a decision of the Party Central Committee, for various reasons 25 of the remaining 327 persons had not been invited to attend the plenum. They were: Wang Guofan (Hebei); Yu Hongliang (Heilongjiang); Jiang Liyin (Fujian); Geng Qichang, Du Xueran and Du Xi (Henan); Wu Guixian (Shaanxi); Wei Fengying

(Liaoning); Feng Zhanwu (Jilin); Qilin Wangdan (Yunnan); Jienan Bu'er (Xinjiang Uygur Autonomous Region); Liu Xingyuan, Kong Shiquan, Reng Sizhong, Liu Guangtao, Huang Ronghai, Jiang Xieyuan, Chen Xianrui, Wu Zhong and Zhang Jihua (PLA); and Cao Die'ou from a central department, as well as Jiu Jianxun, Guo Yufeng, Xie Xuegong, and Zhong Fuxiang who would be assigned new posts by the Party Central Committee. The 327 people minus 37 people added up to 302 attendees. (Using this figure as the base number, the ratio of the members of the Party Central Committee who were invited to the Central Work Conference to all the members of the Party Central Committee attending the Third Plenum was slightly more than 45 percent.) On the list, 21 people asked to be absent because they had other things to attend to or asked for sick leave. A total of 169 members of the Party Central Committee actually attended the Third Plenum, accounting for 84 percent of the 201 members of the Party Central Committee, far higher than the number required for formal decisions.

The Third Plenum was convened to provide legal authorization for matters that had been prepared at the Central Work Conference. Therefore, the name list was very important. This was why it had been prepared along much stricter lines than the ones employed for the Work Conference.

Nine persons on the name list for the Third Plenum were designated as non-voting members. They were: Song Renqiong, Huang Kecheng, Huang Huoqing, Hu Qiaomu, Han Guang, Zhou Hui, Wang Renzhong, and Xi Zhongxun. The Central Work Conference proposed that all of them be elected to the Party Central Committee. Furthermore, once the Plenum passed the resolution electing them members of the Party Central Committee, they became participants in the plenum with both speaking and voting rights.

Zeng Tao, Hu Jiwei, and I, and perhaps a few others as well, were not members of the Party Central Committee. Yet, probably because of the press of work we were asked to remain at the Jingxi Hotel after the Central Work Conference. I cannot find a proper title for us, so let me call us "non-formal, non-voting members." Such non-formal members were not included on the name list. I noticed that Li Xin and some others associated with the General Office of the

Committee for Compiling and Publishing Chairman Mao Zedong's Works seemed not to be staying at the Jingxi Hotel.

The list that I read on the morning of December 18 contained the same six regional groups as those at the Central Work Conference. Also unchanged were the conveners of these groups and the members of the Party Central Committee assigned to each group. There were just a few more members in each group than at the Work Conference. For example, the number of members of the Northwest China Group increased from 35 to 44. With the addition of Song Renqiong and Wang Renzhong, who attended the Plenum as formal non-voting members, our group numbered 46. I was not placed on the formal name list, but, according to the usual practice, I automatically went to the Northwest China Group.

Convocation of the Third Plenum
of the 11TH Party Central Committee

The participants in the plenum spent all day December 18 reading the documents from the Central Work Conference and listening to the transmission of the speeches made by Deng Xiaoping, Ye Jianying, and Hua Guofeng at the closing session. There was no thematic report at the plenum. Judging from the contents of the speeches of the three central leaders, the participants all knew that Deng's speech actually served as the thematic report for the plenum because it expounded the Party's line, principles, and policies in a brilliant and all-round manner, as well as dealing with the organizational issue.

The first plenary session of the Third Plenum was held in the Jingxi Hotel on the evening of December 18. At this meeting Hua Guofeng spoke of how the plenum would proceed, what was its agenda, and so forth. These were the same remarks he had already made at the closing session of the Central Work Conference, and his speech was quite short. Judging by its content, it was evidently not the thematic report for the Third Plenum.

On December 19, all the groups continued reading documents. The Northwest China Group was the first to begin discussions. From December 20 to 22, all groups held discussions. My impression was that the resolution on electing new members of the Central Committee and the Political Bureau, and on electing Chen Yun as a vice-chairman of the Central Committee had been adopted before other resolutions were put to the vote at the first plenary session. I remember that plenary sessions of the Third Plenum were held only on the first and the last days, and all other meetings were classified as group meetings.

The content of the three days of group meetings could be summarized in the following four points. First, members of the Central Committee, who had attended the Work Conference and delivered speeches, briefed those Central Committee members who had not. Second, all participants declared their stands on the speeches of the central leaders at the closing session of the conference; on electing new members of the Central Committee and the Political Bureau; on electing a new vice-chairman of the Central Committee; on the establishment of the Central Commission for Discipline Inspection; and on the name list of candidates for membership on the Central Commission for Discipline Inspection. Third, as at the Central Work Conference, participants aired their views on the "two whatevers," "practice is the sole criterion for testing truth," redressing the framed, false, and wrong cases, and the case of Kang Sheng. Fourth, participants voiced their positions on the draft communiqué of the Third Plenum, and proposed various revisions to the draft.

Many matters were discussed in the three days of group meetings, but there were no longer any differences of opinion. At the meetings participants continued to make critical comments about Wang Dongxing and some other comrades and presented new facts that had not been revealed before.

A plenary session was held on the evening of the last day. The plenary session first adopted the resolution on electing new members of the Central Committee, new members of the Political Bureau, and members of the Political Bureau Standing Committee, and a new vice-chairman of the Central Committee. It also adopted in principle the two documents regarding agriculture and the arrangements for the national economic plan for the 1979–1980 period and the communiqué of the plenum. Before being elected, those attending the plenum as formal non-voting members did not have voting rights, but right after their election, they could vote and participated in the election of members of the Central Commission for Discipline

Inspection. The election result showed that the 100 candidates for membership on the Central Commission for Discipline Inspection, who were on the candidate name list, were all elected. Chen Yun was elected the first secretary of the commission, Deng Yingchao, the second secretary, Hu Yaobang, the third secretary, and Huang Kecheng, the executive secretary. Eleven people were elected deputy secretaries, and another 23 people Standing Committee members. Chen Yun addressed the meeting after his election.

I was not given any specific responsibility at the Third Plenum. Bulletins were issued, and the total number of bulletins from the six groups just equaled the number of one group's bulletins at the Central Work Conference. As it took little time to read the bulletins, I spent five relatively relaxing days.

During the Third Plenum I suddenly thought of one thing I originally wanted to have done, namely, to build an office building for the Chinese Academy of Social Sciences. We sent Deputy Secretary-General Du Ganquan to Hong Kong for a study tour. After returning to Beijing, Du brought back a housing sale advertisement put up by a real estate agent in Yuen Long, Kowloon, Hong Kong. The advertisement inspired my idea that in Shenzhen we could build apartments like those described in the advertisement and sell them to Kowloon residents. We could relax exit restrictions at the Luowu checkpoint entrance to Shenzhen, simplifying procedures for Kowloon and Hong Kong residents who would become the owners of these apartments. Consequently, differential land rents for land in Shenzhen resulting from the distance from the market would be linked to land rents in Kowloon and Hong Kong. This way we would be able to substantially increase land rents in Shenzhen, becoming socialist "landlords," reaping profit without effort. Xi Zhongxun then served as the first secretary of the Guangdong Provincial Party Committee. One night I went to his room to tell him my idea. He listened to my proposal, and was very interested. He asked Jiao Linyi, then a secretary of the Guangdong Provincial Party Committee who had not attended the Central Work Conference but who was at the Third Plenum, to visit me along with his secretary. They came, listened, and took notes. Later, I learned that after returning to Guangdong, Xi Zhongxun, and Jiao Linyi transmitted my idea to the cadres at lower levels. My proposal was regarded as one of the origins of the special economic zone in Shenzhen. Of course, this was a matter irrelevant to the Third Plenum. I mentioned it only to suggest that I was then fairly free. By contrast, during the Central Work Conference, I could not have imagined spending time doing such a thing.

Election of The Central Commission for Discipline Inspection and Chen Yun's Speech

It was at the Third Plenum that I read the name list of candidates for membership on the Central Commission for Discipline Inspection. After the three secretaries, namely, Chen Yun, Deng Yingchao, and Hu Yaobang, came the executive secretary, Huang Kecheng. There were also 11 deputy secretaries: Wang Heshou, Wang Congwu, Liu Shunyuan, Zhang Qilong, Yuan Renyuan, Zhang Yun, Guo Shuzhong, Ma Guorui, Li Yimang, Wei Wenbo, and Zhang Ce. There were also 23 Standing Committee members: Zhou Yang, Zhang Ziyi, Shuai Mengqi, Li Chuli, Wu Xinyu, Wang Weigang, Li Shiying, Zeng Yongquan, Cao Ying, Han Guang, Liu Jianzhang, Liu Lanbo, Kong Xiangzhen, Zhou Zhongying, Ma Huizhi, Liu Xing, Wang Hefeng, Yan Xiufeng, Lu Jianren, Fang Zhichun, Cao Guanghua, Fu Qiutao, and Tang Tianji. I knew most of the 38 secretaries and the Standing Committee members. Except for Ma Guorui, who was my age, they were all older than I. Twenty years later, 61 members of the commission elected then are still alive. So, there has been an increase in the number of such members who are younger than I. For example, Wang Ruoshui was fifty-two years old then, 10 years younger than I. The name list was adopted with applause. I did not have voting rights, but I still applauded warmly.

On the closing day, December 22, 1978, Chen Yun gave a speech. Since he was not a Standing Committee member at the Work Conference, he did not address the plenary sessions there, but at the Third Plenum he was a vice-chairman of the Central Committee. In his speech, he expressed his views on the Central Work Conference. He said, "I think that the Third Plenum and the Central Work Conference convened earlier were a great success. On the basis of Marxism-Leninism and Mao Zedong Thought, all of us have emancipated our minds, spoken without reservation, fully restored and carried forward inner-Party democracy and the Party's line of seeking truth from facts, its mass line and its fine work style of making criticism and self-criticism, earnestly discussed some problems existing inside the Party and enhanced unity.

"The plenum has effectively realized 'a political situation in which we have both centralism and democracy, both discipline and freedom, both unity of will and personal ease of mind, and liveliness' as advocated by Comrade Mao Zedong. Moreover, the plenum has decided that it is imperative to spread this practice to the whole Party, the whole army, and people of all ethnic groups across the country. Now we are holding a meeting at the central level. We still have plenty of work to do before spreading the practice to the whole Party, the whole army, and peoples of all ethnic groups across the country. We are likely to encounter all sorts of problems.

"In the rectification movement in Yan'an, Comrade Mao Zedong first held a rectification meeting involving scores of senior cadres, which lasted for several months. At the meeting everyone made face-to-face criticisms and self-criticisms by name and earnestly summarized experience and lessons since the founding of our Party. On this basis the Resolution on Certain Historical Questions[1] was written. Later, the Seventh Party Congress was convened. As a result, all comrades in the Party were united as one and we achieved victory in the War of Resistance against Japanese Aggression and in the War of Liberation. In 1957, Comrade Mao Zedong called on the whole Party to achieve a political situation that was both relaxed and lively. Because of interference of various kinds, his call had not been achieved for years. This requirement was also written into the Party Constitutions adopted by the Ninth and Tenth Party Congresses, but it still failed to become a reality.

"Now the Party Central Committee headed by Comrade Hua Guofeng has started us off well. So long as we persist, it is likely to become a reality throughout the country. This will certainly play a significant role in ensuring stability and unity and achieving the four modernizations."

Chen Yun's speech at the Third Plenum constituted an assessment of the Central Work Conference. He used just a few short sentences to express thanks to the plenum for electing him first secretary of the Central Commission for Discipline Inspection, a member of the Political Bureau and of its Standing Committee, and a vice-chairman of the Central Committee. Chen Yun also thanked the comrades attending the Work Conference and the plenum for their trust in him. He pledged to devote his best efforts to his responsibilities.

Appointments and Dismissals of Senior Cadres after the Third Plenum

On December 25, 1978, the third day after the conclusion of the Third Plenum, a Political Bureau meeting was convened at which Hu Yaobang was named secretary-general of the Central Committee and, concurrently, head of the Publicity Department. Hu was relieved of his previous post as Head of the Organization Department. The decision of the Political Bureau did not mention Hu's position as deputy president of the Party School, which he held concurrently. At the same time he was named secretary-general, Hu Qiaomu and Yao Yilin were appointed as the Deputy Secretaries-General. Hu Qiaomu also served concurrently as the director of the General Office of the Committee for Compiling and Publishing Chairman Mao Zedong's Works. Yao Yilin served concurrently as the director of the General Office of the Central Committee. Song Renqiong served as the head of the Organization Department, and Feng Wenbin served as the first deputy director of the General Office of the Central Committee.

Wang Dongxing was removed from the various posts he had held concurrently. He would no longer serve as director of the General Office of the Central Committee, director of the Central Guards Bureau, and secretary of the Party Committee of the bureau, Political Commissar, and Secretary of the Party Committee of the 8341 Unit, director of the General Office of the Committee for Compiling and Publishing Chairman Mao Zedong's Works, or secretary of the Party Committee of the General Office of the committee. Wang Dongxing had served also as a vice-chairman of the Central Committee and as a Political Bureau Standing Committee member. All this was in line with the proposal made by all six regional groups of the Central Work Conference and approved, specifically, by Hua

Guofeng, Ye Jianying, Deng Xiaoping, and Li Xiannian. It was unnecessary for the Third Plenum to discuss and decide on this matter. A formal decision was made at a Political Bureau meeting with the newly elected members attending, held after the Third Plenum. As a result, the leading body of the Central Committee emerged with a new look. The changes in the membership of the Political Bureau and its Standing Committee embodied the principle of "entrance only and no exits." However, in terms of both the number of members and real power, the leading body could now implement in all particulars the guidelines set by the Central Work Conference and the Third Plenum.

CONCLUDING REMARKS

The preceding chapters have related in considerable detail the historical turning point that I personally experienced in 1978. In conclusion, I would like to consider the significance of this turn. First let me quote the Resolution on Certain Historical Questions of our Party Since the Founding of the People's Republic of China issued in 1981 by the Sixth Plenum of the 11th Central Committee. This is the first formal document to make an assessment of the historical significance of the Third Plenum, which I still prefer to call more accurately "the Third Plenum of the 11th Central Committee and the Central Work Conference that made all the preparations for the Third Plenum."

The 26th section of the Resolution declares that "the Third Plenum of the 11th Central Committee that convened in December 1978 constituted a great turn of far-reaching significance in our Party's history. It was the biggest turn since the founding of the People's Republic of China." From 1949 when the People's Republic of China was founded to 1978, the Chinese Communist Party went through a full 36 years of history, during which many major events took place. Yet the Resolution pointed out that the Third Plenum marked a great turn of far-reaching significance in our Party's history. This conclusion was only reached over two years after the Third Plenum had occurred. Obviously, the decision to make this historical turn was entirely correct. Today, we can and should elaborate further on that historical turn.

I would like to offer the following basic viewpoints. First, in my view, it is not only a historical turn for the Party, it is a historical turn for Chinese society as well. Although the Communist Party is the ruling party leading the effort to achieve social progress for the country, its history is inseparable from the history of Chinese society. We should acknowledge that that remark in the Resolution is correct. But the history of our Party and that of Chinese society are not synonymous. They are, after all, two different concepts. But only an historical turn that gives rise to great social progress in China can be considered a great historical turn.

Second, that historical turn is a turn from one historical phase to another. This requires us to examine the historical phase the society was in before and after the two meetings convened in 1978. An historical turn cannot simply be understood in terms of a conference. It becomes significant because of the changes in society it helps bring about. The narrative and assessment of historical facts provided by the Resolution adopted in 1981 constitute materials for examining this broader significance by comparing the situation before and after the Third Plenum. It seems to me, however, that the Resolution did not provide adequate theoretical perspective and thus was not sufficiently forceful.

Here I should mention the incident described by the theoretical community as "the storm over historical phases" that occurred in 1979. After the Third Plenum, the first persons to raise the theoretical question of the phase of social development after 1949 were Su Shaozhi and Feng Lanrui, who jointly submitted a paper to the meeting in 1979 to discuss theoretical principles. Their paper expressed the view that present-day Chinese society could only be described as an "underdeveloped socialist society," since it had not reached the first phase of Communism as referred to by Marx in Critique of the Gotha Program or of socialist society as referred to by Lenin in State and Revolution. After the paper was published in Economic Studies, some comrades asserted that Su and Feng had denied that China was a socialist society, thus generating a storm of protest. I do not want to evaluate this storm here.

I have to mention this matter because Hu Qiaomu, a principal writer of the Resolution, did not pay attention to the fact that the historical changes in the Communist Party and in Chinese society wrought by the Third Plenum were of a piece. He failed to value the questions raised by Su and Feng in their joint academic paper and did not support the academic debate about the question of the socialist development phase. Instead, without mentioning their names, in the Resolution he criticized the two scholars for raising the question regarding China's socialist development phase after the victory of the democratic revolution in China. The fact that the 1981 Resolution did not thoroughly elaborate on the historical turn at the Third Plenum was an accurate reflection of Hu Qiaomu's thinking.

The sentence in the 1981 Resolution saying that China was in the primary stage of socialism was the outcome of a debate between Hu Qiaomu and myself. I took the side of the two scholars, Su and Feng, and opposed the sentences in the Resolution criticizing them for raising the question of China's development stage. However, I thought that stating China was "in the primary stage of socialism" was better than referring to "underdeveloped socialism." My view was that the Central Committee should affirm that China was still in this primary stage of socialist society. I thought it imperative to affirm the great significance of discussing the question of what stage of socialist development China currently found itself in. It was only after sharp debates that the following sentences were inserted in Section 33: "Although our socialist system is still in the primary stage, beyond any doubt China has instituted the socialist system and entered socialist society. Any view that negates this basic fact is wrong." At any rate, for the first time the wording "China is in the primary stage of socialism" appeared in a document of the Party Central Committee.

Yet I was still dissatisfied with the Resolution because it contained the two characters "jin guan" (although) before the phrase "China is in the primary stage of socialism." Moreover, the "primary stage" was written into the Resolution to highlight that it is "beyond any doubt" that China has a socialist system. To my way of thinking, this was certainly not "beyond any doubt." I myself was not convinced that China had a "socialist society" during the 22 years from 1956 to 1978, a period characterized by economic stagnation, political turmoil, cultural decay, and a population living in poverty and distress. The section titled "Strive to Promote a High Level of Socialist Ethical and Cultural Progress" in the third section of the report to the 12th Party Congress held in 1982 contained the sentence, "China's socialist society is now still in the primary development stage, underdeveloped economically and culturally." This sentence was the fruit of my proposal and had been approved by Hu Yaobang. No dispute erupted at that time. By then a step forward had been taken, with the "primary stage" no longer viewed as a reflection of a socialist society but as a forthright recognition of the reality. It was not until 1986, at the Sixth Plenum of the 12th Central Committee that the "primary stage of socialism" began to be taken as a theoretical perspective to guide the solution of actual problems and was written into a resolution of the Party.

Now I shall attempt to expound on that historical turn by applying the concept of the primary stage of socialism in China. In 1981 when I proposed the concept of the "primary stage of socialism in China," I felt that it was really difficult to find an appropriate label for Chinese society after the completion of the three great transformations was announced prematurely in 1956. After pondering the question for a long time, I concluded that I could not find a proper label for Chinese society at the time. So, I had no recourse but to call it a socialist society. But what kind of socialist society was it? Since the level of its productive forces was so low and its production standard was not genuinely advanced, I had to regard the socialism as a "premature baby" that had not become mature in its mother's womb and was congenitally deficient. If a premature baby were given special care, it would grow into a fairly healthy child. But Chinese socialism was given extremely improper care. The Eighth Party Congress in 1956 was on the whole good. However, the general line laid down by the Eighth Party Congress was followed for only about one year before being abandoned. A political struggle against Rightists was waged in the summer of 1957. This premature baby was not given good care. No emphasis was put on construction. Instead stress was on the socialist revolution on the political and ideological fronts. Time and again, extremely strong but wrongly prescribed medicine was administered to the premature baby. Turbulent political campaigns were launched one after another.

The year 1958 saw the pursuit of the "three great red banners," namely, the general line, the "great leap forward," and the people's commune, in total disregard of the objective forces and laws governing social development. This brought huge losses to the Chinese people. The struggle against Peng Dehuai was waged at the Lushan plenum in 1959. This was followed by the struggle against "Right-opportunism." Subsequently, the large-scale so-called "socialist education movement" was carried out in the countryside and in all fields, to "criticize capitalist-roaders inside the Party." The movement eventually evolved into the ten-year Cultural Revolution.

In this unprecedented Cultural Revolution, genuine Marxist theory and practice was labeled "counterrevolutionary revisionism." Promoting production was condemned as "attacking" proletarian politics. The idea "to each according to his work" was attacked with a new, specially created, derogatory label, "only for production"; it was criticized for producing the new bourgeoisie. Veteran Party members who had been working hard and faithfully for dozens of years for the Chinese revolution and socialist construction were labeled "capitalist-roaders" and were overthrown and trampled upon. The chairman of the People's Republic of China, the general secretary of the Party Central Committee, and quite a few vice-premiers of the State Council, vice-chairmen of the Central Military Commission, those holding the rank of marshal and senior general, and those holding positions as Standing Committee members of the Central Military Commission were persecuted cruelly. Some were even persecuted to death. Although there were some people who were not criticized, even they could not carry out normal work. They were partially "overthrown" or were cold-shouldered. Conspirators including Lin Biao, Kang Sheng, and the "Gang of Four" wielded the power of the Central Committee and ran amuck.

During the 20 years after 1957, many persons who had been the dregs of society resurfaced to carry out rebellion, and they worked hand-in-glove with a tiny number of opportunists inside the Party in total defiance of the law. The pursuit of such a line and principles mired China's economy, political affairs, and society in a perpetual crisis. The leadership of the Party Central Committee kept aggravating the crisis. At the time, most people, including ordinary cadres and senior cadres inside the Party, did not know that the supreme power of the Party and state was wielded by a supreme leader, a man advanced in age and weak, who could not carry out normal work because of serious illnesses. He was actually manipulated and controlled by the "Gang of Four" and their followers who claimed that he was an "idol for exhibition."

China's destiny was in great danger and China was going along a path that was leading our Party and state to perdition. If we say that Chinese society during the 20 years from 1957, when the struggle against Rightists was waged, to October 6, 1976, when the "Gang of

Four" was smashed, could still be called socialist society, it was a socialist society characterized by economic stagnation, political unrest, cultural decay, and a population condemned to living in poverty and distress. I refer to this stage as the "initial phase" of the primary stage of socialism in China. This is a phase with a very special meaning. Then it was not adequate to describe it as a premature baby. It was older. In those 20 years it became a deformed child, extremely weak and on the verge of death.

In October 1976, Hua Guofeng, Ye Jianying, and others took resolute action to smash the "Gang of Four." The downfall of the "Gang of Four" was an unqualified blessing in Chinese history because it turned China around. In the two years between the downfall of the "Gang of Four" and the convocation of the Central Work Conference, the "Gang of Four" and their followers had been exposed and criticized, a large number of veteran cadres who had been persecuted and inhibited during the Cultural Revolution were reinstated, and economic construction had begun to get back on track. But problems had not been solved. The erroneous thought guiding China during the 20 years from 1957 to 1976 was far from being thoroughly corrected. All the documents of the Central Committee and the speeches of the leaders still stressed Mao Zedong's view that it had been necessary to launch the "Great Cultural Revolution" and echoed his opinion on "continuing the revolution under the dictatorship of the proletariat." Despite the people's call to correct the mistakes of the Cultural Revolution and the wrong decisions made during the Cultural Revolution, the Central Committee still urged cadres and the masses to have "proper regard for the Great Proletarian Cultural Revolution." In the view of the vast number of cadres and masses, "proper regard for the Great Proletarian Cultural Revolution" would have been to criticize it. As more and more people took a genuinely correct approach toward the Cultural Revolution, the Central Committee required everyone to take a stand affirming the Cultural Revolution, asserting that this was the only correct attitude. Nevertheless, people at the time did not follow what was written in the document. Furthermore, the document had already announced the victorious ending of the Cultural Revolution. Even so, the Party's documents, such as the report to the 11th Party

Congress, continued to affirm the "Great Proletarian Cultural Revolution." Supporters of the Cultural Revolution could use these statements to resist setting things right. At a meeting to discuss the issue of "to each according to his work," some people opposed my using well-known facts to criticize and repudiate the "Gang of Four" by quoting the sentences contained in the report to the 11th Congress. Moreover, those people attempting to relaunch the Cultural Revolution might still invoke these words as a "theoretical" weapon. Therefore, the two years from October 6, 1976 to December 1978 can be regarded as the transitional phase between the first phase (the initial phase) of the primary stage of socialism and the second phase (the reform phase) of the primary stage of socialism. It is only from 1979, following the convocation of the Third Plenum, that the primary stage of socialism in China entered the "reform phase." The two meetings in 1978 constituted the turn from this transitional phase to the second phase, and, more broadly, marked the shift from the first to the second phase.

Twenty years have passed since 1978. The more time has elapsed, the more obvious is the significance of the Third Plenum as a great historical turning point. I wrote above that the participants in the Central Work Conference did not spend much time discussing the reforms. The hot topics at the conference were opposing the "two whatevers," politically and ideologically, by invoking "practice as the sole criterion for testing truth"; rehabilitating the nature of the (1976) Tiananmen Incident; and redressing major framed, false, and wrong cases of a number of important senior cadres inside the Party. This required the reshuffling of high-level cadres in leading Party organizations. These were all problems that had to be solved promptly. In the meantime, the ideological and political lines defined by the Third Plenum had a long-term impact. Over the past two decades, China has been pressing ahead step by step in its reform and the process of opening has achieved increasingly greater success in the economic and cultural spheres.

I recall that in early 1978 I met a delegation of Japanese social scientists in the office of the Chinese Academy of Social Sciences. I told the visitors, "China has made great progress ideologically and politically. At present you probably can't discern the progress while walking on the streets in Beijing. But in less then eight or ten years, you will be able to notice this change." I added, "All of us are scientists advocating reason. Our reason can first realize things that we cannot yet perceive. In my mind's eye I can see the progress China will make. I have complete confidence in this." I asked them whether they could accept my view and whether their understanding tallied with mine. The Japanese professors supported my view. We turned out to be correct. China has scored rapid progress in construction since the Third Plenum, and changes quickly became evident on the streets in Beijing.

Some places in the forefront of reform and opening up have experienced even greater changes. One example is the Pearl River Delta in Guangdong Province, Shenzhen in particular. During the Central Work Conference, at a Standing Committee meeting with group conveners, Deng Xiaoping said that a number of areas could achieve prosperity sooner than other areas. Shenzhen was the first such place that Deng mentioned. It was in Shenzhen that a modern city was built from the ground up shortly after the Third Plenum was over.

So many events have occurred in the 20 years since the Third Plenum. In this concluding chapter I do not want to talk about all these questions. I just want to touch upon the reforms and development in China in these years. I attended all the Congresses and all the plenums of the Central Committee held from the Third Plenum of the 11th Central Committee in 1978 to the 15th Party Congress in 1992. (I attended the 12th Party Congress in 1982. I no longer attended all the plenums of Party Central Committee after the 14th and 15th Congresses. I attended the 15th Congress as a non-voting member.) I want to write a few sentences about each congress to portray the features of reforms and development in the second phase of the primary stage of socialism in China.

The 12th Congress held in 1982 summarized six years of historical victory after the downfall of the "Gang of Four" in 1976. The mission of this congress was to further eliminate factors left over from the Cultural Revolution and create in an all-round way a new situation in socialist modernization. The congress set the objective of quadrupling the combined value of China's agricultural and industrial output between 1981 and the end of the twentieth century. With respect to reforms, it affirmed the development of various kinds of economic organizations. Prior to the 12th Congress the Central Committee had already affirmed the socialist nature of the household-based contract responsibility system linking output to the personal income that had been introduced in rural areas. After the 12th Congress the Central Committee issued several documents to affirm the reform in instituting the household-based contract responsibility system linking output to personal income. The report to the 12th Congress emphasized the principle of emphasizing the planned economy as the main force and viewing market regulation as a subsidiary force. However, the academic community's proposal on developing a "socialist commodity economy" was not adopted. The Central Committee document only allowed the market to regulate the production and circulation of certain products. The Third Plenum of the 12th Central Committee held in 1984 adopted a decision on the reform of the economic structure, and affirmed the idea that the development of a commodity economy was a phase that China could not transcend, thus taking another step forward in the direction of a market economy.

The central task of the Thirteenth Congress held in 1987 was to accelerate and deepen reforms. It further defined the basic principles concerning the future course of reform of the economic and political structures. The Congress further elaborated the idea that China was in the primary stage of socialism and regarded it as the foundation on which a correct line and correct policies could be formulated. The Thirteenth Congress stated our Party's basic line to build socialism with Chinese characteristics during the primary stage of socialism. In line with China's national conditions, the Congress stressed that the adequate development of a commodity economy was the sine qua non for achieving the socialization and modernization of production. It also explicitly defined the criterion for productive forces, "Everything that is conducive to the development of productive forces accords with people's fundamental interests and thus is required by socialism or permitted by socialism. Everything that is detrimental to the development of productive forces runs counter to scientific socialism and is not permitted by socialism." It noted that,

217

"Abandoning the criterion of productive forces and judging life by abstract principle and fantasy can only ruin the reputation of Marxism." Compared to 1978 and the Third Plenum, the 13th Congress made great advances in the course of expounding Deng Xiaoping's thinking on building socialism with Chinese characteristics and defining the guiding thinking for China's reforms and opening up.

The convocation of the 14th Party Congress in 1992 followed the talks that Deng Xiaoping gave while inspecting south China. The greatest contribution of the 14th Congress lay in proposing the establishment of a socialist market economic structure, thus solving in principle the most important and fundamental problem in China's economic structure. This was not an easy step to take. The 14th Congress still stated, in accordance with traditional thinking, that a market economy was peculiar to capitalism only, whereas a planned economy was the basic characteristic of a socialist economy. In view of this traditional concept, in the talks Deng Xiaoping gave while inspecting south China, he pointed out that a planned economy was not equivalent to socialism. He said this was because there was also planning under capitalism and that a market economy was not equivalent to capitalism because there was a market under socialism. The 14th Congress held that developing practice and deepening understanding required that we state explicitly that the objective of China's economic restructuring was to establish a socialist market economic structure, in order to help further emancipate and develop productive forces. This decision constituted a substantial breakthrough for China's economic restructuring.

The 15th Party Congress held in 1997 achieved a new breakthrough in the economy of socialist ownership. It affirmed that the common development of the economy with the public ownership as the foundation and the co-existence of multiple forms of ownership was the basic economic system in the primary stage of socialism.

The significance of the Third Plenum as an historical turning point has been constantly confirmed and enhanced in the 20 years that followed. The Third Plenum as an historical turning point can also be placed in the perspective of three "30-year" periods. It is actually quite a coincidence. It was exactly 30 years from the launching of the May 4th Movement in 1919 to the founding of the People's Republic of China. These 30 years witnessed the victory won in China's democratic revolution. It was also 30 years from 1949 to the Third Plenum convened in 1978. This is the 30 years in which China advanced along the socialist road in a zigzag manner before everyone finally realized the necessity of carrying out socialist restructuring. I expect and also wish that the third "30," that is, from 1979 to 2008, be the period when this socialist economic restructuring will be basically completed and the first post-reform Constitution formulated. At the 14th Congress held in 1992, after 14 years of reform, the reform objective was defined as establishing a socialist market economic structure and a consensus on the desirability of a market economy was reached in both theory and practice. This could be considered a great and decisive victory won in economic restructuring.

Two major problems in economic restructuring remain to be solved. The first is to solve the problem of the structure of ownership; the other is to solve the problem of distribution. The 14th and 15th Congresses and even the earlier 12th and 13th Congresses touched on the two problems, but did not solve them theoretically. The problems still need in-depth study and discussion. I believe these two major problems can and should be basically solved by 2008. In the 10 years from now to 2008, two national congresses of the Party will he convened, one in 2002 and the other in 2007. It is entirely possible and feasible to basically complete China's economic restructuring in this time frame. Of course, to solve the two problems within 10 years creates time pressure. Furthermore, as no adequate in-depth theoretical study of the two problems has been done and as there are different views in the theoretical community, the timetable for thoroughly solving the problems has not yet been established. But I have only said that economic restructuring should be completed by and large, and have not said that the reform of the socialist structure as a whole should be completed. In short, I have not said that the reform of the socialist political structure, the cultural and educational systems, and other social systems should also be completed during this period. Even for economic restructuring, I have only said that it should be completed in the main, not that it should be completed thoroughly. This means that I have left room for the wording of the third "30 years." Maybe it will require the fourth 30 years to finish the course of reforms and to formulate the second post-reform Constitution.

The second phase of the primary stage of socialism that China entered upon after the Third Plenum may perhaps be regarded as a transitional phase. Conceivably, at a certain juncture in the future there will be a new turning point. Compared to the turn that occurred at the Third Plenum of the 11th Congress, this turn would entirely be a phase in the historical development of Chinese society, and quite different from what we are referring to now. There is no point in discussing this further

NOTES

Preface

[1] The article titled "Practice Is the Sole Criterion for Testing Truth" was first printed on May 10, 1978, in the Lilun dongtai (Theoretical development), an internal magazine of the Central Party School. On the following day, May 11, the Guangming Daily reprinted the article in the name of its special commentator. The article reiterated the basic tenet of the Marxist theory of knowledge, that is, practice is the sole criterion for testing truth. It pointed out very clearly that the ideological shackles imposed on people by the "Gang of Four" were far from being completely eliminated, that it was unwise to use an existing formula to restrict, pressure, and eliminate and cut on the infinitely rich rapidly developing revolutionary practice, and that it was imperative to dare to study new problems raised by new practices. The article produced an enormous reverberation throughout the country, initiating an ideological emancipation movement focusing on the great debate about the issue of the criterion for testing truth.

[2] Deng Xiaoping then served as a vice-chairman of the Party Central Committee, a vice-chairman of the Military Commission of the Party Central Committee, a vice-premier of the State Council, the chairman of the National Committee of the Chinese People's Political Consultative Conference, and the chief of the General Staff of the Chinese People's Liberation Army.

[3] Hua Guofeng then served as the chairman of the Party Central Committee, the chairman of the Military Commission of the Party Central Committee, and the premier of the State Council.

[4] Ye Jianying then served as a vice-chairman of the Party Central Committee, a vice-chairman of the Military Commission of the Party Central Committee, and the chairman of the Standing Committee of the National People's Congress.

[5] Being "large in size and collective in nature" refers to the basic characteristic of the people's communes, which constituted China's rural organizational system that was begun in 1958. "Large" referred to the large scale of the rural people's communes, with 4,000-5,000 to 10,000-20,000 rural families usually forming one commune, equaling the size of one town previously. The so-called "collective" meant a high degree of collectivization of rural people's communes, with the usual merger into one commune, of scores and even some 100 cooperatives with different economic conditions and different levels of incomes, and with all of their assets turned over to the commune. Unified accounting and distribution were practiced within a commune, which also practiced the partial supply system—a system of payment in kind. After the 1960s, this system was adjusted. The rural people's commune system fundamentally did not conform to the reality of China's rural areas and had a serious negative impact in practice. So it was abolished after 1984.

[6] The Tiananmen Incident refers to the large-scale protest movement that occurred on Tiananmen Square in early April 1976 to mourn Zhou Enlai and oppose the "Gang of Four." The movement in essence supported the correct leadership represented by Deng Xiaoping and laid the popular foundation for smashing the "Gang of Four" later that same year. At the time of the incident, the Political Bureau and Mao Zedong rendered an erroneous judgment on the nature of the incident, regarding it as a "counterrevolutionary incident" and removed Deng Xiaoping from all the posts he had held inside and outside the Party.

[7] Fixing farm output quotas for each household was an operational and managerial form for agricultural production introduced experimentally after 1956 when collectivization was completed in China's rural areas. On the basis of the public ownership of the means of production, it featured production carried out with rural households as the basic unit, set the amount of farm products to be delivered to the state and collectives, and left the surplus products after the delivery in the hands of rural households. This operational and managerial form began to be tried out by farmers on their own in the late 1950s with obvious practical results. Nevertheless, after 1957 this form was criticized repeatedly as representing a "capitalist tendency." After 1978, farmers began once again to adopt this form on their own, which gradually obtained approval and legalization and was explicitly affirmed as a socialist operational and managerial form.

Chapter 1

[1] Jiang Qing was Mao Zedong's wife. She served as a deputy head of the Central Cultural Revolution Group in the early period of the Cultural Revolution and later as a member of the Political Bureau of the Ninth and 10th Central Committees. During the Great Cultural Revolution, she organized and led a counterrevolutionary clique which aimed at seizing the supreme power of the Party and state. She engaged in conspiratorial activities, promoted turmoil, and persecuted a large number of Party and state leaders and well-known public figures. In July 1977, the Third Plenum of the 10th Central Committee adopted a decision to expel Jiang Qing from the Party. In January of 1981, she was sentenced to death by the Special Court of the Supreme People's Court of the People's Republic of China, with two years' probation, and was deprived of political rights for life. In January of 1983, the Criminal Judicial Court of the Supreme People's Court, according to law, reduced her sentence to life imprisonment while reaffirming the deprivation of her political rights for life.

[2] Mao Yuanxin is a nephew of Mao Zedong's. During the Cultural Revolution, he served as a member of the Central Committee, Secretary of the Liaoning Provincial Party Committee and Chairman of the Liaoning Provincial Revolutionary Committee. From the second half of 1975 to September 1976, he served as a "liaison official" between Mao Zedong and the Political Bureau. He was arrested and sentenced to

prison terms according to law for joining the counterrevolutionary clique headed by Jiang Qing.

3 Li Xiannian was a member of the Political Bureau of the Ninth and 10th Central Committees. He then served as a vice-chairman of the Central Committee and a vice-premier of the State Council.

4 Placing somebody "under isolated examination" is in effect house arrest. This measure was taken toward cadres whom the Party and government regarded as having committed serious mistakes. They did not enjoy freedom of movement while they were being disciplined.

5 Zhang Chunqiao served as a deputy head of the Central Cultural Revolution Group in the early period of the Cultural Revolution, a member of the Political Bureau of the Ninth and 10th Central Committees, a member of the Political Bureau Standing Committee of the 10th Central Committee, a vice-premier of the State Council and the director of the General Political Department of the Chinese People's Liberation Army. During the Cultural Revolution, he organized and led a counterrevolutionary clique together with Jiang Qing for the purpose of seizing the supreme power of the Party and state. He engaged in conspiratorial activities, created turmoil, and persecuted a large number of Party and state leaders and other well-known people. In July of 1977, the Third Plenum of the 10th Central Committee expelled Zhang Chunqiao from the Party. In January 1981, he was sentenced to death by the Special Court of the Supreme People's Court of the People's Republic of China, with two years' probation; he was deprived of his political rights for life. In January 1983, the Criminal Judicial Court of the Supreme People's Court, according to law, reduced his verdict to life imprisonment. The original sentence depriving him of political rights for life remained unchanged.

6 Yao Wenyuan served as a member of the Central Cultural Revolution Group in the early period of the Cultural Revolution, and later as a member of the Political Bureau of the Ninth and 10th Central Committees. During the Cultural Revolution, he was a principal member of the Jiang Qing Counterrevolutionary Clique. With the aim of seizing the supreme power of the Party and state, he engaged in conspiratorial activities, created turmoil, and persecuted a large number of Party and state leaders and other well-known people. In July 1977, the Third Plenum of the 10th Central Committee expelled him from the Party. In January 1981, he was sentenced to 20 years in prison by the Special Court of the Supreme People's Court of the People's Republic of China. He was deprived of his political rights for life.

7 Wang Hongwen was a worker with the Shanghai State-Run No. 17 Cotton Textile Mill. In the early period of the Cultural Revolution, he organized the "Shanghai Workers' Revolutionary Rebellion General Headquarters" and served as the principal leader of the organization. Later, he served as a vice-chairman of the Shanghai Municipal Revolutionary Committee. He was a member of the Ninth Party Central Committee and a vice-chairman of the 10th Central Committee. He took an active part in the conspiratorial activities of the Jiang Qing Counterrevolutionary Clique to seize

the supreme power of the Party and state, promoting turmoil, and persecuting a large number of Party and state leaders and well-known public figures. In July 1977, the Third Plenum of the 10th Central Committee expelled him from the Party. In January 1981, he was sentenced to life imprisonment by the Special Court of the Supreme People's Court of the People's Republic of China, with his political rights deprived for life.

[8] Wang Dongxing then served as vice-chairman of the Central Committee, director of the General Office of the Committee for Compiling and Publishing Chairman Mao Zedong's Works and secretary of its Party Committee, director of the General Office of the Central Committee and secretary of its Party Committee, director of the Central Guards Bureau and the secretary of its Party Committee, and Political Commissar and secretary of the Party Committee of the 8341 Unit.

[9] Established in late October of 1976, the "Group of the Central Publicity Departments" was a leading body in charge of publicity work, with Wang Dongxing assuming overall responsibility. The other members were Geng Biao, Li Xin, Zhu Muzhi, Hua Nan, and Wang Shu, with Geng Biao serving as the principal leader.

[10] Li Xin served as a secretary to Kang Sheng, a deputy director of the General Office of the Central Committee, a member of the "Group of the Central Publicity Departments" and a deputy director of the General Office of the Committee for Compiling and Publishing Chairman Mao Zedong's Works.

[11] Guo Yufeng then served as the Head of the Organization Department of the Central Committee.

[12] The "five red elements" refers to people from the five types of "good" families: workers, poor and lower peasants, revolutionary cadres, revolutionary servicemen, and revolutionary intellectuals.

[13] Red guards were the student organization established on their own initiative by the students of middle schools and universities to carry out rebellion in the early period of the Cultural Revolution.

[14] "Destroying old ideas, old culture, old customs, and old habits" was the slogan raised and action taken during the Cultural Revolution to negate and repudiate traditional things (such as the names of old stores, commodity trademarks, street names, and school names), cultural collections, including books, ancient codes and records, artistic works, scenic spots and historical sites, and costumes and attire. The so-called "four olds" referred to old ideas, old culture, old customs, and old habits.

[15] "Appraising Legalists and criticizing Confucianists" was the slogan raised in the movement to "criticize Lin Biao and Confucianists." Legalists and Confucianists stood for different academic schools in the Spring and Autumn Warring State period in ancient China, and put forward different propositions politically. Jiang Qing and her followers distorted history, arguing that the struggle between Legalists and Confucianists had continued since ancient times. They indirectly criticized Zhou Enlai

and others, instigating people to "catch the great modern Confucianist," and attacking Zhou Enlai, Deng Xiaoping, and others.

[16] Zhang Yufeng started working at Mao Zedong's side in the 1970s, taking care of his personal needs and then serving as his confidential secretary.

[17] Wu De then served as a member of the Political Bureau, a vice-chairman of the Standing Committee of the National People's Congress, first secretary of the Beijing Municipal Party Committee, and chairman of the Beijing Municipal Revolutionary Committee.

[18] Chen Yun was a member of the Central Committee and a vice-chairman of the Standing Committee of the National People's Congress.

[19] Wang Zhen was a member of the Party Central Committee and a vice-premier of the State Council.

[20] Li Chang was vice-president of the Chinese Academy of Sciences.

[21] The State Council Political Research Office, an institution attached directly to the State Council, was officially established in July 1975, in accordance with a proposal by Deng Xiaoping who was its head. It played a significant role in the general rectification in 1975 led by Deng Xiaoping. It was severely criticized in the movement to "criticize Deng Xiaoping and attack the Right-deviation tendency to reverse the verdicts." It was renamed the State Council Research Office in 1978. After 1979, it was incorporated into the Investigation and Study Office of the General Office of the Party Central Committee.

[22] Fang Yi was a member of the Political Bureau, a vice-premier of the State Council, and concurrently the minister of the State Science and Technology Commission and the president of the Chinese Academy of Sciences.

[23] Before Lin Biao fled the country on September 13, 1971, while meeting a number of leading cadres on his inspection tour of southern China, Mao Zedong said that the Party had a history of 10 struggles against incorrect policy lines: (1) Chen Duxiu's Right-Opportunist line; (2) Qu Qiubai's "Left" putschist line; (3) Li Lisan's "Left" adventurist line; (4) Luo Zhanglong's Right-splittist line; (5) Wang Ming's "Left" dogmatist line; (6) Zhang Guotao's Right-splittist line; (7) Gao Gang-Rao Shushi anti-Party alliance; (8) Peng Dehuai's Right opportunist anti-Party clique; (9) Liu Shaoqi's counterrevolutionary line; and (10) the struggle at the 1970 Lushan Plenum. The Lushan meeting referred to here was the Third Plenum of the Ninth Central Committee held in 1970 at Lushan. At the meeting Mao Zedong criticized Chen Boda by name. As Chen Boda was a follower of Lin Biao, Mao thereby also criticized Lin Biao without mentioning his name.

[24] Hu Yaobang had served as first secretary of the Central Committee of the Chinese Communist Youth League before the Cultural Revolution. In July 1975, during the all-round rectification led by Deng Xiaoping, he was sent to the Chinese Academy of Sciences to lead the rectification there. He was severely criticized in the movement to

"criticize Deng Xiaoping and attack the Right-deviationist tendency toward reversing the verdict."

[25] Hu Fuming was a teacher at the Philosophy Department of Nanjing University and wrote the first draft of the article titled, "Practice Is the Sole Criterion for Testing Truth."

[26] Hu Qiaomu was the principal leader of the State Council Research Office and the president of the Chinese Academy of Social Sciences.

[27] Zhang Pinghua was Head of the Publicity Department of the Central Committee. [Editor's note: This is the new official translation of the Party department formerly translated as the "Propaganda Department."]

[28] Xiong Fu was editor-in-chief of Red Flag, and a deputy director of the General Office of the Committee for Compiling and Publishing Chairman Mao Zedong's Works.

[29] Dukes and princes were the aristocracy under imperial rule. This refers to the Party and government leaders of various provinces, municipalities under the direct administration of the central government, and autonomous regions.

[30] Wei Guoqing was vice-chairman of the Standing Committee of the National People's Congress, vice-chairman of the National Committee of the Chinese People's Political Consultative Conference, Standing Committee member of the Military Commission of the Party Central Committee, director of the General Political Department of the Chinese People's Liberation Army, first secretary of the Guangdong Provincial Party Committee, and chairman of the Guangdong Provincial Revolutionary Committee.

[31] Wu Lanfu was vice-chairman of the Standing Committee of the National People's Congress, vice-chairmen of the National Committee of the Chinese People's Political Consultative Conference, and head of the United Front Work Department of the Party Central Committee.

[32] Liu Bocheng was vice-chairman of the Military Commission of the Central Committee and a vice-chairman of the Standing Committee of the National People's Congress.

[33] Xu Shiyou was a member of the Standing Committee of the Military Commission of the Party Central Committee and Commander of the Guangzhou Military Area Command of the Chinese People's Liberation Army.

[34] Ji Dengkui was a vice-premier of the State Council.

[35] Su Zhenhua was a Standing Committee member of the Military Commission of the Central Committee, political commissar of the PLA Navy, first secretary of the Shanghai Municipal Party Committee and chairman of the Shanghai Municipal Revolutionary Committee.

[36] Li Desheng was commander of the Shenyang Military Area Command.

[37] Yu Qiuli was a vice-premier of the State Council and concurrently the minister in charge of the State Planning Commission.

[38] Zhang Tingfa was a Standing Committee member of the Military Commission of the Central Committee and commander of the PLA Air Force.

[39] Chen Yonggui was a vice-premier of the State Council, known for advocating the Dazhai model, based on a highly collectivized agricultural brigade in a very poor area.

[40] Chen Xilian was a vice-premier of the State Council, a Standing Committee member of the Military Commission of the Central Committee, and commander of the Beijing Military Area Command.

[41] Geng Biao was a vice-premier of the State Council and head of the International Liaison Department of the Central Committee.

[42] Nie Rongzhen was a vice-chairman of the Military Commission of the Central Committee.

[43] Ni Zhifu was president of the All-China Federation of Trade Unions, second secretary of the Beijing Municipal Party Committee, a vice-chairman of the Beijing Municipal Revolutionary Committee, second secretary of the Shanghai Municipal Party Committee, and first vice-chairman of the Shanghai Municipal Revolutionary Committee.

[44] Xu Xiangqian was a vice-chairman of the Military Commission of the Central Committee, a vice-premier of the State Council and concurrently National Defense Minister.

[45] Peng Chong was a vice-chairman of the National Committee of the Chinese People's Political Consultative Conference, third secretary of the Shanghai Municipal Party Committee, and second vice-chairman of the Shanghai Municipal Revolutionary Committee.

[46] Chen Muhua was a vice-premier of the State Council.

[47] Zhao Ziyang was a vice-chairman of the National Committee of the Chinese People's Political Consultative Conference, first secretary of the Sichuan Provincial Party Committee, and chairman of the Sichuan Provincial Revolutionary Committee.

[48] Sai Fuding was a vice-chairman of the Standing Committee of the National People's Congress, first secretary of the Xinjiang Uigur Autonomous Regional Party Committee, and first political commissar of the Xinjiang Military Area Command.

[49] The 7,000-person conference refers to the enlarged Work Conference of the Central Committee convened from January 10 to February 7, 1962, with more than 7,000 people attending.

[50] Xi Zhongxun was secretary of the Guangdong Provincial Party Committee.

[51] Song Renqiong was a vice-chairman of the National Committee of the Chinese People's Political Consultative Conference.

[52] Wang Renzhong was the second secretary of the Shaanxi Provincial Party Committee and first vice-chairman of the Shaanxi Provincial Revolutionary Committee.

Chapter 2

[1] "Double attacks" refers to the attacks on the remaining forces supporting the "Gang of Four" and the attack on sabotage activities of class enemies.

[2] Lin Hujia was first secretary of the Beijing Municipal Party Committee and chairman of the Beijing Municipal Revolutionary Committee.

[3] Liu Zihou was first secretary of the Hebei Provincial Party Committee and chairman of the Hebei Provincial Revolutionary Committee.

[4] Luo Qingchang was head of the Investigation Department of the Central Committee.

[5] Qin Jiwei was first political commissar of the Beijing Military Area Command of the Chinese People's Liberation Army.

[6] Wang Enmao was first secretary of the Jilin Provincial Party Committee and chairman of the Jilin Provincial Revolutionary Committee.

[7] Ren Zhongyi was first secretary of the Liaoning Provincial Party Committee and chairman of the Liaoning Provincial Revolutionary Committee.

[8] Tang Ke was minister of the Metallurgical Industry.

[9] Yang Yong was a Standing Committee member of the Military Commission of the Central Committee and chief of staff of the People's Liberation Army.

[10] Wan Li was first secretary of the Anhui Provincial Party Committee and chairman of the Anhui Provincial Revolutionary Committee.

[11] Bai Rubing was first secretary of the Shandong Provincial Party Committee and chairman of the Shandong Provincial Revolutionary Committee.

[12] Nie Fengzhi was commander of the Nanjing Military Area Command of the Chinese People's Liberation Army.

[13] Duan Junyi was first secretary of the Henan Provincial Party Committee and chairman of the Henan Provincial Revolutionary Committee.

[14] Mao Zhiyong was first secretary of the Hunan Provincial Party Committee and chairman of the Hunan Provincial Revolutionary Committee.

[15] Huang Hua was the Minister of Foreign Affairs.

[16] Yang Dezhi was a Standing Committee member of the Military Commission of the Central Committee and commander of the Wuhan Military Area Command of the Chinese People's Liberation Army.

17 An Pingsheng was first secretary of the Yunnan Provincial Party Committee and chairman of the Yunnan Provincial Revolutionary Committee.

18 Wang Feng was first secretary of the Xinjiang Uigur Autonomous Regional Party Committee and chairman of the Xinjiang Uigur Autonomous Regional Revolutionary Committee.

19 Huo Shilian was first secretary of the Ningxia Hui Autonomous Regional Party Committee and chairman of the Ningxia Hui Autonomous Regional Revolutionary Committee.

20 Xiao Hua was first political commissar of the Lanzhou Military Area Command of the Chinese People's Liberation Army.

21 Zhang Xiangshan then served as a deputy head of the Publicity Department of the Party Central Committee and director of the Central Radio Broadcasting Bureau.

22 Zeng Tao was president of the Xinhua News Agency.

23 Hua Nan was editor-in-chief of the Liberation Army Daily.

24 Hu Sheng was a deputy director of the General Office of the Committee for Compiling and Publishing Chairman Mao Zedong's Works under the Party Central Committee.

25 Wu Lengxi was a deputy director of the General Office of the Committee for Compiling and Publishing Chairman Mao Zedong's Works under the Central Committee.

26 Hu Jiwei was the editor-in-chief of the People's Daily.

27 Zhang Yaoci was a deputy director of the General Office of the Central Committee.

28 Yang Xiguang was the editor-in-chief of Guangming Daily.

29 Wang Huide was the director of the Compilation and Translation Bureau of the Central Committee.

30 Li Ruishan was the first secretary of the Shaanxi Provincial Party Committee and chairman of the Shaanxi Provincial Revolutionary Committee.

31 Yu Mingtao was the secretary of the Shaanxi Provincial Party Committee and a vice-chairman of the Shaanxi Provincial Revolutionary Committee.

32 Song Ping was first secretary of the Gansu Provincial Party Committee and chairman of the Gansu Provincial Revolutionary Committee.

33 Li Dengying was secretary of the Gansu Provincial Party Committee.

34 Shao Jingwa was secretary of the Ningxia Hui Autonomous Regional Party Committee and a vice-chairman of the Ningxia Hui Autonomous Regional Revolutionary Committee.

[35] Song Zhihe was secretary of the Xinjiang Uigur Autonomous Regional Party Committee and vice-chairman of the Xinjiang Uigur Autonomous Regional Revolutionary Committee.

[36] Tan Qilong was first secretary of the Qinghai Provincial Party Committee and chairman of the Qinghai Provincial Revolutionary Committee.

[37] Zhao Haifeng was secretary of the Qinghai Provincial Party Committee and vice-chairman of the Qinghai Provincial Revolutionary Committee.

[38] Liu Zhen was commander of the Xinjiang Military Area Command of the Chinese People's Liberation Army.

[39] Guo Linxiang was second political commissar of the Xinjiang Military Area Command of the Chinese People's Liberation Army.

[40] Han Xianchu was a Standing Committee member of the Military Commission of the Party Central Committee and commander of the Lanzhou Military Area Command of the Chinese People's Liberation Army.

[41] Li Shuiqing was commander of the Second Artillery Forces of the Chinese People's Liberation Army.

[42] Chen Heqiao was political commissar of the Second Artillery Forces of the Chinese People's Liberation Army

[43] Mo Wenhua was political commissar of the Armored Forces of the Chinese People's Liberation Army

[44] Liu Wei was minister of the Second Ministry of the Machine-Building Industry.

[45] Zhang Zhen was minister of the Fifth Ministry of the Machine-Building Industry.

[46] Zhang Jingfu was the Minister of Finance.

[47] Jiang Yizhen was the Minister of Health.

[48] Yao Yilin was head of the State Council Financial and Trade Group.

[49] Li Renjun was a vice-minister of the State Planning Commission.

[50] Kang Sheng was an alternate member of the Political Bureau, a member of the Secretariat, and a member of the Political Bureau Standing Committee of the Eighth Central Committee. He also was a member of the Political Bureau Standing Committee of the Ninth Central Committee and a vice-chairman of the Tenth Central Committee. During the Cultural Revolution, along with Lin Biao, Jiang Qing, and others, he engaged in conspiratorial activities to usurp the leadership of the Party and power, and persecuted a large number of Party and state leaders, senior Party and government leaders, and well-known public figures. He died of illness in 1975. He was posthumously expelled from the Party in 1980.

Chapter 3

[1] "Cutting off the capitalist tail" was a "Left" economic policy pursued from the late 1950s to the late 1970s. Private plots of farm households, household-based sideline production, and rural open markets that were still retained after socialist transformation was completed in rural areas were defined as the "remnants" of "capitalism" in rural areas and were banned. This policy, slogan, and practice were known as "cutting off the capitalist tail."

[2] "Zhao san mu si" or "zhao si mu san" refers to an ancient Chinese story. Once upon a time a man playing with monkeys used acorns to feed his monkeys. When he told the monkeys that he would give three acorns to each monkey in the morning and four in the evening, all the monkeys became upset. Then he told them that he would give four acorns to each monkey in the morning and three in the evening, to the delight of all the monkeys. The original metaphorical meaning of the fables is that smart people are good at devising various means. Later, the metaphor came to mean caprice. I use it here in its original meaning.

[3] Tie Ying was first secretary of the Zhejiang Provincial Party Committee and Chairman of the Zhejiang Provincial Revolutionary Committee.

[4] Wang Qian was first secretary of the Shanxi Provincial Party Committee and chairman of the Shanxi Provincial Revolutionary Committee.

[5] Liu Jingping was secretary of the Inner Mongolia Autonomous Regional Party Committee and vice-chairman of the Inner Mongolia Autonomous Regional Provincial Revolutionary Committee.

[6] Jiang Weiqing was first secretary of the Jiangxi Provincial Party Committee and chairman of the Jiangxi Provincial Revolutionary Committee.

[7] Ma Xingyuan was secretary of the Fujian Provincial Party Committee and vice-chairman of the Fujian Provincial Revolutionary Committee.

[8] Zhang Shiying was deputy secretary of the Jilin Provincial Party Committee and vice-chairman of the Jilin Provincial Revolutionary Committee.

[9] Chen Puru was secretary of the Liaoning Provincial Party Committee and vice-chairman of the Liaoning Provincial Revolutionary Committee.

[10] Li Yimang was deputy head of the International Liaison Department of the Central Committee.

[11] Qiao Shi was a deputy head of the International Liaison Department of the Central Committee.

[12] Ma Hong was deputy secretary-general of the Chinese Academy of Social Sciences.

Chapter 4

[1] The "case of the renegade group of 61 members" was a major wrong case trumped up by Lin Biao, Jiang Qing, and others during the Cultural Revolution. Around 1931, because of the search and arrests by the police of the Guomindang government and information provided by renegades, many cadres of the Northern Bureau of the Party Central Committee were thrown into a prison, where they remained faithful to the Party and unyielding. In 1936, the Central Committee and the Northern Bureau of the Central Committee instructed Bo Yibo and 60 others in prison to leave the prison by performing the procedures as stipulated by the enemy, for the purpose of beefing up the Party's strength and increasing its cadres. In August 1966, Kang Sheng brought up this matter again, accusing them of collaborating with the Guomindang to gain release. Instigated by Jiang Qing and others, the movement to "catch renegades" (who collaborated with the enemy) was launched everywhere. The aforementioned 1936 case in which the circumstances were clear and procedures had been properly followed without any problems was branded the case of a "renegade group." In March of 1967, the Central Committee erroneously printed and distributed the "Material Concerning the Capitulation and Traitorous Activity of Bo Yibo, An Ziwen, Yang Xianzhen, and Others," labeling the 61 persons as members of a "renegade group." From then on, a number of leading cadres involved in the case were persecuted cruelly, with some persecuted to death.

[2] Bo Yibo was an alternate member of the Political Bureau of the Eighth Central Committee, vice-premier of the State Council, and concurrently minister in charge of the State Economic Commission. During the Cultural Revolution he was vilified as a "renegade" and persecuted by Lin Biao, Jiang Qing, and others.

[3] In the early period of the Cultural Revolution, Tao Zhu served as a member of the Political Bureau Standing Committee of the Central Committee, a member of the Secretariat of the Central Committee, vice-premier of the State Council, and head of the Propaganda Department (later, the official translation was changed to the Publicity Department) of the Party Central Committee. He was later criticized and persecuted by Lin Biao, Jiang Qing, and others. Tao Zhu died in 1969, before he could be cleared of false charges.

[4] Wang Heshou was the minister of the Metallurgical Industry before the Cultural Revolution and was framed and persecuted during the Cultural Revolution by Lin Biao, Jiang Qing, and others.

[5] Peng Dehuai was a member of the Political Bureau of the Eighth Central Committee, vice-chairman of the Military Commission of the Central Committee, and Minister of National Defense. At an enlarged meeting of the Political Bureau convened by the Central Committee at Lushan, Peng Dehuai wrote a letter to Mao Zedong, criticizing the mistakes made in the Great Leap Forward. Mao Zedong erroneously criticized Peng Dehuai. Immediately afterward Peng was removed from his positions as vice-chairman of the Military Commission of the Central Committee, and Minister of

National Defense. During the Cultural Revolution Peng was cruelly persecuted by Lin Biao, Jiang Qing, and Kang Sheng. He died of illness in 1974, uncleared of false charges.

6 The Central Cultural Revolution Group was set up in May 1966 to lead the Cultural Revolution. Its leader was Chen Boda, its deputy leaders were Jiang Qing, Zhang Chunqiao, Yao Wenyuan, and others, and its advisor was Kang Sheng. In the early period of the Cultural Revolution it functioned for some time in place of the Political Bureau and the Secretariat of the Central Committee.

7 Peng Zhen was a member of the Political Bureau and the Secretariat of the Eighth Central Committee, first secretary of the Beijing Municipal Party Committee and Beijing mayor. Lu Dingyi was an alternate member of the Political Bureau of the Eighth Central Committee, vice-premier of the State Council and head of the Propaganda Department of the Central Committee. Luo Ruiqing was a member of the Secretariat of the Eighth Central Committee, vice-premier of the State Council and Chief of Staff of the Chinese People's Liberation Army. Yang Shangkun was an alternate member of the Secretariat of the Eighth Central Committee and director of the General Office of the Central Committee. At an enlarged meeting of the Political Bureau of the Central Committee held in May 1966, Peng, Lu, Luo, and Yang were mistakenly criticized and accused of forming an "anti-Party clique," and removed from their posts. During the Cultural Revolution they were cruelly persecuted by Lin Biao, Jiang Qing, and others.

8 The "February Adverse Current" is a slanderous wording of the event in which, in early 1967, some senior leaders in the Party criticized and resisted the perverse acts of Lin Biao, Jiang Qing, and others that disrupted the Party and army during the Cultural Revolution. In February 1967, at a brief Political Bureau meeting and a brief meeting of the Military Commission of the Party Central Committee, Tan Zhenlin, Chen Yi, Ye Jianying, Li Fuchun, Li Xiannian, Xu Xianqian, Nie Rongzhen, and others engaged in a sharp debate with Jiang Qing, Chen Boda, Kang Sheng, and Zhang Chunqiao, and pointedly criticized the Central Cultural Revolution Group for conniving and inciting and supporting unrest in various places. After the incident, the Central Cultural Revolution Group reported it to Mao Zedong and vilified the leaders who criticized them. After listening to the report, Mao Zedong sternly condemned these Party, government, and army leaders. Jiang Qing and others smeared the struggle waged by these Party, government, and army leaders by labeling it the "February Adverse Current."

9 Xie Fuzhi was a member of the Political Bureau of the Ninth Central Committee, vice-premier of the State Council and Minister of Public Security. During the Cultural Revolution he took a direct part in the conspiratorial activities of Lin Biao, Jiang Qing, and others to usurp the power of the Party and seize power, and persecuted a large number of senior Party, government, and army leaders and well-known public figures. He died of illness in 1972. After the Cultural Revolution he was posthumously expelled from the Party.

---

[10] Wu Zhong was commander of the Beijing Garrison of the Chinese People's Liberation Army.

[11] Wang Xiaoyu was vice-chairman of the Shandong Provincial Revolutionary Committee during the Cultural Revolution.

[12] During the Cultural Revolution, Wang Huaixiang was a member of the Eighth and Ninth Central Committees as well as of the 10th Central Committee and served as first secretary of the Jilin Provincial Party Committee.

[13] Yu Wusheng Chu (n a silent place) is a modern drama created and staged by the Shanghai Workers' Cultural Palace in 1978. The drama portrayed how ordinary people commemorated Zhou Enlai and fought against the "Gang of Four" in the April 5th Movement of 1976.

[14] The Collection of Tiananmen Poems is an anthology of many poems written during the "April 5th Movement" in 1976 by people wanting to commemorate Zhou Enlai, support Deng Xiaoping, and oppose the "Gang of Four." It was compiled by a number of the teachers and staff from the Beijing No. 2 Foreign Languages Institute.

[15] Jia Tingsan was third secretary of the Beijing Municipal Party Committee and a vice-chairman of the Beijing Municipal Revolutionary Committee.

[16] Han Ying was first secretary of the Central Committee of the Communist Youth League of China.

[17] Hu Qili was secretary of the Central Committee of the Communist Youth League of China.

Chapter 5

[1] Su Shaozhi was an editor with the Theory Department of the People's Daily.

[2] Feng Lanrui was a staff member of the State Council Political Research Office.

[3] Lin Jianqing was a staff member of the State Council Political Research Office.

[4] Xu Chi, a writer, wrote the article "Conjecture of Goldbach," which caused such a great sensation throughout the country that it "drove up the price of the Luoyang paper" making it a bestseller for some time.

[5] Chen Manyuan was president of the Logistics Academy of the Chinese People's Liberation Army.

[6] Zhang Hanzhi was an interpreter, department director in the Ministry of Foreign Affairs, and the widow of Qiao Guanhua.

[7] Ding Zhaozhong is a Chinese American physicist.

[8] Cheng Zihua was the Minister of Civil Affairs.

[9] Before the Cultural Revolution Wang Shiying had served as member of the Central Supervision Commission and a Standing Committee member of the National Committee of the Chinese People's Political Consultative Conference. During the Cultural Revolution, he was slandered as a "renegade" and a "special agent" by Lin Biao, Jiang Qing, Kang Sheng, and others and was cruelly persecuted. He died in 1968 uncleared of a false charge.

[10] Xiao Ke was president of the Military Academy of the Chinese People's Liberation Army.

[11] Ji Pengfei was vice-chairman of the Standing Committee of the National People's Congress.

[12] Wu Qingtong was director of the General Office of the State Council.

[13] Li Baohua was the president of the People's Bank of China.

[14] Zhao Cangbi was Minister of Public Security.

[15] Li Dazhao, a founder of the Party, was arrested and murdered by a warlord of the Feng faction in 1927.

Chapter 6

[1] Tan Zhenlin was vice-chairman of the Standing Committee of the National People's Congress. Before the Cultural Revolution he had served as a member of the Political Bureau, as a member of the secretariat of the Central Committee, and as vice-premier of the State Council. During the Cultural Revolution he was erroneously criticized and persecuted by Lin Biao, Jiang Qing, and others. In 1978, at the request of Red Flag, he wrote an article, "Practice in the Struggle in the Jinggang Mountains and the Development of Mao Zedong Thought," which reflected the view of practice serving as the sole criterion for testing truth.

[2] Zhou Yang was an advisor to the Chinese Academy of Social Sciences.

[3] Shen Baoxiang now serves as a professor at the Central Party School. In 1978, he was an editor with the Editorial Board of Lilun dongtai (Theoretical development) journal published by the Central Party School. His work Zhenli biaojun wenti taolun shimo (The full story of the discussion about the issue of the criterion for testing truth) was published by the China Youth Publishing House in 1998.

[4] I carefully read The Full Story of the Discussion about the Issue of the Criterion for Testing Truth, which had been given to me as a gift by the China Youth Publishing House. The author, Shen Baoxiang, took part in the work then, thereby acquiring personal experience. In recent years he has collected a large amount of data in this regard. His hard work deserves our praise.

It is impossible for any researcher—no matter how diligent—to collect a complete range of relevant data with nothing missing and to grasp accurately the essence of events and people. It is entirely understandable and excusable that there are some shortcomings in the book. I am sorry that a person like me with a fairly good knowledge of that discussion does not have time to do special research in this area and still less to write a special book in this regard. So, I was very delighted to read this book. Since I did not have the slightest idea about the writing of the book and did not know the author, I was sorry that I was unable to be of any help to the author before he finished writing his book. After reading the book, I felt even more strongly that I should offer the author some data and lend a helping hand. Better late then never. But as I was too busy, I was not able to take up my pen until now. Yet I still can write about only one event, namely, matters associated with the discussion about the issue of the criterion for testing truth held at the Central Work Conference convened in 1978, as reference for the researchers, including Shen Baoxiang, who are studying this issue.

Chapter 7

[1] Hu Deping is Hu Yaobang's son.

Chapter 8

[1] "Gong jian fa" is an abbreviation for public security departments, procurators, and courts.

[2] The "Palace of the King of Hell of the General Political Department" is a slanderous reference to the General Political Department of the Chinese People's Liberation Army.

[3] Wu Faxian was a member of the Political Bureau of the Ninth Central Committee and the commander of the Air Force of the Chinese People's Liberation Army. He was a principal member of the Lin Biao Clique. During the Cultural Revolution he took a direct part in the conspiratorial activities of the Lin Biao CliqueLin Biao Clique to usurp the leadership of the Party and seize state power, and persecuted a large number of senior leaders of the Party, government, and army and well-known public figures. After the "September 13th" incident in 1971, he was placed under isolated examination and was expelled from the Party. In 1980, the Special Court of the Supreme People's Court sentenced him to prison on charges of "counterrevolution."

[4] Ye Qun, the wife of Lin Biao, was a member of the Political Bureau of the Ninth Central Committee and a principal member of the Lin Biao Clique. During the Cultural Revolution she took direct part in the conspiratorial activities of the CliqueLin Biao Clique to usurp the leadership of the Party and seize state power, and persecuted a large number of senior leaders of the Party, government and army and well-known public figures. On September 13, 1971, she fled China together with Lin

Biao and others and was killed in a plane crash. She was posthumously expelled from the Party.

5 Li Zuopeng was a member of the Political Bureau of the Ninth Central Committee and the Political Commissar of the Navy of the Chinese People's Liberation Army. He was a principal member of the Lin Biao Clique. During the Cultural Revolution he took direct part in the conspiratorial activities of the Lin Biao Clique to usurp the leadership of the Party and seize state power, and persecuted a large number of senior leaders of the Party, government and army and well-known public figures. After the "September 13th" incident in 1971, he was placed under isolated examination and was expelled from the Party. In 1980, the Special Court of the Supreme People's Court sentenced him to prison on charges of "counter-revolution."

6 Huang Kecheng was a member of the Secretariat of the Eighth Central Committee, the secretary-general of the Military Commission of the Eighth Central Committee and the chief of staff of the Chinese People's Liberation Army. At the enlarged meeting of the Political Bureau at Lushan in 1959, he was severely criticized as a principal member of the "Peng Dehuai anti-Party Clique" for airing views similar to those of Peng Dehuai and for criticizing the "Left" mistakes during the Great Leap Forward. He was dismissed from all the posts he had held. He was cruelly persecuted during the Cultural Revolution.

7 Tan Zhen was a member of the Secretariat of the Eighth Central Committee and the Director of the General Political Department of the Chinese People's Liberation Army. He was attacked by Lin Biao for criticizing Lin's practice of "empty politics" in 1960. He was dismissed from his post as a member of the Secretariat of the Party Central Committee at the Tenth Plenum of the Eighth Central Committee held in September of 1962.

8 Li Rui was a vice-minister of Water Resources and the Power Industry and a part-time secretary of Mao Zedong. At an enlarged meeting of the Political Bureau at Lushan in 1959, he was severely criticized as a principal member of the "Peng Dehuai anti-Party Clique" for voicing views similar to those of Peng Dehuai and for criticizing the "Left" mistakes made in the Great Leap Forward, and was expelled from the Party. He was persecuted during the Cultural Revolution.

9 Rao Shushi was an early head of the Organization Department of the Party Central Committee. He was expelled from the Party for engaging in conspiratorial activities in 1953 together with Gao Gang aimed at usurping the leadership of the Party and seizing state power. Later, he was sentenced to a prison term for committing a "counterrevolutionary" crime. He died of illness in prison in 1975.

10 Pan Hannian served successively as head of the Social Department and the United Front Work Department of the East China Bureau of the Central Committee and the Shanghai Municipal Party Committee, as third secretary of the Shanghai Municipal Party Committee, and as vice-mayor of Shanghai. In 1955, he was placed in custody for examination in connection with the so-called "hidden traitor" case. In 1963, he was

erroneously determined to be a "hidden traitor" and was sentenced to a prison term. In 1982, the Party Central Committee issued a circular, announcing his rehabilitation.

[11] Ma Mingfang was deputy secretary of the Northwest China Bureau of the Central Committee and deputy head of the Organization Department of the Central Committee.

[12] Zhang Ziyi served as deputy head of the Propaganda Department of the Central Committee before the Cultural Revolution.

[13] Yang Zhihua, the wife of Qu Qiubai, was Minister of the Textile Industry before the Cultural Revolution.

[14] Qiu Huizuo was a member of the Political Bureau of the Ninth Central Committee and director of the General Logistics Department of the Chinese People's Liberation Army. He was a principal member of the Lin Biao Clique. During the Cultural Revolution he took a direct part in the conspiratorial activities of the Lin Biao Clique to usurp the leadership of the Party and seize state power, and persecuted a large number of senior leaders of the Party, government, and army and well-known public figures. After Lin Biao's plane crash on September 13, 1971, Qiu was placed under isolated examination and was expelled from the Party. In 1980, the Special Court of the Supreme People's Court sentenced him to prison term on charges of "counterrevolution."

[15] Liu Shikun is a pianist.

[16] Liu Zhijian was deputy director of the General Political Department of the Chinese People's Liberation Army before the Cultural Revolution.

Chapter 9

[1] Rong Yiren was the former general manager of the General Management Office of the Shanghai Shenxin Textile Company. Later he served as vice-chairman of the National Committee of the Chinese People's Political Consultative Conference and chairman of the All-China Federation of Industry and Commerce. He was for many years regarded as a model former capitalist cooperating with the government.

[2] The "three workstyles" refer to linking theory to practice, forging close relations with the masses, and criticism and self-criticism. Mao Zedong was the first to summarize the three workstyles.

Chapter 10

[1] The Beiping Military Mediation Department was also known as the Beiping Military Mediation Executive Department, established in 1946 by the Party and the Guomindang in accordance with the cease-fire agreement signed by the two sides on

January 10, 1946. **[Editor's Note: The name "Beiping" was changed to "Beijing" (northern capital) when the communists established their capital there in 1949.]** It consisted of one representative of the Guomindang Government, one representative of the CPC, and one representative of the U.S. Government. It had a number of executive groups under it that were authorized to carry out mediation at the sites of military clashes in order to implement the cease-fire agreement. Ye Jianying served as the representative of the Party in the Military Mediation Department. The Beiping Military Mediation Executive Department was abolished in 1947.

2 The book Since the Third Plenum—Collection of Important has two editions: one is *Since the Third Plenum – Selected Important Documents of the Party,* and the other is *Since the Third Plenum – Collection of Important Documents of the Party.* Both were compiled by the Party Literature Research Center of the Party Central Committee and published by the People's Publishing House in 1982.

Chapter 12

1 Yang Chengwu was deputy chief of staff of the Chinese People's Liberation Army.

2 *Tian Dao – Zhou Hui yu Lushan hui yi* (The Doctrine of Heaven—Zhou Hui and the Lushan Meeting) was written jointly by Quan Tingchi and Huang Lina and published by the Guangdong Tourism Publishing House in 1997.

Chapter 13

1 The Resolution on Certain Historical Questions was adopted by the Seventh Plenum of the Sixth Central Committee on April 20, 1945. The resolution mainly addressed historical issues arising from the founding of the Party in 1921 to 1945.

INDEX

Index

DENG XIAOPING SHAKES THE WORLD

*An Eyewitness Account of China's Party Work Conference
and the Third Plenum (November–December 1978)*

Yu Guangyuan was born in 1915 and graduated in physics from Qinghua University. He was a participant in the December 9th movement (1935), was one of the organizers of the National Liberation Pioneers (Mingxian), which was intended to broaden the anti-Japanese alliance, and joined the CCP shortly before the Japanese invasion. From 1937 to 1982 he held a variety of positions and was struggled against and sent to a May 7th Cadre School during the Cultural Revolution. In 1975 Yu was assigned as a senior member of the Party Research Office of the State Council, and later of the Political Research Office and concurrently a deputy president of the Chinese Academy of Social Sciences and a deputy director of the Science and Technology Commission of the State Council; he worked closely with Deng Xiaoping in Deng's periods of ascendancy.

Ezra F. Vogel teaches at Harvard University and is former Director of the John King Fairbank Center.

Steven I. Levine teaches at the University of North Carolina, Chapel Hill, and is Interim Director of the Carolina Asia Center.

Voices of Asia

Steven I. Levine, Imprint Editor

Voices of Asia presents important books in the social sciences and the humanities by leading contemporary Asian writers in English translation. By making available work which would otherwise be accessible to only a very small number of Western specialists, Voices facilitates a two-way flow of knowledge between Asia and the West.

Steven I. Levine teaches Asian history at the University of North Carolina at Chapel Hill and is the interim Director of the Carolina Asia Center. He received his AB in Politics from Brandeis University and Ph.D. in Government and Far Eastern Languages from Harvard University. He has taught at the University of Michigan, Duke University, The American University, the Defense Intelligence College, Columbia University, and Merrimack College. He served as a Consultant and Social Scientist at the Rand Corporation; as Director, Center for Slavic, Eurasian and East European Studies, University of North Carolina at Chapel Hill; and as Resident Director, Duke Study in China Program, Bejing and Nanjing.

CPSIA information can be obtained
at www.ICGtesting.com
Printed in the USA
BVOW06*1132171117
500685BV00011B/146/P